On Singing Onstage

On Singing Onstage

David Craig

SCHIRMER BOOKS
A Division of Macmillan Publishing Co., Inc.
NEW YORK

Schirmer Books
A Division of Macmillan Publishing Co., Inc.
866 Third Avenue, New York, N.Y. 10022

Collier Macmillan Canada, Ltd.

Library of Congress Catalog Card Number: 78–8820

Printed in the United States of America

printing number
 2 3 4 5 6 7 8 9 10

Library of Congress Cataloging in Publication Data

Craig, David.
    On singing onstage.

    1. Singing—Instruction and study.   2. Musical revue,
comedy, etc.   I. Title.
MT820.C788   782.8'1'071   78–8820
ISBN   0–02–870580–7 pbk.
ISBN   0–02–8707510–6

To my wife
who taught me that theatre,
like comedy,
is no laughing matter

Contents

Acknowledgments

I would like to express my gratitude to Gary Carver, my pianist and good friend, to Henry Polic II, who granted me the use of his creative technical work, to Leonard Gershe and Henry Marks, who aided me in securing rights to certain lyrics, to Tony Stecheson, music encyclopedist and proprietor of Hollywood Sheet Music, to Ellen Geer, Marge Champion Sagal, James Mitchell, and Robert Windeler, all of whom furnished me with valuable feedback, and to Enid Unatin, Penny Rice, and Ruth Oberdorfer, who transferred a muddle of manuscript into a model of typed clarity.

Foreword

Lee Grant

David Craig observes in his first chapter that the American actor is addicted to teachers. All of our lives, at all stages of our careers, we explore new disciplines simply to learn new crafts as the necessity to work confronts us. What if, God forbid, you were offered a musical and couldn't sing?

Like eternal children we are forever being tutored for Great Examinations and Great Expectations, trying to mold ourselves into whatever it is "they" want us to be. When my husband, Joey, was a dancer, he wrote on his resumé that his height was 5'9" to 6'2"—whatever it is "they" want us to be.

I first heard of David's classes when we were in that period on Broadway when musicals were "in" and plays were "out." Dramas were opening and closing out of town. I couldn't work yet in television or film because of the Blacklist. I had to be able to sing in order to stay in a shrinking profession. My previous singing experiences had been traumatic and I was earning my own living by teaching acting. I entered David's class with fear and caution.

In his Introductory Class, for purposes of demonstration, David has graduate students perform. I cannot tell you what it is like to see an ordinary actor, an ordinary extraordinary actor, perform after working with David. The mystery of it! Why is she doing that? How sure she is of herself! Why is she looking there? Now there? And the singing seems to take care of itself—the voice follows the thoughts. The concentration is not on the voice! A person in total command is on the stage, an elegant, interesting person who is telling me something through a song I'd heard a hundred cliché times before, but telling me in a way that I'd never heard or seen before. My fear left as I felt a pure hunger to be able to do that thing myself—that particular hunger that makes one want to act, to create, in the first place.

There is a great psychological difference between actors and entertainers. Actors need a situation, a play, and other characters to buffer them from the audience. The actor works for solitude in public, creating an area the audience shouldn't enter, where we are free to create and to re-create life. We feel impossibly exposed and uncertain in an entertaining posture. David Craig recognizes this dichotomy and, using the actor's tools, shows us the way to create our own privacy and invent characters that we need while we are doing this monologue called song. His approach is unique, image breaking. For those of us who were still terrified of singing, his class was the Second Coming.

The fact is, I was so enamored of David's classes that I haunted them. I attended his sessions three seasons in a row until he gently pried my fingers loose from my chair and told me it was time to go out into the world. I think he was wrong. If I could, I'd be there still.

As you come to know David through his book, you will treasure him as I do. He is not a teacher who encourages mystery. The mystery is one's talent. It exists or it doesn't. He is a master at creating exercises and tasks that release that talent; tasks that are measurable, that he can estimate you have carried out or have not carried out.

His work is taxing and inventive, and so is he—caustic when you are self-indulgent, loving when you achieve; a Papa-bird training and protecting the faint-of-heart until the day he pushes you to stand on your wobbly legs to fly.

David is also a snob in the very best sense. He brings to all his students a fierce conviction about who is a talent and who is not. When he works himself up about it it's a terrible beauty, and pure oxygen to me because he cares. He maintains a highly rigid set of values and is so charming and witty that, even when I don't agree with him, I laugh.

When you've read a book you've cherished and reluctantly turned the last page, it's good to call a friend and say, "You're so lucky you haven't read this—it's all ahead of you."

It's all ahead of you.

Preface

Sweeter than any sung
My songs that found no tongue; . . .

John Greenleaf Whittier

It would seem to be daring to choose to write a book about performing techniques in the musical theatre at a time when it is
demonstrably in a sorry state of sterility. Certainly the health
chart of this arm of the fabulous invalid indicates a serious illness, while that of the legitimate theatre of comedy and drama
continues to present a healthy and vital picture. Regional
theatres have rooted themselves throughout the country with
fertile results and, in consequence, have broken the old saw
that Broadway is the sole provider of meaningful works for the
stage. Indeed, theatre centers in Los Angeles, San Francisco,
New Haven, Washington, Minneapolis, Houston, and other
cities are burgeoning. Classical drama, considered box-office
poison in New York City, very often sells out in the hinterlands
where runs are limited, critics harmless, and stars merely
celestial.

Musicals, however, are more mechanical in their contrivance. They depend to a large degree on technical know-how
and professional talent pools that cluster for economic warmth
in New York. Like prides of lions who stay their lives in and
around their birthsite, the musical community (composers,
librettists, lyricists, publishers, and the countless related groups
that comprise the creative and interpretive aggregate) does not
venture far afield from the Broadway scene. California has
seen some action due to the westward flight of musicians,
writers, directors, choreographers, actors, singers, and dancers
seeking possible employment seven months a year in the television industry. But despite this influx of talent, no musical piece
of any great distinction or consequence has emerged from the
West Coast, preferring, as it does, another revival of a standard
piece to an innovative and/or original work.

The playwright beginning a career need not leave his
hometown. He or she can write a play, submit it to the local
theatre group, see it produced, and learn from the experience.
University drama departments, theatre organizations affiliated
with universities, and regional theatres are often eager for new
material and greet with affection that which is less safe. What

Broadway dare not afford they can afford to dare. There is even a degree of personal promotion in the mounting of new, difficult plays and special imports that may attract the New York drama critics who, with a favorable review, focus national attention on an otherwise unknown theatre. When that happens, everyone has and eats his cake. Far from Broadway, working in what once were considered "salt mines," the director and actors have both their freedom and their fame.

But the composer, lyricist, and librettist are less fortunate. Each is forever in search of the other two to create a viable partnership, and each comes to New York to move among his own kind and to play a game whose playing fields have always been laid out on Broadway. On that street musicals have matured, like the ages of man, starting from their origins with *The Black Crook* (1866) and *A Trip To Chinatown* (1880s); proceeding through the fin de siècle period of English Savoy, French, and Viennese imports; then on to the youthful beginning of a pastiche expertly created by Victor Herbert from middle-European sources leavened with an emerging native statement. Representative of the succeeding era was Jerome Kern, whose *Girl from Utah* (1914) and Princess Theatre musicals introduced simpler but more credible plots studded with less eclectic and a more seminal American tonality at a time when Romberg and Friml were still profitably plowing operetta fields. The next phase combined the mindless adolescence of the librettos of the early twenties with ravishing scores by the Gershwins, Rodgers and Hart, Berlin, and Porter; then came the depression years, with the radical *The Cradle Will Rock* and the benign satire of *Of Thee I Sing, Let 'Em Eat Cake*, and *I'd Rather Be Right* balanced by the aristocratic Porter of *Anything Goes* and *Jubilee*; followed by the more mature sophistication of the same composer's *Kiss Me, Kate* and the regional celebrations of Rodgers and Hammerstein's *Oklahoma!* and *Carousel* and Loesser's *Guys and Dolls*, presaged two decades before by Kern's *Showboat* and Gershwin's magnum opus *Porgy and Bess*. The middle years of *My Fair Lady* and *West Side Story* have led inevitably to Sondheim's autumnal *Follies* and today's flirtations with the senility of mimetic revivals.

It is inarguable that musical theatre pieces of the excellence of *Company* and *A Little Night Music* are born in our marketplace, and they do recall and reaffirm the splendor of the past and of the genre itself, but the odds are against their auguring a future proliferation. High costs of production and touring stifle the producer's desire to innovate. Even the most conservative race becomes hazardous to run. Entrants check in expensively and, should they fail, check out even more dearly. With each failure unconscious restraints affect the writer and composer, restraints that may possibly proscribe material they would otherwise have elected to treat for the musical stage. The implicit recognition that there is a certain safety in adaptations of such proven properties as plays and films reduces the gamble but unfortunately narrows the cut of the swath.

In recent years musicals have been, on occasion, produced away from New York, but they are advertised as "Broadway-bound" as if any other destination would imply a less significant product. They boast, more often than not, a heavy box-office name, and may even recoup their enormous costs before arriving in New York. Produced wisely and well, road showing can realize large profits and result in a lucrative Broadway run, but the journey is arduous and, like spawning salmon, many do not make it. It must be added that these productions are seldom concerned with originality of concept and execution. They may present to road audiences stars of great appeal, but few "name" performers can guarantee the giant ticket sales that would justify their huge salaries. Fewer still are willing to commit themselves to the harshness of touring, the aesthetic friction created by the need to play in houses that seat three, four, and even twelve thousand people, and, finally, to the long-term contracts producers demand, a priori, before they can consider the package.

The road was appreciably swelled in the late sixties by the arrival of the rock musical. *Hair,* first produced Off-Off-Broadway, shifted to the Broadway stage and sired a minor spate of lucrative national companies. *Jesus Christ, Superstar* and *Godspell* similarly reprised themselves, and with phenomenal success. In the case of *Hair,* productions were birthed that were less national than municipal. Los Angeles, San Francisco, Chicago, Philadelphia, and Detroit all hosted their own versions of the piece in an open-end arrangement not synonymous with touring companies as generally defined. *Godspell* road showed and one of its companies barnstormed with one-nighters, a throwback to the twenties, when operettas traveled the country with awesome durability.

Statistically, then, there is an irony here. While fewer new musicals are produced on Broadway, the road survives from year to year with no significant waning. Rock musicals have acted as a stimulus but, even as this is written, one can detect the signs of approaching decline.

The slow grinding down of distinctive product has resulted in an inevitable loss of creative and interpretive talent. With the exception of Stephen Sondheim (who writes with equal continuum and success for the stage) and Burton Lane, Jerry Bock and Sheldon Harnick, Frederick Loewe, Alan Jay Lerner, John Kander and Fred Ebb, Cy Coleman, and a scant few others, America listens to theatre music out of the past. Apart from contemporary and folk-rock material, singers continue to record and/or perform "standards," decking them out in new sounds and accompaniment.

The musical theatre gave birth to, defined, and molded artists as unique as Astaire, Merman, Lahr, Martin, Fields, the Howard and Marx Brothers, Clark, Benny, Allen, Lillie, Lawrence, Coward, Brice, Raye, Walker, and many more, but extraordinary talents like these cannot be replenished and replaced in an almost barren breeding ground. Standing in for them in most musicals produced successfully today are television and cinema stars, whose ability to sing, dance, or even act is subservient to their power to attract a curious public into the theatre. They are not in their natural element and comparisons with sui generis performers who spent their lives perfecting their work on the stage would be unfair.

All of this is profoundly depressing when one considers that musicals were once this country's most indigenously valuable theatre statement. Even with today's infertility, I doubt that London or the Continent can duplicate with as much invention of script, score, mise-en-scène, and conceptual direction our *Fiddler on the Roof, Gypsy, Company, A Funny Thing Happened on the Way to the Forum,* and *A Little Night Music.* Although this fabulous invalid who sings and dances may be ailing, it makes extravagant and unique statements.

The continuing decrease in the number of musicals specifically written for the stage has not, however, reduced the hordes of young people eager to enter the profession. A persistent interest in the crafts of singing and dancing finds the actor and the dancer studying with a voice teacher and/or coach and, for reasons of survival, the singer and the dancer invading professional acting classes. This irony of supply exceeding demand is not entirely the result of a simple imbalance between product and labor force. In the last thirty years there has been a growing need for the performer to leave the exclusivity of one work area and to consider the wisdom of gaining other proficiencies if he or she intends to survive in an ever-shrinking marketplace. In just one generation it is now manifest that no one today can hope for consistent employment unless he widens his range of technical ability, at least enough to *pass* in two out of the three angles in the actor-singer-dancer triangle.

Up to and into the early forties the segregation between a "legit" and a "musical" career was total. In the late thirties, when I first dreamed of making my way in musical comedy,[1] it was a light year apart from its other half, and fraternization was almost unknown. I do not ever recall meeting an actor professionally, and on the rare occasion when we met socially there was a benign disdain implicit in the greeting, the actor holding the opinion that he was considerably higher up the achievement ladder than the hoofer, the belter, the comic, and the denizens of Shubert operetta country. As in all class societies, there was a pecking order on both sides of the line. At the top was the "serious" actor intent upon the classic theatre as his goal. Following him was the less weighty and less honored player appearing in the then-current light comedies, although there was a hierarchy even within this sector, with a Coward, Behrman, or Barry play adding considerably more tone to one's dossier than a *Dear Ruth, Time Out for Ginger,* or *John Loves Mary.* The penultimate position was held by the radio actor, whose technique was regarded as shallow and concerned with verbal facility. In the last position was the presumptively skill-less movie actor.

On the musical front, despite similar grading, there was then, and I think there still is, more democracy and respect among performers. Singers and dancers applaud good work more readily because it is more immediately measurable. But viewed as parts of a whole, even leading entertainers were never thought of as actors. Merman sang, Astaire danced, Lahr clowned. A star of note was referred to as a "comedian" or a "comedienne" (remember, it was musical *comedy* then), without the specificity the French bring to those words. Below them, but still musical-oriented, were the gypsies (or professional chorus performers), who are still a distinct tribe today, although this endangered breed is shuffling off like the buffalo.

But always there was this separation between the actor and the musical performer. (An apparent exception like Walter Huston appeared successfully in the Weill-Anderson *Knickerbocker Holiday* [1938], but he had been a vaudevillian and could be considered, even then, a hybrid.) Has the intermingling among actors, singers, and dancers that began in the forties and continues with unflagging zeal erased the indulgent sense of superiority on the part of the one toward the other two? I think the answer must be "yes." One cannot mock what

---

[1] The more elegant moniker "musical theatre" was not heard until a few years later when, among other values, a somewhat self-conscious critical significance was attached to the work of Rodgers and Hammerstein, Weill, Bernstein, DeMille, and Robbins. Often what was meaningful replaced what was comic, and the new identification was less a pretension than a fact.

is so difficult to learn. No actor comes close to the kind of relentless labor basic to the dancer's training and the singer's ceaseless vocal exercising. But there lingers on the other side of the footlights an audience, a body of critics, and, more inexcusably, producers and directors who continue to patronize what is sung and danced. There are ticket buyers who will attend a trivial play rather than a musical of distinction; reviewers who lavishly overpraise actors of little or no ability who hobble through a musical, but reserve harsher judgments for the musical artist able and courageous enough to venture into a "legit" experience; and hirers who eschew the singer/dancer who can act with evident and equal ability but give employment to the actor who can barely sing or dance.

Examples of this provincial attitude abound and can be found even in the reviews of the Broadway critics. Lauren Bacall and Katharine Hepburn—two actresses of note, but with actually little singing and dancing talent—appeared, respectively, in the successful production of *Applause!* and the not-so-enduring *Coco.* One critic waxed of Miss Bacall: "She sings with all the misty beauty of an on-tune fog-horn; she never misses a note and although her voice is not pretty, it does have the true beauty [sic] of unforgettability." Of Miss Hepburn it was said: "Her singing voice is unique . . . a neat mixture of faith, love, and laryngitis; unforgettable, unbelievable, and delightful." With this in mind, I suggest listening critically to the singing in the albums of *Coco* and *Applause!* and evaluating the case for the contrary. On the other side of the fence, when musical-comedy star Gwen Verdon ventured into a nonmusical play, the uncompromising critic wrote: "The acting of the entire cast, including, I fear, Miss Verdon, was so indescribably bad that I do not intend to describe it." And finally, after famed comedienne and character actress Nancy Walker appeared in *The Cherry Orchard,* one reviewer responded that her "Charlotta sounded as appropriate as a Bronx taxi-driver in Mozart and got her laughs in precisely that fashion." It makes one wonder whether a severe case of amusia deafens the otherwise severe critic when he enters a theatre that houses a musical production.

These are the bleak facts, but there is also reason for optimism. Quite apart from the value to the actor/singer/dancer who stretches his technical range, a consequent advantage of desegregation devolves onto the writer, director, and choreographer. Today the creators of a musical can hope to find casts who are more protean and who will illuminate more sophisticated scripts and scores. Sondheim's *Company,* staged by Harold Prince and Michael Bennett, exemplifies this exquisite meshing of complicated elements. Richard Kiley in *Man of La Mancha*, Richard Burton in *Camelot*, Gwen Verdon in *Sweet Charity*, Barbara Harris in *On a Clear Day You Can See Forever*, Rex Harrison in *My Fair Lady*, Robert Preston in *The Music Man*, Alexis Smith in *Follies*, and Joel Grey in *Cabaret* represent a new and more multifaceted entertainer.

Performers like these have exposed an element increasingly present in the new show business: *study*. In the first three decades of the twentieth century the legitimate and musical comedy theatre, vaudeville, nightclubs, and burlesque all furnished rich working grounds for the young performer not only to hone and polish his skills, but with a living demonstration of an older generation evidencing the meaning of excellence, a standard that could be and distinctly was passed on. With the slow demise of product those methods of learning were denied the new arrival, and study took their place. I do not want to imply that study has not always been a part of the young artist's early years. Singers and dancers require instruction and actors have formed groups in which their craft could be sharpened. But study was not the sine qua non for a career. A safe assumption can even be made that consistent work in front of audiences created actors and entertainers of far greater skill than do multitudes of teachers in the acting emporia.

As study per se established itself as the sole available method of learning stage techniques, it splintered into many schools and became a thing of awesome complexity. Now the actor required not only an acting teacher but singing and dancing instructors as well. Singers already involved in serious vocal instruction sought out acting and dancing teachers who could help them to move and to project text. Dancers, by tradition the hardest workers of all, faced an even greater task. They would, of course, continue to dance, but they were also compelled to set aside the rigid language of the dance and to relearn more realistic physical expression and, further, to add the alien element of sound, spoken and sung, to their range.

Nor could anyone ignore the need for this all-inclusive training. Competition demanded it. Choruses that once required only beauty and an ability to tap dance or sing a "doo-wah doo-wah" vocal arrangement now were comprised of ballet dancers able enough to be included in major ballet companies (such as Herbert Ross, Janet Reed, and Tommy Rall, all of whom appeared in *Look, Ma, I'm Dancin'!* in 1948) and singers of brilliance and wide vocal range (the chorus of the 1952 Broadway revival of *Of Thee I Sing*, for which I was vocal arranger, included tenor James McCracken, who has since become the opera world's reigning Otello).

There is another factor contributing to the growing demand for study specifically concerned with the musical theatre: Scratch an actor and you will find a frustrated singer. It is a fascinating fact that most actors seem to nurse a dream of invading musicals. As their fields of possible employment alter from the theatre to television, remuneration moves in inverse ratio to the personal joy they derive from their work. Commercials, movies, and situation comedies are necessary for survival, but they are not such stuff as dreams are made on. Participation in the musical theatre can restore a "glamour" to the dream. It must also be remembered that success in a musical will generate by tenfold the notoriety and consequent career values the actor might achieve in even a hit play.

Most actors would be almost as pleased to appear in a musical as they would a play of Shakespeare's. Songs are soliloquies, and both forms of playwriting have similar horizontal and vertical elements. Also, mise-en-scène, design, costuming, music (both orchestral and vocal), and choreography all combine to achieve a heightened theatre condition. Musicals, as in the case of the plays of Shakespeare, belong preeminently on the stage.

The inevitable strain placed upon the small but expert teaching community in New York was not diminished by this added fact: Many "serious" teachers were unwilling to teach anyone not particularly gifted in the teacher's sphere of interest. The serious ballet instructor had neither the time nor the inclination to train actors and singers with little or no natural grace. And, in fact, the student was not seeking so stringent a technique, but one that would be of more limited and immediate use. Singing teachers, traditionally able to work only in private, had even less time to sell, and could not be blamed for preferring to instruct someone with a probable future in opera and concert halls.

However, the insatiable demand inevitably gave rise to a supply that could fulfill it. Today there are, for the hiring, singing teachers who coach and coaches who will add a dollop of vocal technique to an hour of "give me more on the word *love*"; there are acting teachers who will edit an actor's singing performance; and there are dance teachers who operate quasi-gymnasia where actors can keep in shape without the bother of learning a plié or a time-step. Indeed, the ascension of teachers of the performing arts has brought to some of them a certain cachet. The actor's biography in a playbill and in a resumé that once listed only work credits now informs the audience and the hirer of the names of those with whom he has studied.

I think too much is made of all this schooling. Young people seem to me to have added to the need to learn an illusion that study fills the void created by unemployment. In the race to "collect" teachers they study far too much, often far too long, and certainly far too expensively. Their zeal is so intense that it may even permit the preclusion of work unless the job is deemed, by them or their management or the current fashion, to be "advantageous."

Clearly I am not speaking here to the beginner. He should and must learn whatever he can of the techniques of his chosen craft, but one inevitable fact cannot be denied: One teacher's concept of "how to" can be and often is in opposition to another school of thought. Because the buyer is seeking a credo, he must beware that a "how to" here and a "how to" there can, in rival establishments, be more a "how *really* to" or, worse, a "how not to." The instructor's efficiency score is another modifying qualification. One student may understand a teacher's explication of an interior thought/emotion process while another student may not. But when the student and teacher are compatible and the student acquires the technique (the means) to "do" (the ends), it is time to bid that instructor and further study of the subject goodbye. Flitting from this studio to that, from this singing teacher to that one, and from this dance class to another in the misdirected conceit that this accretion of information broadens and further molds one's talents is a fanciful error. I except the "workshop" from this notion of diminished returns from further study. From my observation of its function it furnishes a hall in which a body of professionals, chosen by an elected slate of officers, performs plays, scenes, and exercises. That is the workshop's function. In actuality it can be educative, but the experience is proctored, not tutored, by peers.

Let me attempt further to define this somewhat unfashionable theory. When a beginner wants to learn how to do something, he searches for the teacher who teaches it, and from the start their roles are clearly defined. When that student has learned to perform that which he originally asked of the teacher, those roles become blurred. No longer is he asking "how to" do something, but rather what the teacher *thinks* of his *performance* of it. Such judgments, necessarily subjective, are dangerous in both the creative and interpretive arts and must be kept to a minimum. Their importance is undeniable when the artist lends a reluctant ear to what the hirer, the agent, and the audience may think, because their opinions influence and inevitably govern his career. But those judgments, set apart from the mercantile laws of buying and selling, are often no more valid than the teacher's appraisal.

Finally, the artist is his own most severe critic; it is his burden and his anguish. Is one ever good enough? What could have made my performance better? What could have been done to make it the best? In any learning process Oscar Hammerstein's "There's a hill beyond a hill beyond a hill beyond a hill. . ." obtains. How to perform is mastered throughout a lifetime. It begins with the help of a teacher but must take its leave of the studio atmosphere, no matter how sophisticated a verisimilitude of the marketplace it may be, and move out and into a work situation.

I am reminded of a story, possibly apocryphal, told about the late Ivor Novello, master of English operetta. Throughout the years, during auditions for each of his shows, a woman would appear among the many aspirants to sing for him. She was inept but rejection never discouraged her; with every new production, there she was again, older but no better. At last, after yet another appalling audition, out of pity and a grudging regard for her persistence, he instructed his stage manager to inform the by now old woman that there was a job for her in his new musical. Upon hearing the news, however, she refused the offer and confessed that she only liked to audition, wanted nothing more, thanked them all, and left the theatre.

Yes, we may study in order to achieve work, but it is only through work, whether with good, indifferent, or even bad actors and directors, before good, indifferent, and often disinterested audiences, that we learn to assess ourselves. Of urgent importance is attending performances and ceaselessly attempting to measure the work you witness. Listen, reject, and even borrow from those you esteem. From Tyrone Guthrie: "No art is completely original. We all learn, borrow, steal, if you like, from another. But if this is theft, then all are thieves who have the wit to profit from another's experience."

George Kaufman once said to me that he did not believe anyone could learn anything about the doing of something in our profession, and when I confessed that I was learning a great deal from working with him, he suggested that I was only learning what *not* to do, which was something quite different. (For resolution of this claimed conviction, see chapter 17.)

An artist's credo belongs to his late years, or made lapidary after his death. Much of this handbook is devoted to seeking to define the undefinable. It offers only a possible device to make less discomforting the terror the actor and the dancer endure when they must sing what they have to say, a device molded through many years and filtered down and texturized by those who have worked with it. For the singer it may reprise what he knows already. If the reader is not a beginner, discard what has no value for you. Substantively, it is meant to be read by knowledgeable actors who are beginning a flirtation with the musical theatre. Whenever I can use a term more comprehensible to the actor than to the singer, I shall use it.

There are three divisions in my classes that separate the work each actor accomplishes in my studio: The First and Second Classes, each about eight weeks long, are concerned with the techniques outlined in the Contents. The Third Class, a watershed that all actors filter into, is concerned solely with performance. How long the individual remains in that class is determined by personal work methods, attendance record (one never knows when a part may come up), and, of course, that elusive element—talent.

I want to affirm my gratitude to all the actors, dancers, and singers with whom I have worked. It is thirty years since I began to attempt a definition of what singing is about for those who had never interpreted anything but spoken text. Since this work has generally been shared with artists well into their careers, I have been fortunate to have taught some of our best American actors. The caliber of a teacher's performance is mirrored by the quality of his students. The high standards achieved and maintained in my studio are the result of their skills and talents. I am in their debt.

On Singing Onstage

Introduction

Although the actor is the primary target for whom this book is intended, its tenets are equally applicable to a wider range of readers. I have taught many dancers and singers and, if they have had some acting experience and/or training, there is much here that can be helpful. I think, however, the actor is uppermost in my mind because he has, through the years, been responsible for the particular path my classes have taken. His questions provoked the answers. Had the class been peopled more with singers it would have resulted in something quite different—perhaps as valid but, nevertheless, different.

As for the dancer, I am happiest when I am fortunate enough to be working with one who has acted and sung before we meet. Of all the citizens in our business none is so serious and uncompromising a worker. No actor or singer defines labor with such relentless and un-self-conscious dedication. But the singer and the dancer live in a world where music is not a bugaboo. They are not threatened by its mystery, since it is a major element of what their art interprets and illuminates.

The actor's musical innocence is what impels me to single him out both in the text and burden of this volume. A knowledge of music, with its sublime but compelling tyranny, is *not* required background for the reader. *The text of the song is everything.* If you can hear pitch and rhythm this book is for you. My intention is to help transform the actor into an actor/singer without robbing him of what he knows he knows.

Whenever the need for example or assignment requires a lyric or a song, I have chosen material written for the theatre. This, in itself, does not require justification, but the reason for the choice is elementary. There is no *either-or* in electing a particular song the actor/singer will use for an audition. The stage requires vocal sound, a lyric with some degree of urbanity, and the diction needed to articulate it. The song is a "costume" designed to advertise the appearance and the talent of the performer.

Either it does this or it doesn't. If it doesn't, a better choice must be made, and always one is faced with the same supply source: the theatre. No matter the extent of one's affection for the rock scene, this music is not intended for the stage but for the record buyer. Mainstream songs are written for voices with no vocal training and with words one is more likely to hear up-country than downstage. Their accompaniments on record may be masterpieces of aural splendor but, shorn of them, the songs betray a melodic-harmonic inanity. As audition material they are valueless. Although they may possess a strong dramatic statement, they do not present the wide range the hirer needs to hear for determining the performer's vocal gamut.

A most important motive for staying with show tunes, in both my classes and in this book, is that, though dated, they remain published and therefore available. The reader and the student can obtain copies of theatre songs in sheet music and collections. The rock, pop-rock, punk-rock, country-western, and soul music we hear on record may have a first printing but rarely will it receive the long life on paper that the show tune enjoys. However, in all cases where I employ lyrics to define technical work, a knowledge of the song is not necessary. Again, the actor is made more comfortable sailing the charted waters of *script*.

I do not pretend to be happy teaching material that lives in a strange time warp. Often the words of a show tune are inimical to social and sexist changes. On occasion I find a song that allows the performer to sing a "script" written by and for a contemporary. It may even offer sufficient vocal grist for the audition mill, and it will be worked in class. But the major supply source remains the tune that came into being during the first half of this century. This time warp is more disturbing to me than it is to the students, for they seem to be in the grip of an inexplicable nostalgia for theatre music. In 1975 I was invited to lecture at the Southwest Theatre Conference that convened in and around the University of Tulsa in Tulsa, Oklahoma. On my last evening there I witnessed a revue performed by the senior students of the University Drama Department that contained not one "now" song, and further stretched my incredulity by working quite creditably within the bailiwick of Noel Coward! In the summer of 1977 Ethel Merman appeared in the Hollywood Bowl before a sold-out house of nearly eighteen thousand, a large fraction of whom, being under the age of thirty-five, could not have been witness to her work in the theatre. She sang a program of songs written for her by Porter, Gershwin, Berlin, and others, some of which were from shows almost fifty years old but all of which received tumultuous ovations.

This yearning for yesterday's show tunes indicates not only the hollow left unfilled by rock music but also the paucity of *supply*, one that should augment the old with the newer sound. The extraordinary popularity of Stephen Sondheim's "Send in the Clowns" implies that the song found an across-the-board acceptance from both theatre audiences and the record-buying public. The *demand* is still there. However, outrageous production costs that limit the number of musicals do not provide a favorable environment for new work. What seem to be called for are new techniques of production that eliminate or minimize the all-or-nothing gamble that nowadays must ride on a single show that can reach a cost of a million dollars. Joseph Papp's Public Theatre succored Michael Bennett's *A Chorus Line* in a workshop situation for over a year and, long before that, the minimusical *The Fantasticks* opened in a minitheatre Off-Broadway (at minimal cost). The latter, written by Harvey Schmidt and Tom Jones, opened in May of 1960 and still thrives in the same theatre. Perhaps the methods by which these shows were produced point the way to a renascence in the musical theatre. Until then, forward to yesterday.

In the technique sections I have included, contrary to their usual lineup, lists of *Don't's* and *Do's*. My purpose is this: What *not* to do defines margins beyond which error lies. Before the student attempts the ice, *don't's* are the red flags marking dangerous areas on the rink. Once those perimeters are drawn, *do's* fill the spaces they have defined.

Last, I caution the reader to remember that we are attempting to explain the inexplicable. Words and descriptions are necessities but not always clarifications. Michael Chehhov, in his volume *To The Actor,* offers this memo:

The abstruse nature of the subject [acting] requires not only concentrated reading, not alone clear understanding, but co-operation with the author. For that which could easily be made comprehensible by personal contact and demonstration, must of necessity depend on mere words and intellectual concepts. . . . Unfortunately, there is no other way to co-operate: the technique of acting can never be properly understood without practicing it.[1]

To this comforting caution I would add that "mere words" create rules with their own exceptions, and that these exceptions, in turn, have *their* own validity. But the charting must begin somewhere, I have chosen as a starting point that place of transition wherein the actor's text, the script of his play, becomes the actor/singer's lyric, which is the script of his song.

---

[1] From "Memo to the Reader" (New York: Harper & Row, 1953).

1 Techniques

Chapter 1

Words as Script

*As I understand it, some actors, perhaps most actors,
work on the theme first, on the idea first, on what
they are. I work on something else. I work on words,
nothing but words.*

Paul Muni

The actor who has begun to sing emerges for the first
apprehensive weeks during which he settled for survival and little else, and then, like a rocket clearing the
Van Allen belt, eases off and expends his energy on an
assessment of the scene. His first complaint concerns the
narrow and banal subject matter he sings about in a
familiar blizzard of words and titles that seem to blend
together. For instance, the anguished chagrin of "I Love
Her (Him) but She (He) Doesn't Love Me," "He (She) Loves
Me but I Don't Love Him (Her)," or "Why Doesn't
Anybody Love Me?" is balanced off, in placating an-
tipodes, with the blithe promise of "What a Day this Has
Been but Tomorrow Will Be Lovelier on that Great Come-
and-Get-It Day When You Can See Forever and All Your
Fords Will be Buicks Mañana."
And then there is love, requited and un-; presumptive
pie-in-the-sky times; didactic instruction on how to be
happy (*Get Happy!*) for "You Only Have One Life to Live
so Why Not Sing All Your Blues Away because the Devil
Is Afraid of Music." An added suggestion is proferred, if

one can dance as well as sing, to "Pick Yourself Up,"
"Change Partners," and "Cheek to Cheek" do "The Con-
tinental," "The Piccolino," Ball the Jack, Conga, Tango,
Rhumba, Bossa Nova, Hustle, Slow Dance, Soft-Shoe,
Polka, Rock and/or Roll (hard and soft), do the one- or the
two-step in Top Hat, White Tie, and Tails, and, step by
step, Build a Stairway to Paradise. Or do you prefer to
raise your voice in praise of musical instruments? You
can sing of Pete's piccolo, Yuba's tuba, Joe's banjo ("The
Banjo that Man Joe Played"—Porter), Freddie's, Mischa's,
Jascha's, Toscha's, and Sacha's fiddle, or of your love of
the piano ("I love to stop right beside an upright or a high-
toned baby grand"—Berlin*), or of a "Happy Hunting
Horn" (Rodgers and Hart), slapping that Bass ("Slap
Away Your Trouble"—Gershwin), or tootling on the
"Ocarina" (Berlin), while you exhort someone to "Strike
Up the Band" (Gershwin) and "Beat Out Dat Rhythm on a
Drum" (Hammerstein).

Do you have the blues? You can have them redun-
dantly in St. Louis, Memphis, Kansas City, on Basin
Street, Beale Street, or even on the Blue Danube ("When
the band is playing the song that keeps them swaying, the
Blue Danube Blues"—Anne Caldwell), as well as in the
night, "In the Wee Small Hours of the Morning,"
specifically even at a quarter to three, on a "Lazy After-
noon," "In the Blue of Evening," or "When the sun comes
out and the rain stops beating on your windowpane" in
all that "Stormy Weather" (both by Arlen).

Tautological paeans can be directed toward the likes
of Alice, Amy, Amanda, Angela, Angelina, Bedelia ("I
want to steal ya"), Caroline, Carolina, Cecelia, Chloe,
Cinderella ("Here's a Kiss for . . ."), Circe ("Who
showed men no mercy"), Cornelia, Dina, Diana,
Dorothea, Edith ("She possessed what every man
needeth"), Fedora, Frankie, Fred ("I'm in love with a girl
named . . ."), Gertie, La Gioconda, Hannah, Irma
("She's heaven on terra firma"), Isabella, Jennie, Lana,
Laura, a Lady (unnamed from Spain), Lina, Liza, Lisa,
Shanghai Lil, Lili Marlene, Lou, Louise, and Louisa, Lor-
raine, Lucy, Lucretia, Lydia (the tattooed lady), Mary,

---

* "I Love a Piano," music and lyrics by Irving Berlin, from *Stop! Look! Listen!* (1915).
Copyright © 1915 Irving Berlin. Copyright © renewed Irving Berlin. Reprinted by permission of Irving Berlin Music Corporation.

Marie, Maria and Marietta, Margot, Marcella, Melinda, Momo, Nancy (". . . with the Laughing Face"), Nina (". . . from Argentina") and Niña ("I'll be having Neurasthenia till I make ya mine!"), Olivia, Ophelia, Peg, Psyche (along with "Venus and Cleo, her melodies are in my key"), Rebecca, Rose, Rosie and Rosabella, Ruby, Rita ("Nothing sweeta!"), Roxanne, Sadie, Sappho, Stella, Sylvia ("Who is she?"), Sue, Venetia, Virginia (". . . the devil's in ya!"), Mrs. Worthington and her daughter (name withheld), Miss Otis, and finally, in package deals, the Sabines ("Them Sobbin' Women") and the Lorelei.

The list of men is less adulative. Women sing of their beastliness ("Jim never ever sends me pretty flowers"); their flaws ("Bill," whose "Form and face are not the kind that you would find in a statue"); their hopeless enslavement to them ("Won't you turn that new leaf over so your baby can be your slave, oh, Why Can't You Behave?"); their mastery over them ("Dinner for one, please, James"); their anonymity ("Tom, Dick, or Harry" and a nameless Lamplighter); their incompetency ("Sam you made the pants too long!"); their heartlessness ("Most gentlemen don't like love—They just like to kick it around!"); their faithlessness ("Frankie and Johnny"); their passion for roaming ("Come Home, Joe, Come Home") or the succinct wrap-up ("The Gentleman Is a Dope!").

Some degree of admiration is conferred on "Bojangles," both "of Harlem" and the jailbird philosopher; political hyperbole is lavished on all presidential candidates in a frenzy of partisan fiction, but those words are heard only quadrennially. Royalty is sometimes sung about either biographically ("Solomon," "Napoleon," Anne Boleyn "With 'er 'ead tucked underneath 'er arm," and "Dubarry") or autobiographically (by Good Queen Bess—"I'm Elizabeth the Virgin Queen, don't laugh!"); and by the Duke of Plaza Toro, the Mikado himself, the Sheik of Araby, and a Vagabond King; a lyric may even find a lady boasting of her amours with the Baron de Signac, the Duke of Ferrara, and the King of the Belgians, but the list is nowhere near as long or affectionate as the male's praise of the opposite gender. The imbalance may be a seminal indication of women's latterday emergence and a declaration of their own bill of rights.

Further, you can sing of your fondness for New York, Oklahoma, Tennessee, Carolina, Californi-ay, Texas, Missouri, Hawaii, Georgia, Lousiana (both of its Purchase and the Hayrides therein), Maine (". . . is the main thing"), Vermont, Rhode Island (". . . is famous for you!"), Iowa ("Oh, I know all I owe dear old Iowa!"), Connecticut, and Mississippi ("M . . I . . S . . S . . I . . S . . S . . I . . P . . P . . I"). In all these songs, though the title changes, the burden of the lyric remains the same.

Narrowing *that* down, there are lyrics to extol New York, New York ("The Bronx is up and the Battery's down"), its East Side and its West Side, Broadway ("Give My Regards to . . ."), Herald Square ("Remember me to . . ."), Forty-second Street, Fifth Avenue (on which "The photographers will snap us"), the Bowery, New Rochelle ("I met my mademoiselle in . . ."), Yonkers (". . . Where true love conquers in the wilds") and further East, West, and South: Chicago ("My kind of town, Chicago is . . ."), Hollywood ("Hooray for . . ."), Miami ("Moon over . . ."), New Orleans, Paris ("April in . . ."), London, Rome, Naples, Capri (" 'Twas on the Isle of . . ."), Venice, Rio de Janeiro ("Flying Down to . . ."), Ipanema, Manakura ("The Moon of . . ."), Kialakakoo ("I want to go back to my little grass shack in . . ."), and a region just "South of the Border down Mexico Way."

The list of names of people and places is considerably longer. However, the point is this: even maximum length does not alter the minimum of variety. The actor, then, is justified in his complaint about existing show music. Early in their careers a distinct and unmistakable revelation occurs to all those who sing: They have sung it all before.

The contemporary lyric scene, though less rigid in its meter and rhyme, appears no more rich in subject matter. The emergence of the woman lyricist, writing from the inside, so to speak, can slant the need to love and/or be loved toward the less abject subject of aloneness, a state of being endured by both men and women. When this broader base is applied to the old Tin Pan Alley tenets, one can see how far we have come in banishing the sexist handicaps placed on women in the sung battle of the sexes (see chapter 7). This genre is not as commonplace as the times permit: recidivism exists even in the marketplace of popular song. However, here is a stunning example of the best of the new look—Dory Previn's "The Lady with the Braid":

Would you care to stay till sunrise?
It's completely your decision:
It's just that goin' home is such a ride,
    such a ride.
Goin' home is such a ride
Goin' home is such a ride
Isn't goin' home a lo-lonely ride?
Would you hang your denim jacket
Near the poster by Picasso?
Do you sleep on the left side or the right?
    or the right?
Would you mind if I leave on the light?
Would you mind if it isn't too bright?
Now, I need the window open
So, if you happen to get chilly
There's this coverlet my cousin hand-crocheted—
    hand-crocheted:
Do you mind if the edges are frayed?
Would you like to unfasten my braid?
Now, I'll make you, in the mornin'
A cup of homemade coffee,
I will sweeten it with honey and with cream,
When you sleep, do you have dreams?
You can read the early paper
And I can watch you while you shave
Oh God! The mirror's cracked!
When you leave, will you come back?
You don't have to answer that at all
The bathroom door is just across the hall
You've got an extra towel on the rack
On the paisley-patterned-paper wall
There's a comb on the shelf
I papered that wall myself . . .
    that wall myself . . .
Would you care to stay till sunrise?
Now it's completely your decision:
It's just the night cuts through me like a knife,
    Like a knife . . .
Would you care to stay awhile and save my life?
Would you care to stay awhile and save my life?
I don't know what made me say that

I've got this funny sense of humor
You know I could not be down-hearted if I tried,
    if I tried . . .
It's just that goin' home is such a ride.
Goin' home is such a ride
Goin' home is such a ride
Isn't goin' home a lo-lonely ride?
Isn't goin' home a lo-lonely ride?
Isn't goin' home a lo-lonely ride?

Work songs, back- and up-country songs, and protest songs abound today, but Dylan's pen is far less mighty than Brecht's. Artless melodies and innocent harmonic changes lean heavily on electronic accompaniment and heightened rhythmic superstructures to achieve their effects. Bereft of this decibel count, their value simply as songs to be sung on a stage is often negligible. Vocal sophistication would be, in fact, in opposition to the songs' intent. Auditioning them in the theatre with only the aid of a piano would be their betrayal.

The French chanson is somehow more substantial than the American and English popular song. I remember hearing a song about a gorilla who escaped from the town zoo after years of incarceration (Georges Brassens' "La Gorille"). Denied any sexual gratification behind bars, he sets about to resolve his hunger by chasing after the townfolk, who, in turn, are running for their lives. The lyric sang of the ape's effort to catch one of the two slowest runners, an old spinster and the town mayor. Because of the obvious political comment implicit you may well guess who came in last. Piaf sang the same heartbreakers Helen Morgan favored before her, but here again the words and the song-handles, although still pivoting on rejection, are more valuable to the actor than to the singer. "L'Accordioniste," "Les Cloches," "Les Blouses Blanches" all come to mind. And it is no accident that Jacques Brel, alive in Paris, is doing so well in America. His songs, performed by actor/singers, are original and contain enormous emotional and dramatic impact.

For the actor accustomed to the multiplicity of plays published and available to him for study work, there is considerably less variety of subject matter, style, and range on call when he begins to "sing" his words. When Tin Pan Alley and the musical theatre were intimate bedfellows, songs by theatre composers enjoyed great popularity. Thirty, forty, and even fifty years ago, what Broadway was singing soon could be heard nationally and even internationally. Recordings (both vocal and instrumental), vaudeville, nightclubs, and dance bands brought national renown to the names and work of Herbert, Kern, Berlin, the Gershwins, Rodgers, Porter, and many others. Today musical scores do not enjoy anything like that kind of popularity. The recording industry is busy elsewhere, with a product for a younger record buyer, and show albums of Broadway successes are rarely, if ever, plugged. Only musicals that have an extraordinary triumph on Broadway, tour extensively, and are ultimately filmed and seen internationally can hope to receive the mass play once lavished on all scores written for the New York stage. *My Fair Lady, West Side Story,* and *The Sound of Music,* to name but a few, are in this category, and although their scores are vastly successful, I wonder how many listeners can tell you who wrote them.

CATEGORIES OF LYRICS

When an actor "reads" for a play he is given scenes the director has extracted from the manuscript. The actor is able to give himself an objective and to play the scene intelligibly because he has scanned the scene or, given more time, studied the whole play in order to comprehend its parts. When a lyric is sung out of context at an audition or, for that matter, anywhere, any choice the actor makes is valid if it works and the song lives. However, no one wants to be told "Do it any way you care to." Let me try to narrow this realm of choice to infinity minus four.

All lyrics can be categorized, essentially, into four groupings: the subjective, the objective, the narrative, and the instructive.

Subjective

Here, as an example, are the words of Oscar Hammerstein:

Why was I born? Why am I living?
What do I get? What am I giving?
Why do I want a thing I daren't hope for?
What can I hope for?
I wish I knew.
Why do I try to draw you near me?
Why do I cry? You never hear me
I'm a poor fool but what can I do?
Why was I born to love you?

I readily admit to card stacking, but only to make the point obvious to the eye. Underlining the first person singular pronoun wherever it appears emphasizes its prevalence, which, in this lyric, connotes an almost neurotic self-concern. The lyric is further weakened by questions that remain rhetorical until the last line. The performer is denied even the motive of puzzlement—it seems she *knew why* all along. *One dare not sing a subjective lyric subjectively.* The actor/singer must allow her mouth to speak (sing) the words while she runs ahead with all available equipment to *objectivize* the text, since the audience, deprived of a demanded involvement, will all too willingly surrender to disinterest. Attention must be paid, the wail and the whine traded in for wit, self-humor, and maintaining cool, and the audience (the "you") made to *care* why she (the "I") was born.

Today the image of the maudlin, gin-soaked chanteuse is as demoded as the black-faced minstrel and, for a time, heavily subjective material went out of style. But the heartbroken archetype has not disappeared, only put away her bottle. She lingers among us, sober but no less self-oriented (see Previn's "The Girl with the Braid".) The red flag is still up on the rink. Skaters, beware.

Objective

The most famous of the genre (perhaps worded a little unfamiliarly), from the pen of Cole Porter:

You're the top, <u>you're</u> the breasts of Venus
You're the top, <u>you're</u> King Kong's penis
You're the torrid heat of a bedroom suite in use
You're a high colonic, a Pinkham tonic, <u>you're</u>
    self-abuse![1]

The integral word in objective lyrics is "you." In this example it appears like an organ point in each line. The trap here is that the "you" (the listener) receives all the attention while the "I" (the singer) is no more interesting than the bearer of any message, even one this amusing. Indeed, the actor can "phone it in" and achieve the same audience reaction. *Objective lyrics require all the SUB-JECTIVIZING the performer can invent to keep attention focused on him.* The audience will *hear* the words if they are clearly articulated. What they must *see* is the effect of the explicit "you" on the implicit "I." In this particular song the actor/singer inherits the full weight of Porter's wit and the majesty of his rhyming skill. The performer is not always this lucky. He may have wished for an elegant lyric, but one as striking as this one can do him in. To diminish the effect of Porter on the ear, one must magnify what meets the eye. In other words: fight back.

Narrative

A fool sat beneath an olive tree and a wondrous thought
    had he
So, he rose and he told it to the sky
And where was I? Behind the tree. I overheard his reverie.
"Why be content with an olive when you could have the tree?
Why be content to be nothing when there's nothing you
    couldn't be?
Why be contented with one olive tree when you could have a
    whole olive grove?
Why be content with a grove when you could have
    the world?"
The fool stood beneath the olive tree,
"What a wondrous thought!," said he, "but alas, it is very
    very deep."

---

[1] This scatalogical version has been credited to Cole Porter. I have no reason to doubt the master's touch. The song has seven (!) respectable published choruses. In "You're the Top," music and lyrics by Cole Porter, from *Anything Goes* (1934).

And then he yawned and went to sleep,
Because, you see, he was a fool.

Like the subjective lyric, with which it has much in common, the narrative song once enjoyed great popularity. "The Babbitt and the Bromide," "Tess' Torch Song," Loesser's setting for Hans Christian Andersen's "The Ugly Duckling," "The Emperor's Clothes," and "Frankie and Johnnie" all come to mind. Contemporary music has revived the form and brought it new success: "Taxi," "Bojangles,""Ode to Billy Joe," and much of John Prine's work. Narratives sung, unfortunately, are no different from narratives spoken. They require one helluva storyteller. Despite protests to the contrary, no one really wants to *hear* a tale. The best way to put a child to sleep is to *tell* him a story. Sit him in a chair, *act* it out, allow him to *see* the story, and you have your audience in the preferred state: wide awake. When the Caliph in *Kismet* threatens to amputate the hands of Hajj the Beggar, the beleagured poet sings "Gesticulate." As a professional storyteller whose livelihood depends upon his skill, he knows such brutal punishment will place him not only *hors de combat* but on welfare.

Since narrative songs by their peculiar nature are only for the exceptional performer, one must be adroit enough to be both *narrator* and what one *is narrating* to get any mileage out of them. A physical style, a certain grace, and a deft wit are essentials. The late Noel Coward, Danny Kaye and Jacques Brel himself have made beautiful moments with these particular talents. In the theatre the narrative song often has appeared in revues, shows with no connecting plot but merely consisting of an unrelated series of songs, dances, and sketches. It was begun by a singer standing downstage left or right but, as a safety factor, the curtains soon parted to reveal the choreographer's version of the tale. As audition material I would give this sort of lyric wide berth. The corps de ballet that should be upstage of you represents a large part of the action.

Instructive

> I say to me every morning,
> "You've only one life to live
> So why be done in? Let's let the sun in,
> And gloom can jump in the riv.
> No use to beat on the doldrums
> Let's be imaginative
> Each day is numbered, no good when slumbered
> With only one life to live.
> Why let the goblins upset you?
> One smile and see how they run,
> And what does worrying net you?
> Nothing! The thing is to have fun!
> All this may sound kind of hackneyed
> But it's the best I can give.
> Soon comes December, so please remember
> You've only one life to live.
> Just one life to live!"

By far the most tedious to attend, and not much less so to perform, is the instructive lyric. The domain of the sermon is the pulpit where those present can reject or accept the counsel. "How to" dicta (even this volume) belong on bookshelves, where the reader reserves the right to buy them or pass them by. When sermons are sung the moral tone creates a distance between the stage and the audience that only performers of great charm and persuasion can erase. If the words possess a degree of self-criticism and wit the song is more palatable, of course, but when these elements are absent the actor/ singer must create them or he appears arrogant and didactic. (It is interesting to note that Ira Gershwin's "One Life to Live" is performed by the leading lady, quite literally, on a soapbox.) Speaking only for myself, I prefer to stay away from this kind of lyric. Songs such as the harmless "Put on a Happy Face," the self-righteous "Carefully Taught," the rhapsodic "Make Someone Happy," or the pseudoreligious "You'll Never Walk Alone" are first rate—when it is the next man singing them, and not me.

A subcategory of the instructive lyric that I equally do not recommend for audition purposes is the one of defiant threat or promise. I shall refrain from offering a complete chorus, for each title is self-explicative: "Don't Rain on my Parade," "I'm the Greatest Star," and "You're Gonna Hear from Me!" If sing them you must, be sure you have been heard from already, and with approval and affection.

SHEET MUSIC

The script of a song is obtainable in its published form, paired with its melody, and commonly referred to as *sheet music* (see chapter 2). Once you are in possession of the sheet music, it is always wise to write the lyric down, apart from its musical line and time signature (see chapter 3, under "From Lyric"). Now you can see it without its covering. For the actor/singer intent upon performing the song, this act permits a first discovery of what the words say, what they may mean (see chapter 12), rhyme structures, and the particular verticality—as opposed to the horizontal nature of dialogue—of the soliloquy.[2]

The lyric often, but not always, is composed of a Verse followed by a Chorus. The latter may be referred to as the Refrain, and it is broken down into arbitrary divisions called "8's," described in chapter 2.

Some random thoughts on the words you read printed in the sheet music you buy:

1 Unlike the book-publishing business, which now furnishes readers with material no longer smuggled through customs, sheet music still is bowdlerized. "Hell" becomes "h—," Hart's "Couldn't sleep, and wouldn't sleep, until I could sleep where I shouldn't sleep" becomes "Couldn't sleep, and wouldn't sleep, when love came and told me I shouldn't sleep."

God, thusly named, is "out" but "the gods" are "in,"

---

[2] Dialogue, as it moves the story ahead and delineates character, can be said to perform its function on a horizontal plane. A soliloquy (in Elizabethan drama, Moliére, opera, and song) stops the horizontal movement and states its case vertically. In all cases it is most effective when its function is to reveal how the character feels about what has just happened and what *may* happen by virtue of the revelation; ideally, it should not be heard by anyone but the audience.

sometimes to the destruction of an internal rhyme, as in the case of Sondheim's:

Do I hear a waltz?
Very odd, but I hear a waltz
There isn't a band and I don't understand it at all!
I don't hear a waltz,
Oh my God, there it goes again . . .

The published sheet music replaces the final line with "Oh my lord, there it goes again," which is cutting the name of the deity with a fine-tooth comb. I imagine all this was meant to keep sheet music a family affair that allowed mother, father, the kiddies, and Aunt Polly to stand at the piano and play and sing without distraction. Should the actor correct it? Yes.

2 Be prepared, when shopping for a particular song, to be told by your local music-store proprietor that it is either not published or out of print. A first printing of a few songs from a new musical is standard procedure. Unless a song "takes off" and becomes enormously popular, rarely is there a second printing. A recent innovation in music publishing has been selections of songs from a score in one binding, and you may have to buy them all to get the one you want. Secondhand music stores are alternative caches of published music difficult to find elsewhere, or you can write to the publisher and request a copy of a song not on the shelf of your neighborhood music shop. You can, in extremis, copy the lyric from the show album as it is being sung and have a musical friend write a lead sheet (the melodic line and the basic chords that go with it) for you, but it is important to remember that you may *not*, without permission of the publisher, *perform the song professionally* if you have come by it in this manner because it is *not* published. This permission is also required if you have rewritten the lyric by parodying or tampering with it in any way.

3 Should you learn the Verse? Yes, by all means. If

you are auditioning for a "white contract" role (as a principal, distinguished from the pink contract signed by members of the chorus), I know of no director who will request that you sing just the Chorus. This suggestion is often heard at auditions for the singing chorus, where time is short and the writers and musical director are more interested in voice and vocal range. When I held auditions for a choral ensemble I often asked for a scale to be sung, and the last "8" (explained in chapter 2) of the song brought in by the singer. I do not recall that being insufficient as a judgment of the singer for the job. However, when the book of a musical is being cast, the time allotted to each actor/singer on the day's schedule of auditions should be sufficient to allow for the singing of both the Verse and the Chorus of a song.

Just as exposition in a play makes it possible for us to know the who, what, where, when, and why of a situation (without it we could not "take sides") before we are presented with the attack of the play, the Verse of a lyric gives the Chorus specificity. It affords a reference for the Refrain and diminishes the generality of the lyric when it is taken out of its context. It is important to remember that songs from theatre scores usually are written for a most particular reason, to develop the character and/or plot, to be sung by a particular character in a particular situation at a particular time and place. Removing a song from that placement leaves a "space" where once the scene gave the lyric credence and drama. If one considers the dialogue preceding the song as a steadily rising horizontal line moving inevitably toward the verticality of the song, its excision makes most difficult the singer's task of making the song rise. The Verse is an aid in pushing the Chorus up and over. (For further explanation see chapter 7, following "Exercise Two: The Vamp.")

However, exposition in a play or song (Verse), although necessary, is a necessary evil. Information is not dramatic. To *move it*, it is worth considering singing the Verse in *ad-lib* (an expression that signifies the *singing of words as scored melodically but out of tempo*). If you are puzzled about a proper ad-lib reading, *say* the line first, then *sing* it exactly as you have said it. A knowledgeable composer would be aware of this phrasing possibility and would score a Verse with a melody either simple enough to permit it or one specifically designed for it.[3] Inevitably one gains a certain grace in ad-lib singing. You learn to *move* a line of little interest or a repeat of one already said (sung) and slow down to give time and clarity to lines that must be heard because of their increased importance. Speaking the line first limits the inclination to pour out heart and voice on unimportant words (like "a," "an," "and," "then," and so on) that happen to fall on notes the singer loves to sing.

4   The illusion must be that a song is created line by line by the performer while it is being sung and, in fact, that it never existed until that moment when, proceeding *from* moment *to* moment, the singer creates a statement large enough to sing instead of to speak. If there are words in the lyric you do not understand, look them up, learn their meaning, and perfect their pronunciation. It is, after all, *your* choice of language.

ANALYSIS OF A LYRIC

The following lyric is written by Lorenz Hart. Let us analyze it as a script we might sing:

VERSE   A, B, C, D, E, F, G, I never learned to spell, at least not well.
1, 2, 3, 4, 5, 6, 7, I never learned to count a great amount.
But my busy mind is burning to use what learning I've got.
I won't waste any time,
I'll strike while the iron is hot:

CHORUS   If they asked me I could write a book
About the way you walk, and whisper, and look.
I could write a preface on how we met
So the world would never forget.
And the simple secret of the plot
Is just to tell them that I love you a lot.
And the world discovers as my book ends
How to make two lovers of friends.

"I Could Write a Book," music and lyrics by Richard Rodgers and Lorenz Hart, from *Pal Joey* (1940). Copyright©1940 by Chappell & Co., Inc. Copyright renewed. International copyright secured. All rights reserved. Used by permission.

[3] Cole Porter's Verse for "Night and Day" achieves the monotone of the "Tick tick tock of the stately clock" while at the same time freeing the singer of an enslavement to the 4/4 time signature.

Like all well-written ballad lyrics when parted from their musical line, this one appears over-lean and un-complicated. Inhibit an inclination to judge it too harshly and remember that it is not poetry but light verse intend-ed to be sung (see chapter 3). In this case it is about "love," to be sure, but it shuns sentiment and a head-on verbalizing of the "I love you" statement by employing the novelist's terms of reference; although it is not stun-ningly original, it has consistent motion.

The Verse is pure exposition. Without it, the Chorus loses its point of reference. A writer confessing an ability to write a book announces only what is expected of him. In this case it is the Verse that informs. The man is not only *not* a writer, but undereducated as well. Additional information occurs in the last two lines of the Chorus, for only then do we learn the singer and the lady under discussion are, at present, "friends" but not yet "lovers." By saving this information until the last moment of the Chorus, there is a plot point that insures tension and in-terest through and until the end.

Because the Verse is expositional, we elect to sing it in ad-lib. I have said that speaking a line before you sing it gives you the sense of the language. You will find that some lines will be sung faster because they are less in-teresting, while others will be slower in delivery because of their importance. How fast is fast and how slow is slow? Howard Lindsay once described "speed" in the theatre in terms of interest rather than motion. All of us have endured a fast-paced farce that moves like a glacier through an endless evening. The *slowness* of the event is in no way affected by the rapid-fire delivery of the dialogue or all that running about. The play lacks interest and is therefore slow. Conversely, Harold Pinter's *The Homecoming* progresses in stately rhythms made even slower by stretches of silences, and yet we are enthralled. It moves with remarkable *speed*.

As we begin an ad-lib singing of the Verse of "I Could Write a Book," there is no reason not to move the first two lines with some degree of speed. Since we can assume our audience speaks the language we are speak-ing, our alphabet is theirs. We would not say "A . . . F . . . R . . . B . . L . . . T . . . W . . . H" or

"1 . . . 4 . . . 9 . . . 3 . . . 6 . . . 2 . . . 8,"
which might be interesting, but that is, of course, another
song. Warning: It is important to remember that your accompanist, whether he is a pianist, guitarist, or conductor
of the orchestra, also speaks the same language you do.
Capricious readings only make his job more troublesome,
since he has enough of a task *staying* with you when you
are scored in ad-lib.

The third line of the Verse begins with the ubiquitous
"But." If I were to list, in descending order of importance,
the words that theatre and contemporary lyricists call
upon most often, they would probably be: I, me, you,
love, dream, free, man (boy), girl (woman), and but. The
first eight words appear in Verses and Choruses alike, but
"but" in a Verse is almost as certain as death and taxes.
When it appears, small though it may be, the lyric starts
moving from first into second gear. The use of "but" to
shift gears, like the shift that impels a car's thrust, excites
the exposition to make its point, to stop dawdling with
generality and get on to what is specific. It follows, then,
that when the "but" appears the speed of your ad-lib
slows down, because you are about to say what is more
important to hear.

"I won't waste any time" can be quickened again.
The rule here is quite simple. A slow line achieves greater
importance when it is sandwiched between two faster
ones. In this case:

(FASTER)	1, 2, 3, 4, 5, 6, 7, I never learned to count a great amount
(SLOWER)	*But* my busy mind is burning to use what learning I've got
(FASTER)	I won't waste any time . . .

The last line of the Verse, "I'll strike while the iron is
hot," when followed by a Chorus to be sung *a tempo* (at
the designated rate of motion), should be broken in as
many places as possible without destroying sense. An effort must be made to keep the rhythm of the first line of
the Chorus from arriving too unexpectedly. As in the car
allusion, it is as though we must shift from overdrive to
third, second, first, and finally into neutral to keep the

vehicle from jerking when we stop. In telegram prose, then, the line reads something like this:

I won't waste any time [stop]
I'll strike [stop]
While the iron [stop] is hot [stop]:

> The stops are glottal stops and not acting beats (see chapter 3, under "The Glottal Stop"). The tempo arrives on the last word of the Verse, namely, "hot." The singing of the Chorus is straightforward, but should be phrased according to the examples in chapter 3.
> Three cautionary notes are in order.

1   "Walk and whisper and look": Each verb should be clearly articulated and spotlighted or the line sounds like the name of a brokerage firm.

2   "Book ends": A glottal stop is needed between the two words to distinguish them from brackets designed to hold up a row of books (see chapter 17, under "Bad English—Good Lyrics").

3   The penultimate word "of": You will probably want to go out of tempo in the next to the last bar of the Chorus, the bar that includes the words "Lovers of." Remember, you may take as long as you want to say anything when you are not in tempo if your talents are able to make silence meaningful, but once you have taken that silence after "How to make two lovers," get on with it. The orchestra is poised to go back into tempo on the word "friends." Lingering on the word "of" exposes you to the double jeopardy of senselessness and a muffed downbeat.

> The actor beginning to sing may consider music an enemy, but the words are his script and their illumination is paramount, no less than when he merely *speaks* them in a play. When he *sings* them, they should be his friend. Script is, after all, what he knows he knows.

Chapter 2

Music, the Other Script

Songs without words are best.

George DuMaurier

For the nonsinger just beginning to sing, music is an alien language. In the preceding chapter I discussed the words one sings. This initial task of dealing with words as lyrics (or poetry) was easier than lyrics sung with music for two reasons: First, the text is finally just text, and it is the actor's profession to negotiate with it. Second, the words are in English, and English is the language he speaks. But music, as in the case of any foreign tongue, possesses new symbols, styles of expression, and even a new "grammar." It is not my purpose here to dwell on musical theory, harmony, ear training, and sight singing. I am only concerned with the performance of that which is sung. I will try, therefore, to deal with what is relevant.

If we agree that music is a different language from the one we speak, it is an absorbing fact that, unlike other foreign languages, we hear it and are subjected to it, consciously and subconsciously, from babyhood on, every day of our lives. And although we may not speak it well, we all speak it with facility and even enjoy a fractional comprehension of it. No musicianship is required to identify a ballad, a lullaby, a blues, or an acid-rock instrumental, and most of us can limp our way through a duet with whomever we hear singing, on record, live or in a disco, or with our dancing partner. Nor do we require more than a moment to categorize any kind of music, vocal or instrumental, that we hear. This may not seem significant but I want to make the point that none of us, even the most abject beginner, is totally alien to the language of music when we first begin to sing.

It is also of interest to the actor/singer to learn that each composer "speaks" music with different accents, personal and distinctive, in much the same manner that playwrights do. The actor does not play Odets as he plays Sheridan, Shakespeare as he would Chekhov, or Pirandello as he would Neil Simon. His task, among many, is to duplicate the tonality of the play. It is no less so when he sings. Just as, in more serious (appalling word!) music, Mozart is not interpreted in the manner of Tschaikowsky, Chopin as Beethoven, or Stravinsky as Strauss, theatre-music composers leave their signatures on everything they write. Among the more "standard" composers, Gershwin, Rodgers (more with Hart than with Hammerstein), Porter (in his more playful moods), Berlin, early Lane, and Loesser wrote and write most often for performers rather than singers. The actor can feel comfortable singing their songs with a minimum of strain and overt display of vocal inadequacy. But Kern, Arlen, Loewe, Rodgers (in his operetta settings of some of Hammerstein's work), Bernstein, the more lavish Porter, Schwartz, and latter-day Lane are all distinctly more sumptuous melodists who require voices adequate enough to "sing" them as well as "play" them. This is, of course, a general observation. But if your singing is not of a high degree of musical splendor, pick up with care the work of these men. They are not the best friends of actors whose voices are not their calling cards.

In the work of the younger composers such as Bock, Kander, Coleman, Herman, and Sondheim, among others, you will always find material you can sing, but each of them may lean more heavily on an organic musical statement when the subject matter of the book for which they compose demands it. If they score a more "pop" sound, as in the case of Sondheim's *Company,* the less-than-musical singer is more able to sing the score, whereas the Sondheim of *A Little Night Music* may call for greater vocal resources. Again, discretion is protection. Your singing, as in the case of all foreign languages, absolutely identifies you as an abject beginner, a resident immigrant, or a native son.

The sheet music you buy contains both the music and the text of the song. The preceding chapter dealt with words. Here are some random thoughts on music.

1 It is important to know that the exact composition as set down by the composer is rarely rendered in the sheet music. Nor was it meant to be. It is a reduced version of the song, with its harmonies made uncomplicated enough for the least-equipped pianist to play. Unlike the music scored for voice by the more classic composers (such as the lieder of Hugo Wolf or Schubert or the chansons of Fauré, Debussy, or Poulenc), which is printed with the composer's specific intentions and is to be sung accordingly, learning a song from its sheet-music copy requires no such fidelity. You are using an instrumental rather than a vocal copy. Anything that will help to lard flesh back onto this flimsy skeleton is permissible. Short of outright alteration of the melody (though even that is considered only a venial sin), you are free to interpret the song in whatever manner you feel will best service the essential statement. The term "arrangement" is nothing but the personal signature of the arranger of the song.

2 The sheet music of the show tune is not only a simplification but often a truncation of the song as it is performed in the theatre. Verses and Interludes may be cut down or even edited out.

3 Key changes may be made that permit a song originally scored for a tenor or a soprano to be within the range of a baritone or a contralto. The melody remains the same no matter the key in which it is sung.

4 Time signatures and note values are often altered to give a less formidable look to the published version of the song.

Let us use the same song we employed when we spoke of words as a model of what you will find when you purchase sheet music: Rodgers and Hart's "I Could Write a Book." If you have no access to a copy of it there should still be no difficulty in understanding what I say.

All songs, this one included, begin with a few bars of music that possess no accompanying lyric. This is the *Vamp* or the *Intro* (Introduction). The terms are interchangeable. How many bars make an Intro? One, two, three, four, six, eight . . . as many as deemed needed, but two or four bars are generally what you will see. Sometimes the Vamp is the creation of the composer and can be considered an organic part of the song. But just as often it is a stale musical phrase invented by a nameless copyist and has no significance. Its only function is to herald, at its end, the arrival of the vocal beginning of the tune.

THE VAMP

Whether you use the Vamp printed on the sheet music or one created by you or your arranger, one thing is certain: You cannot live without it. Even though the Vamp has three basic functions, only one is considered essential to the singer. In descending order of importance they are:

1 The Vamp sets the key in which the song will be sung. Unless the singer has perfect pitch and can pick his starting note out of the air by *thinking* it, there are eighty-eight possible starting notes from which to choose. The Vamp specifies which key, and often which note, you want.

2 The Vamp decrees, before you start to sing, the tempo in which the script will reach the ear of the auditor. No Vamp is ever designed to fool the audience. If the song is fast, the Vamp is equally and exactly that fast. If it is slow, the Intro is just as slow. No one would deliberately begin "I Got Rhythm" with a solemn, plodding Intro, or preface "Some Enchanted Evening" with a brisk upbeat Vamp.

3 Finally, a Vamp can function as a *scenic designer*. By creative scoring it achieves, in a minimum time span, a color, an environment, and even a musical/dramatic setting for the singer's state of heart and mind.

Can we live without the last two of these functions? Most definitely, yes. It is not necessary that the audience hear the tempo in which you will be singing the script.

And *you* know whether the song will be fast, slow, or moderate in its rhythmic statement. As for the scenic contribution a Vamp might make, we might like it but we most certainly can do without it. In fact, in the last twenty-five years Vamps have almost disappeared in the theatre; the arrival of the *Belltone* has taken their place. The Belltone is self-explanatory. One instrument gives the starting note, and that is all. Often, in the body of the show, this permits dialogue to melt into song without a Vamp destroying or interrupting the flow. In an audition, I strongly suggest forgetting the Belltone as a means of beginning a song. You may not hear it when it emerges from the orchestra pit, and there is nothing more pitiable than two Belltones.

If the minimal Vamp (Belltone) is not valuable under audition conditions, how maximal a Vamp does one need? The simplest answer is this:

What is the first line you will be speaking (singing) and how much time do you require to prepare (ideate) before you say it? It is obvious that you need little time if a song begins with "ABCD. . . ," "Once upon a time," or "My name is . . . ." But the song may begin more profoundly: "My sister just died . . . " Or provocatively: "I'm a boy named Sue" or "I'm in love with a girl named Fred." More time, then, is needed. An ancillary consideration: The time it takes to say something as devastating as "My sister just died" is the same whether or not I receive an accompanying musical Vamp. In fact, less music followed by a silence that *I* fill before I begin to sing can have tremendous impact. There are silences possessed of a valuable noise. The choices of an accompaniment to that silence is mine to make. It is my decision whether the audience will have any musical distraction.

THE VERSE

The Verse follows the Vamp and is the first vocalizing of the song's text. In the preceding chapter I spoke of its value to the actor/singer: needed expository information that, in turn, brings specificity to the statement of the Chorus. The Verse seldom embodies strong musical content. It is ad-libbed without effort because its melody is simple. In the case of "I Could Write a Book" the first eight bars are sung on almost one note; a simpler musical line cannot be invented. With Rodgers' genius for setting words to music, the musical value increases as the lyric begins its ascent from the third line to the end of the Verse.

A warning: I speak only in the general sense. There are many exceptions. Gershwin's Verses are often more interesting than his Choruses. When melodic, harmonic, and rhythmic sophistication informs the Verse, it tends to surrender complexity as it shifts into the Chorus. Vernon Duke wrote Verses as complicated as his Choruses are simple. They seem to be an unintentional attempt to bridge his life as Vladimir Dukelsky in the symphony hall with the more vulgar Duke of Tin Pan Alley. But rarely does a first-rate song possess a Verse more satisfying than its Chorus.[1]

The third and fourth lines of the Verse are sometimes called the "vest" of the Verse, but this term seems restricted to the writer. I have never heard a singer use it in the theatre.

The body of the song, in the sheet music, is, of course the Chorus, the Refrain, or, rarely, the Burthen.

THE CHORUS

The Chorus is constructed of themes contained within a certain number of bars. The song is composed of "8"s, a number that relates to the sum total of bars required by the statement of the theme. The number "8" is often deceptive, since counting the bars may reveal fewer or more than eight bars in that first melodic statement, but "8" remains the given name. A song is generally thirty-two bars in length, so the Chorus can be considered to be made up of four "8"s. Oddly, when the composer tends

---

[1] The Chorus of Gershwin's "The Man I Love" was originally the Verse to a nameless song none of us has ever heard. As reported by Ira Gershwin in *Lyrics on Several Occasions* (New York: Viking, 1959), the melody was too heavyweight as a Verse. Somewhat modified and with a new Verse of its own, it was added to the score of *Lady, Be Good,* this time as a Chorus. The inversion must have been a sound one; as a Chorus it became a major standard in the Gershwin folio.

not to write in the rigid mold of the thirty-two-bar song form (Arlen, Sondheim, and some of the younger composers come to mind), the Chorus sections are still called "8"s. Singers are not concerned with mathematical truth here, and the word has shifted from the specific to a general trade name, much like Aspirin.

If we call the first eight bars of the Chorus by the letter name "A," when the second eight bars are the same theme (e.g., "The Man I Love") they are also designated "A." The third eight bars, called the *Bridge* or the *Release,* state a new musical theme and are given a new letter: "B." The final eight bars are a restatement of the first and second "8"s, with some variation, and are referred to as "A." "The Man I Love" is, in form, *AABA.* So is "Where or When," "Blue Skies," "Smoke Gets in Your Eyes," and thousands of other songs we hear every day.

In the case of "I Could Write a Book," the second "8" is *not* a reprise of the first "8" but the statement of a new theme. It is, therefore, labeled "B." The third "8" again recalls the first eight bars and we use "A" to describe it. The fourth, or more correctly the last, "8" is a reprise of the second eight bars (again, with variation), and it is so dubbed "B." This song, in form, is *ABAB.* So is "Embraceable You," "How High the Moon," "Happiness Is Jes' a Thing Called Joe," and many others. Two minor points of order:

1   The third "8" in an ABAB is never called the Bridge or the Release, since this song form does not possess one. It is simply the third "8."

2   It is valuable for the actor/singer to familiarize himself with this terminology. Asked to "take it" from the second "8," he should be able, without confusion, to sing: "I could write a preface on how we met," and so on.

RIDEOUT

Every Chorus ends with a *Rideout.* It serves as a reverse Vamp and can range in length from one to many bars. Like the Vamp, it is recognizable on the sheet music as musical footage without an accompanying lyric. It is born at the exact moment when the final syllable of the lyric begins. Where the Vamp achieves an ascent into the song, the Rideout permits the singer his descent. Whereas the Vamp is somewhat less alien to the actor/singer (the idea of taking time before he speaks is irrefutable), the Rideout implies that nothing more will be said/sung. The need to ideate at this point is a mechanical one and probably represents the only time in singing when one must fall back on "reacting" to what has just been said/sung. Rideouts and their performance will be discussed later.

The Rideout, like the Vamp, can be any length you choose. In the sheet music it is seldom longer than four bars. In the theatre, however, its extensions can be as endless as they often seem. The "Roxy Rideout" (the exact history of the name is unknown to me, but a fair guess would link it to the extension upon extension required to clear the stage of a multitudinous chorus of dancers) is the longest of the breed, and it works with Pavlovian effect upon an audience. They hear it begin at the precise moment the singer launches into the last word and, like a dog salivating at the sound of a bell, they will applaud. I have heard songs achieve ovations that, shorn of this insistent and clamorous Rideout, would have died with little or no audience response attending the death. If all this guaranteed affection can be bought for the price of a Roxy Rideout, should you tack it on to what you sing at an audition? No. I have said that it incites applause. At an audition the theatre is empty save for the staff listening to you. Even if they felt that kind of affection for your work, they would not be guilty of an overt demonstration that might plague them at contract-haggling time. Unless you can hear an ovation in your mind that will sustain your joy and unbridled energy through the course of a lengthy Rideout, I would eschew it and come in and down simply. That applause you heard when you turned up the imaginary audience may not have matched the reaction of those who truly were there to hear you.

"AIR"

The Vamp, the Verse (if there is one), the Chorus (composed of "8"s, usually four in number), with the last "8" followed by the Rideout, constitute the song's sequence as it appears in the sheet-music copy. I have with good reason omitted one element of pure music that is evident on reading the sheet music of the song. It is that musical space without lyric—the "Air"—that appears between each line, between the Verse and the Chorus, between "8"s, and, by virtue of its definition, in the Vamp and Rideout.

"Air" is that interval of time, that interstice between lines, during which the actor/singer must *think his loudest* by creating implicit cues that will make specific and inevitable what immediately follows that silence. With the addition of "Air," the musical shape of the sheet-music copy of the song now reads, in this somewhat absurd fashion:

VAMP	[Air]
VERSE	A,B,C,D,E,F,G, I never learned to spell, at least not well. [Air]
	1,2,3,4,5,6,7, I never learned to count a great amount. [Air]
	But my busy mind is burning to use what learning I've got. [Air]
	I won't waste any time, [Air]
	I'll strike [Air]
	while the iron [Air]
	is hot: [Air]
CHORUS	If they asked me I could write a book [Air]
1ST "8"	About the way you walk, and whisper, and look. [Air]
2ND "8"	I could write a preface on how we met [Air]
	So the world would never forget. [Air]
3RD "8"	And the simple secret of the plot [Air]
	Is just to tell them that I love you a lot. [Air]
LAST "8"	And the world discovers as my books ends [Air]
	How to make two lovers [Air]
	of friends.
RIDEOUT	[Air]

These musical pockets of "Air" are integral. They give mathematical shape to the sung phrase and are to be considered as much a part of the song as the melody. The lack of accompanying lyric in no way diminishes their importance. "Air" comes in all sizes, from the simple

Belltone (the "Air" in the Verse between "I'll strike" and "while the iron") to uncomfortably long musical fills'.

RHYTHMS

Music is binary, consisting of a melody wedded to a rhythmic pulse. Until now we have spoken only of the melody and the words that are superimposed on it. The variety of rhythms that dress melodies is limited. In music not considered "serious," the variations are even fewer. By explanation:

2/4 time signature: This alludes to a bar of music that includes, within that boundary, two beats, each beat with the value of one quarter note or its equivalent. In 2/4 time the downbeat occurs with every alternate beat. The word "upbeat" refers to that pulse immediately preceding the downbeat. In the following the downbeat is underlined and the upbeat undefined: 1, 2, 1, 2, 1, 2, 1, 2, 1, 2, 1, 2. . . .

3/4 time signature: Here there are three beats in each measure or bar, with each beat a quarter note or its equivalent. The downbeat occurs with every fourth pulsation, double underlined. The upbeat, preceding the downbeat, is singly underlined: 1, 2, 3, 1, 2, 3, 1, 2, 3, 1, 2, 3 . . . .

4/4 time signature: This indicates four beats in each measure, each beat receiving the value of a quarter note or its equivalent. The downbeat now is on every fifth beat (1) and the upbeat preceding it on (4): 1, 2, 3, 4, 1, 2, 3, 4, 1, 2, 3, 4. . . .

5/4 time signature: This is not often seen, but when it does occur it is simpler for both the singer and the conductor to think of it as a combination of 3/4 plus 2/4, both within one bar. The downbeat now appears on every sixth beat: 1, 2, 3, 4, 5, 1, 2, 3, 4, 5, (or 1, 2, 3, 1, 2, 1, 2, 3, 1, 2. . .).

6/8 time signature: Each bar has six beats within its measure, and each beat is the equivalent of an eighth note. 6/8 is a variation of 2/4 and is conducted in two pulses, each gesture containing three beats. It would be impossibly frenetic for the conductor to indicate to the orchestra and the singer six beats within each bar: 1, 2, 3, 4, 5, 6, 1, 2, 3, 4, 5, 6. . . .

And that is about the sum total of the rhythms you will meet. There are additional time signatures (6/4, 9/4, and sometimes even 12/4), but they are variations and/or extensions of 3/4 and 4/4 time signatures.

Random thoughts on the above:

2/4: This rhythm is somewhat out of style. Because of the return of the downbeat with such frequency and immediacy, there is about it a certain showtime excitement. "Love Is Sweeping the Country" from *Of Thee I Sing*, for example, is scored in 2/4 time. A dated patina hovers over this time signature, but happily, the present craze for nostalgia is reviving it.

3/4: The waltz. It is important to remember that all waltzes are not, by definition, Viennese or oom pah pah, oom pah pah, oom pah pah. There is a slow stately waltz, called *triste*, in which each of the three beats receives equal stress. "Melinda" from *On a Clear Day You Can See Forever* and "Days Gone By" from *She Loves Me* are examples of the valse triste. There are, too, swing waltzes—"I'm All Smiles," "Bluesette," and "Walk Away"—that are infectious and home-grown American.

4/4: This is by all odds the most common of all time signatures. All fox-trots, ballads, tangos, rhumbas, sambas, bossa novas, congas, rock, disco—almost all pop music that is not a waltz is scored in 4/4 time.

5/4: Rare, but one song comes to mind that owes its wit not only to the lyric but to the time signature in which it is scored: "Sensitivity" from *Once Upon a Mattress*.

6/8: Many marches are written in this rhythm as well as in 4/4 time. Included would be "Seventy-Six Trombones" from *The Music Man*, "Buckle Down Winsocki" from *Best Foot Forward*, "Mr. Goldstone" from *Gypsy*, Irish jigs, and the Scottish "My Mother's Wedding Day" from *Brigadoon*.

In Sondheim's *A Little Night Music* the 3/4 time signature and its variations (6/4, 9/4, and 12/4) constitute the entire tempo structure. The score is a stunning example of the dissembling of a single time signature by variations within the composer's preset constriction. When no constriction is operative we can see that our popular music, with its seeming infinity of melodies, is created on a relatively limited palette of rhythmic patterns. For the beginner actor/singer this can be something of a comfort.

All that remains of this simple analysis of music as it appears on a copy of sheet music is a brief reference to the piano accompaniment and, above the staff, the cryptic symbols for the guitarist to follow. The piano and guitar supports are easy enough for a novice to play and need have no pianistic or harmonic resemblance to the inventive chordal structure of the original song. Albeit they are imprecise, neither has anything to do with the *singing* of the song. When the song is sung without accompaniment it is said to be sung "a cappella" (in chapel style). At an audition, especially for the novice, that is where such unaccompanied performance belongs—in the chapel.

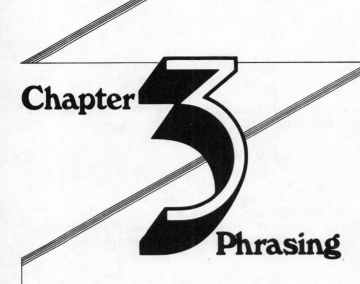

Chapter 3

Phrasing

A world of thought in one translucent phrase.

Henry Carpenter

FROM LYRIC

What a song is *about* is conveyed to an audience by the actor/singer through the personal choices that are the parts of the sum of his performance. What a song *says* is made clear only when it is phrased. One can phrase either from the lyric or from the music, or employ a plotting that draws on both of these elements. I begin with phrasing from lyric on the assumption that the actor/singer will be more comfortable projecting the sense of the script than molding an elegant melodic line.

At the start, I recommend that the lyric be written down, in your own handwriting, to help you experience the look and general tonality of the words and the rhyme structures that become apparent with increased visibility. I caution you that much of what is sung can appear trivial when it is divorced from melody.[1] However, the work of a Nash, Gershwin, Hart, Harburg, Porter, or

---

[1] In his preface to *Lyrics on Several Occasions* (New York: Viking, 1959), p. xi, Ira Gershwin says: "Lyrics are arrived at by fitting words mosaically to music. Any resemblance to actual poetry, living or dead, is highly improbable."

Sondheim can look much like, and even pass for, light verse. An example is this verse by Ogden Nash:

When you look life in the face
There's too much time,
There's too much space.
There's too much future, too much past
Man is so little and the world so vast.
You may fancy yourself as an immortal creature
But you're just the cartoon between a double-feature.

or, from the pen of Cole Porter, the Verse of "Red, Hot and Blue":

Due to the tragic lowness of my brow
All music that's highbrow gets me upset.
I don't like Schubert's music or Schumann's
I'm one of those humans who only goes in
For Berlin, or Vincent Youmans.

But, more often than not, a bare lyric is better clothed in song.

I have chosen as a model lyric, and as a model lyric for phrasing, Lorenz Hart's "The Most Beautiful Girl in the World":

1ST "8" The most beautiful girl in the world
Picks my ties out,
Eats my candy,
Drinks my brandy,
The most beautiful girl in the world.

2ND "8" The most beautiful star in the world
Isn't Garbo,
Isn't Dietrich,
But that sweet trick
Who can make me believe it's a beautiful world.

BRIDGE

Social not a bit,
Nat'ral kind of wit,
She'd shine anywhere,
And she hasn't got platinum hair,

LAST "8"

The most beautiful house in the world
Has a mortgage
What do I care,
It's goodbye care
When my slippers are next to the ones that belong
To the one and only beautiful girl in the world!

Qualitative elements can be observed when the words are separated from the ravishing waltz that accompanies and often dims this lyric, the skeletal leanness of which creates a sumptuous amplitude when the song is sung. It must be clear that the more syllables confined within a bar of music, the more strangled the singing. Excess words do not make for soaring melodies.

There is a wit at work here, with Hart's affection for Savoy rhyming[2] ("Dietrich—sweet trick" as evidence). One cannot concern oneself with singing a rhyme beyond a clear articulation of it. Rhyme, by definition, rhymes, while the performer's thinking, again by definition, is exclusive of rhyme. However, it is important to know where the rhymes are in a lyric—if not to be played, at least to be clearly sung.

There is a balance to the lyric. Its form is AABA, and in the first "8" the lengthy title is set off by three short lines and a restatement of the song's name for balance and the shape of things.

In the second "8" the last line is longer and promotes a swelling that will later be corroborated in the music.

The Bridge could not be tighter, and in the last "8" the build is extended more than before, personalizing the title and avoiding a restatement of it as it appeared in the first "8."

[2] From the Gilbert and Sullivan Savoyard works, but especially for Gilbert's gift for strings of nonstop rhymes.

Further study of the lyric furnishes more valuable information for the actor/singer. Essentially the lyric is expository and objective. *It will need subjectivizing to make it come alive in performance.* Aiding the actor/singer are lines that tell of the personal taste of the performer; comments about the lady under discussion reveal added editorial opinions:

"Picks my ties out": A minor revelation, but nevertheless most men do not permit this, at least not happily.

"Drinks my brandy": A postprandial drink implying a fairly intimate relationship with the lady.

"Who can make me believe it's a beautiful world": Sheer irony in the light of every day's newspaper and TV news.

"Social? not a bit": We know what the gentleman thinks of those who *are*; "Nat'ral kind of wit": of those who *manufacture* it; "and she hasn't got platinum hair": and of those who *have* it.

Plot 1: The Breath Mark

It is understood that phrasing is the placement of words and phrases that, when linked together in a breath arc, make sense of language. These arcs are defined by the inspiration and expiration of a column of breath that, as it passes through the larynx, is employed in the production of vocal sound. Breathing is an involuntary action, but one can husband it or waste it voluntarily. In this first plotting of the phrasing of the lyric I will used a breath mark (✓) to separate each subject and predicate from the next subject and predicate:

The most beautiful girl in the world
Picks my ties out (✓)
Eats my candy (✓) [implied is the title line of the song]
Drinks my brandy (✓) [implied is the title line of the song]
The most beautiful girl in the world (✓)
The most beautiful star in the world
Isn't Garbo (✓)
Isn't Dietrich (✓) [implied is the first line of the 2nd "8"]

But that sweet trick
Who can make me believe it's a beautiful world (✔)
[Is she]
Social? (✔) not a bit (✔)
[She has a]
Nat'ral kind of wit (✔)
She'd shine anywhere
And she hasn't got platinum hair (✔)
The most beautiful house in the world
Has a mortgage (✔)
What do I care (✔)
It's goodbye care
When my slippers are next to the ones that belong
To the one and only beautiful girl in the world. (✔)

Plot 2: The Glottal Stop

After working out this first plotting of the phrasing, call in the pianist and sing through exactly what has been marked. It will be evident that a second plotting is required. There are places where you will not need a breath, and others where you will not have enough of it. These conclusions are not absolutes, for they depend upon your ability to take, sustain, and utilize the breath you take, but within the realm of the obvious changes to be made, the following choices require adjustment:

"Eats my candy" (✔): The breath after this line
is unnecessary. Deprived of it, one can easily
proceed without loss of vocal strength.

"Isn't Dietrich" (✔): The same may be true here,
but a longer line follows it, and discretion
should be the rule. More of that later.

"Social" (✔): This breath is almost impossible to
take, for only one word separates it from
the inspiration at the end of the 2nd "8."

"Has a mortgage" (✔): As with "Eats my
candy," unneeded.

"It's goodbye care": Undermarked for breath *in
this particular case*. Had this been a patter song there would have been little difficulty
in singing all of what follows in the one
breath. Here it is impossible or, worse, self-

conscious to sing all of "It's goodbye care when my
slippers are next to the ones that belong to
the one and only beautiful girl in the world"
in one breath, not forgetting the Rideout,
which demands holding the last word at the top
of the singer's range. A good rule to remember
is to elect to breathe where the least damage
is done to the sense of the text. More often
than not, that will occur immediately
preceding prepositions: "When my slippers are
next (✓) to the ones that belong (✓) to the one
and only beautiful girl (✓) in the world (✓)."
You need not take all three breaths; the
second of the three is apt to be the most valuable,
but the third breath is a distinct possibility in view of the impending demands of
the Rideout.

The breaths that have been removed from the first
plotting must now be replaced with another artifice, since
the motive behind their choice remains valid. Because the
language still requires the same definition, _glottal stops_
are employed as substitutes for the breaths. A glottal stop
is a comma in the voice that interrupts the column of air
as it passes through the larynx.

An added value results from placing a glottal stop
immediately before any word that needs to be _lighted_ and
brought to the attention of the listener. In the Bridge, for
example, a glottal stop between "shine" and "anywhere"
would make it clear that there is nowhere the lady under
discussion would not shine. Similarly, a glottal stop between "got" and "platinum hair" would underline the
gentleman's disaffection for platinum hair.

Between "goodbye" and "care" a glottal stop is required to confirm that the word "care," in _this_ line, is a
noun, and not the verb "care" as it appears in the
preceding line. When this couplet is spoken the accents
fall naturally:

What do _I_ care?
It's goodbye _care_

But when the words are sung, the rhyme "I" and "goodbye," falling on downbeats, disturbs the sense of the

statement. The glottal stop will restore the meaning of the phrase, and in no way damage the singing of it. In this second plotting of the phrasing of the lyric, glottal stops will be indicated by an inserted comma (,):

The most beautiful girl in the world
Picks my ties out (✓)
Eats my candy (,)
Drinks my brandy (✓)
The most beautiful girl in the world (✓)
The most beautiful star in the world
Isn't Garbo (,)
Isn't Dietrich (,)
But that sweet trick (✓)
Who can make me believe it's a beautiful world (✓)
Social (,) not a bit (✓)
Nat'ral kind of wit (✓)
She'd shine (,) anywhere
And she hasn't got (,) platinum hair (✓)
The most beautiful house in the world
Has a mortgage (,)
What do I care (✓)
It's goodbye (,) care
When my slippers are next (✓?) to the ones that belong (✓)
To the one and only beautiful girl (✓) in the world. (✓)

If you are comfortable when singing through this second plotting of the phrasing, it can then be frozen. But if there is still a need for more or less breath, go on to a third plotting. It is important always to give yourself the benefit of the doubt. Remember: One's supply of breath diminishes under the stress of an audition or a performance.

Once you have settled on the final phrasing pattern, I suggest you mark your copy of the music with all breath marks, glottal stops, and important information, just as the actor marks his script with directions and intentions only *he* may be able to decipher. In the case of this particular song, I would mark, in the Bridge, the word "bit." It is scored to be held for two bars, but doing so destroys the onomatopoeic value of the word. I would, therefore, make a point of cutting off the word to give added weight to the lady's inability to behave socially. The vowel "ih" in the words "bit" and "wit" is closed, and when these words are held too long one is brought perilously near to

Bert Lahr's classic imitation of a closed-throat baritone with strangulated vocal production. So although "wit" is not a word that sounds like its meaning, the less it is held the less it plagues you.

Exceptions

There are two distinct exceptions to the ground rules outlined above when *phrasing from lyric* and, like the rules, the exceptions are important to remember:

1 Most important of all, when you need a breath, take one! Turning purple to achieve sane phrasing is insane. Phrasing, and the way it is achieved, is of no importance to an audience. In fact, the more concealed it is, the more successful the singer has been in presenting the text. So breathe when you need to breathe. Remember, however, to do it with your lungs and not your mind. It is not difficult to camouflage the inspiration of breath under the cover of an inspired piece of acting.

2 Never be without sufficient breath to sing and sustain a Rideout. The actor/singer should keep in mind that the nature of a Rideout is alien to his work. He is never asked to hold the last word of a speech, but he almost always does it, to a greater or lesser degree, when he sings. Rideouts can be sung only with an adequate amount of breath, even if that breath must be taken at a place that would appear absurd on paper. For example:

When my slippers are next (✔) to the ones that belong to the one and only beautiful girl in the (✔) world. (✔)

The breath before the last word allows the listener to hear a well-sustained Rideout. What was nonsense to read is effulgently vocal to listen to. As before, the breath should not be advertised.

FROM MUSIC: ALTERNATIVES

Enharmonic Changes

There are many times when music takes precedence over text, for we are, after all, concerned with song and not mere verse. And music speaks its own language. Enharmonic key changes often occur in the melodic line when the voice becomes more of an instrument than a purveyor of script. These enharmonic changes are difficult to describe to the nonmusician, but as an illustration I have chosen two lyrics that should be familiar to the reader:

You are the angel glow
That lights a star,
The dearest things I know
Are what you are.
Someday my happy arms will hold you. . . .

The above is, of course, the Bridge and first line of the last "8" of Hammerstein and Kern's "All the Things You Are." Phrased from lyric, as we have been doing, the plotting would read:

You are the angel glow
That lights a star, (✓)
The dearest things I know
Are what you are. (✓)
Someday my happy arms will hold you. . . .

However, there is an enharmonic change[3] leading out of the last line of the Bridge. In the published copy of the song the word "are" is scored on a G# (the third [mi] of the key of E Major) and the first word of the next bar—the "some" of "someday"—is called A♭ (the fifth [sol] of the key of D♭). The Bridge, having taken a journey in a *relative key* (the *master key* of "All the Things You Are" is D♭), is brought home at once by this simple and exquisite enharmonic modulation. To breathe while the change is occurring would destroy the melodic arc. Sense, then, be damned; do not breathe. Phrasing from lyric yields to the music's claim on your sensibility:

[3] An enharmonic modulation permits a sudden key change by altering the notation without changing the note, e.g.: A♭ becomes G#, F# becomes G♭. The device allows the laws of modulation to be set aside while common tones with dissimilar names are employed to effect an instant key change.

You are the angel glow
That lights a star, (✓)
The dearest things I know (✓)
Are what you are ⌒
⌣Someday my happy arms will hold you (✓) . . . .

By taking the breath in the wrong place (lyrically speaking), after "know" in the third line of the Bridge, you will have enough breath to elide the last word of the Bridge, "are," over into the next line and to swell with the orchestra through the enharmonic change. If you cannot make it all the way through "hold you," grab for a breath after "someday" when the coast is a bit clearer.

A second example:

Long ago and far away,
I dreamed a dream one day
And now that dream is here beside me.
Long the skies were overcast. . . .

Here is the first "8" and the first line of the second "8" of Gershwin and Kern's "Long Ago and Far Away." Phrasing from lyric and disregarding the enharmonic change on the words "beside me" effects this plotting:

Long ago and far away,
I dreamed a dream one day (✓)
And now that dream is here beside me. (✓)
Long the skies were overcast. . . .

Again, however, the enharmonic change that occurs on "beside me" and over the bar into "Long the skies were overcast" can be an elegant musical effect. To gain the value of the enharmonic change the phrasing should be altered as follows:

Long ago and far away, (✓)
I dreamed a dream one day
And now (✓) that dream is here beside me. ⌒
⌣Long the skies were overcast (✓) . . . .

By changing the breath marks to suit the *musical demands* rather than the *lyrical sense* of the script, an awkward plotting of the phrasing on paper becomes a graceful vocal line whose only purpose is to serve the music. In this case, that service takes precedence over the script.

Enharmonic changes, and the demands they make upon the vocalist, live in a country that always speaks the language of music. Phrasing from a purely musical impulse is a valid starting place for anyone who sings well. To learn the variations of choice, the *instrumental* motive behind the singer's intention, and what the singing finally *sounds* like, the best procedure is to listen to good singing. This education is available to you through recordings. In the popular field Frank Sinatra, Ella Fitzgerald, Tony Bennett, Carmen McRae, and Peggy Lee are all singers of sensivity with much to teach you. Eminent jazz instrumentalists are another valuable source. The rock scene should be eschewed, since phrasing in that musical part of the forest is not fundamental to an effective performance. The raw vocal sound (not necessarily sung) is the vital element here, and there is no way I know to study how to do it well. In that sense the rock culture is of small value, for it does not consistently renew or present first-rate vocalism to the younger generation. Sound, fury, unintelligible language all hold center stage, and vocalism, as an end in itself, is of no importance. Thus, it should not surprise the reader that the comparative popularity of the above-mentioned singers continues.

The loss of the small clubs to the discotheque scene has led to a valuable revival of Mabel Mercer's and Bobby Short's recordings; they are the last of a vanishing breed. Cleo Laine has come to us from England, and is extraordinary, but very much one of a kind. Tyrone Guthrie has said that "young artists invariably imitate what they admire." I would agree, and add only that when you model yourself after another, be certain you elect someone whose work is of an excellence.

There is, finally, little to learn from a Streisand or a Vic Damone, unless one can equal her opulent vocalism or the velour of his sound; sound, in both cases, is the thing. This was also true of the late Judy Garland. One can say that the law of inverse ratio is applicable here: *As one's ability to sing decreases, the importance of the text of the song increases.* Ideally, one should be concerned with both. The singer who "sings" with full throat and empty mind must forever remain alert. He is vulnerable to anyone who can sing it better. The artful interpretation of melody and lyric is a fingerprint and, by definition, remains unique.

Over-the-Bar

There are other employable devices for phrasing from music rather than from lyric that can give life to a song. These are *sound* experiences and not easy to describe. One procedure, however, can be set down. Called *over-the-bar* phrasing, it relates to an arbitrary musical arc achieved by the singer's refusal to breathe until the lyric phrase has passed over the bar line—whether or not the sense of the text is served. The following lyric, by Johnny Mercer to music of Harold Arlen, is one in which over-the-bar phrasing can be seen as well as imagined:

I promise you a faithful heart,
One that has always been free.
At night there's a handful of stars
That I pretend belong to me.
I promise you that rich or poor,
I would be happy to share
The arms you have taken possession of.
The sun in the meadow,
The fire in the shadows,
And I promise you I'll be there.

"I Promise You," music and lyrics by Harold Arlen and Johnny Mercer, from *Here Come the Waves* (film, 1944). Copyright © 1944 by Harwin Music Corp. Copyright renewed. Used by permission.

Phrased from lyric, a sensible plotting would be:

I promise you a faithful heart, (✓)
One that has always been free. (✓)

At night there's a handful of stars
That I pretend belong to me. (✔)
I promise you that rich or poor, (✔) [for the vocal demand of
    the following line]
I would be happy to share
The arms you have taken possession of. (✔)
The sun in the meadow, (✔)
The fire in the shadows, (✔)
And I promise you I'll be there. (✔)

Over-the-bar phrasing, regardless of sense, would read:

I promise you a faithful heart,
One (✔) that has always been free.
At night (✔) there's a handful of stars
That I pretend belong to me. (✔)
I promise you that rich or poor, (✔)
I would be happy to share
The arms (✔) you have taken possession of.
The sun (✔) in the meadow,
The fire (✔) in the shadows,
And I promise you I'll be there. (✔)

No reason born of text motivates this phrasing, but it provides a surge of dramatic thrust that will not permit the listener to relax into the arrival of "Air" at the end of the lyric line. Just as interest begins to wane the ear receives new information.

As an example, "I Promise You" is significant only because it permits a number of over-the-bar choices. Most songs are not so accommodating. But when *phrasing from music* is employed once or twice within a plotting that is primarily *phrased from lyric,* it more than pays its way. The aim of all vocalism is that the song gain and hold the attention of the audience. Anything and everything that is artful and organic should be considered when its intention is to achieve interest. Phrasing, from lyric, music, or combinations of both, is a means to that end.

Placed on the music line, it would appear as shown on the accompanying lead sheet (see following page).

I Promise You

I prom - ise you_____ a faith - ful heart,

One that has al - ways been free._____ At

night there's a hand - ful of stars_____ That

I pre - tend be - long to me._____

I prom - ise you_____ that rich or poor, __

I would be hap - py to share_____ The

arms you have ta - ken pos - sess - ion of._____ The

sun on the mea - dow, The fire in the sha - dows, And

I prom - ise you I'll be there._____

Chapter 4
The Audition

Respect all such as sing when all alone.
Robert Browning

Auditions bring two mutually exclusive units into confrontation. On stage is the performer who is there to get a job by showing what he can do; on the other side of the apron is the hirer who elects to buy or to bury. It is a creaky and inefficient system, but nothing more effective has been invented to replace it and we are all, on both sides of the line, stuck with it. If it were feasible for the audition first to divide the wheat from the chaff, then the good from the better, and then to see that the best were hired, there would never be the whisper of a complaint from either corner. But the human factor forbids objective judgment, and the audition rarely produces even the comparative good choice. Great performances in musicals are seldom the result of a sensitive detection of talent hiding within the audition system. More often, the performers the public sees gained employment through recommendation of trusted middlemen or just plain luck. As a teacher I have seen first-rate performers fail to intimate even a fraction of their ability at an audition, and as a quondam hirer I have been taken in by a singer of minor talents whose audition advertised a gift that, later into rehearsals, proved to be nothing but a veneer that masked inferiority.

Auditions or *readings* for a play tend to be more efficient than those for a musical, not only because there are fewer judges but because the material to be read is that which is to be produced. The director and the playwright, only two in number, can confer easily. If the author, who by right of his Dramatists Guild membership holds final veto, is young, the weight is on the director's side. If the playwright is prestigious, the partnership may indicate that imbalance and the choice of cast will mirror that bias. Rarely does the producer carry enough weight to affect changes in those decisions, although he may be in attendance.

THE JUDGES AND THE JUDGED

Auditions for musicals are Towers of Babel. To begin with, what is being sung has nothing to do with the score of the production to be mounted. And where only two judges sit for the casting of a play, now there is often an army in attendance, with all members registering opinions even if they do not have a "vote." It is not impossible to imagine auditioning before the following: a composer; a lyricist; a librettist (or two or three); the director; the choreographer; the musical director (conductor); possibly a choral director; all assistants to these creative people; and, if they are free to stop by that day, assorted staff members such as scenic designers, costume designers, lighting director, orchestrator(s), upper-echelon wives, and, of course, the producer(s).

It is still true that the writers (composer, lyricist, and librettist) hold the veto, but so large an array of creative talent must take on the characteristics of a benign anarchy. They all seem to be clear about what they are *not* looking for, but there is almost no agreement among them that defines what they *are* looking for.

Let me talk further about the judges before discussing the judged with equal candor. It is an incontestable truth that few, if any, of the creative staff know anything about what they are witnessing at an audition, and fewer still can do it. The director of a play may well have been an actor at one point in his career and might be expected to bring knowledge and compassion to the task of auditioning other actors. But this is rare indeed in the musical theatre. I do not want to imply that only someone who can sing, dance, and act is qualified to cast a production, but a Zuleika Dobson ("I don't know anything about it, but I know what I like") demonstrates a preference no more valid than the next man's. When the caster's appraisal of what he sees is based on his own ability to perform it (director/choreographer/singers such as Michael Bennett, Bob Fosse, or Patricia Birch), it is my personal conviction that the game, as is apparent to both sides, is played more fairly.

Another harsh reality: I spoke of compassion because I am so often shocked by the tales that describe the treatment given performers at an audition. Appointment times ignored or delayed for more than an hour without apology, with an inevitable destructive effect on the auditionee's already abraded mental state; interminable waiting in the wings, further exacerbating the spirit; interruptions at the beginning of the song to announce displeasure with the choice when "What are you going to sing?" could have been asked of the performer before he began; interruptions just before the end of the song when a moment or two more would have permitted the singer to complete the audition—all these are commonplace. Pianists supplied by the management are often inept, and the singer can do little but protect himself from assassination by accompaniment. And, finally, callback after callback after callback may be demanded, with the performer's complicity born out of fear that he will appear uncooperative, and thus lose the job.[1]

There are managements less guilty than others. There are directors and casting directors more knowing and compassionate than others. A climate in which the performer can function at his best is desirable to both parties, and the true professional not only knows that but sees to it that it happens.

On the other side of the battle lines stands the actor/singer/dancer, and he is no more a hero than the management is a villain. I have written and helped cast

[1] The Actors' Equity Association ruling allows for four callbacks, after which, if there is need for another, the performer must be paid one-eighth of today's minimum weekly salary of $355 for principal or "white-contract" roles.

musicals, and I can testify that an endless line of third-rate auditions can erode the patience threshold of the most sensitive director, writer, and choreographer. There is an appalling array of unqualified people who come on stage intent, it would seem, upon proving that they do not belong there. And this is more true of musicals than of plays. The number of first-rate actors available to playwrights and the directors of their plays is always a joyous surprise to me, for the sad fact is that quite the opposite condition exists in our part of the forest.

An odd footnote: The actor moving into musicals is affected by the virus. Unwilling to audition for a play unless he has prepared his reading adequately, he is now more than eager to run out on the stage and sing a song he learned an hour before. Why is he disposed to do so overtly that which he cannot do yet, and not inclined to do, off the top of his head, that which he knows *how* to do?

Uta Hagen, in her practical and passionate *Respect for Acting* (New York: Macmillan, 1973, p. 221), has this to say: "The profession of acting has been maligned throughout the ages. . . . To a degree, we are to blame for this opinion. . . . In our longing for dignity, we have not followed through in our work to merit respect for our profession and respect for our own work in that profession."

The actor/singer and the singer are often guilty of this same lack of respect for the musical stage. I exempt the dancer because he is the most serious of artists and never stands accused of anything less than total commitment to his work. Before any performer can justifiably attack the hirer and his tactics, he should first be able to stand on the stage secure in the knowledge that he knows he knows what he is about to perform. Only then can he pray, if he gets the job, that those on the other side of the footlights, whose work has not yet been tested, will be as craftworthy.

The auditionee often blames the irksome circumstances and an implicit hostility in the theatre for the terror that breeds a poor showing. This is a psychological escape hatch to mend a shattered ego. Bad work is the consequence of inadequate preparation. Some nervousness may be expected when possible employment is at stake, but nerves and fear are not synonymous. We are frightened because we do not know what we are going to do. Fear cannot flourish when expertise informs performance. Nervousness is not a destroyer. The truth is that an un-nervous performance can be deadly, while a frightened one bears witness to the cause of the fear—namely, ignorance.

CHOICE OF MATERIAL

Don't's

1   Do not choose a song that has nothing to say. "Isn't This a Lovely Day" is a charming tune when sung and danced by Fred Astaire with the full burden of his history and personal style to sustain it. Lesser mortals, standing in a worklight, need more utilitarian weapons.

2   Do not choose a song that requires contemporary instrumental accompaniment to achieve its effect. Or, if you must, bring that accompaniment with you, played by someone other than yourself.

3   Do not choose a song that loses its vertical interest when performed out of context. "I'm Gonna Wash That Man Right Outta My Hair" is viable when the singer simultaneously sings and shampoos her hair. Deprived of soap and water it is an inanity.

4   Do not choose a song that requires a performance above and beyond what you can deliver. "Rap Tap on Wood," "Shoes with Wings On," and "I Want to be a Dancing Man" are all first-rate lyrics, but not when the actor/singer is nailed to the floor.

5   Never audition without your own pianist. You will find the rationale for exceptions to this advice, but in the end they are invalid. I repeat: Never audition without your own pianist. Your agent, the casting director, or even the stage manager will assure you that there will not only be a pianist at the theater, but that he is the reputed offspring of Marian MacPartland and Emil Gilels, but don't you believe it. And even if it were half-true he could never be expected to know what you are going to do and what will be required. It makes more sense to audition

with a third-rate pianist who knows your work than to sing, without rehearsal, with a first-rate one.

6   Do not sing songs that are currently enjoying great popularity or are overexposed standards. There will be sufficient numbers of competitors that day who will reprise them.

7   Do not choose a song written by a friend or a member of your family. If a song is unknown to a director or composer/lyricist, there is much comfort in being able to say, when asked who wrote it, "Gershwin" or "Sondheim" rather than "My Uncle Harry."

8   Do not sing *signature songs.* You may hold the opinion that your interpretation of "Over the Rainbow," "When the Moon Comes over the Mountain," or "People" surpasses Garland's, Smith's, or Streisand's, but your assessment is debatable. Why afford anyone the opportunity to measure you against the original and court disagreement?

9   Do not, if it is at all possible, choose a song written by the composer for whom you are singing that day. Like playwrights, composers and lyricists have strong notions of how they *see* their material. Yours may be an interesting approach, but again, why risk dissent?

10   Do not make conversation. If you are spoken to, answer, of course. The exchange has probably been initiated to hear your speaking voice. But if there is no reason to chat, do not offer a "hello," a quick weather report, or your interest in the director's health. This may seem a needless cautioning, but in the grip of galloping jitters you will be astonished by your gift for suicide.

Do's

1   Try to ascertain what the management wants to hear. Have your agent call ahead or, if you do not have representation, *you* call. Musical auditions are attended by crowds of aspirants. The task of the director is considerably lightened if you can, by choice of material, simulate quickly what would be required of you if you are given the job.

2   Dress the part. I do not mean that you should rent a costume, but Sally Bowles in *Cabaret* is harder to characterize, in a worklight, if you are in jeans or basic

black dress. Again, because of time limitation, attempt to paint in broad primary strokes that which brings you and the hirer together—the casting of a role.

THE FLAWS WITHIN THE SYSTEM

Auditions are doomed to some degree of failure because there are always those who are more capable in a production than at an audition, and others who audition splendidly but cannot perform half as well when the curtain rises. An audition, after all, can be rehearsed and rehearsed until it is merely that: a singularly rehearsed performance. When the actor/singer on callback is asked to prepare something from the score, his proficiency is more reliably revealed. Often a role is given to someone who auditioned brilliantly and yet, when you see the musical months later, there is only a cipher on stage. You ask youself why A was given the part while B, C, or even D, all three of whom auditioned for the management, were bypassed. Subsequently you may even see B, C, or D play the role in a touring company or in summer stock theatres and have your opinion confirmed. I offer this as an example that affirms the fallibility of the system.

Are there alternatives to the system? Few, unfortunately. It is always valuable in musicals, as well as in plays, when performers come by way of recommendation. Someone on the staff has seen their work and knows what they can do. Or perhaps someone who is aware of talent that may go unseen without commendation brings that actor/singer to the attention of the management. Because this is so, I suggest you *work as much as and wherever you can.* You can never be sure who is watching you. Being "caught in the act," if you are gifted, is far more valuable to you than having to demonstrate your craft under audition conditions, lit by a cold worklight in an empty theatre, alone and . . . by yourself.

There is only one significant achievement for a performer who auditions for any role. That is *not* getting the part, but showing the best you can do that day. The hirers' chore is to cast the musical. Do not confuse the two. Many factors outside your control will condition their choice, and there is no way you can outguess what they have in mind. If they have just decided they are looking for a tall blonde, then a short brunette, no matter how gifted, scores two out on entrance. If a short brunette has been hired to play a role corresponding to the one you are auditioning for, and you are shorter still, there is little you can do about *that*. I am reminded of the agent's admonition to a client on his way to an audition: "Oh, and for God's sake, watch your height!"

Of this I am certain: A good audition never goes unnoticed. It may not achieve immediate employment, but no director, casting agent, or composer/lyricist ever forgets first-rate work. There is just too little of it.

Chapter 5

The Song as It Reflects You

I celebrate myself and sing myself.

Walt Whitman

For the actor and the dancer just beginning to sing, the moment is less a joy than a torment. And their terror is awesome in its self-annihilating power. I have witnessed every variation of stage fright from perspiration to dehydration, from tremors that turn the neophyte into a human aspic to a paralysis equaled only by that of Lot's wife after she turned around. An actress once confessed to me that even her hair was nervous and trembled when she first began to sing in class. In my studio one can decipher who has just finished singing and who is thinking of singing next from the traffic in and out of the restrooms. This would seem to add loss of sphincter control to the list of panic variations inspired by singing.

It is as if one is as naked as a babe, visible to everyone in all one's true and imagined imperfections. It may be of some small comfort to know that this projection has some justification. No more can the actor fall back on the artful dissembling that will make his Hamlet credible, or that, where before the curtain rose stood a mere mortal indistinguishable from any member of the audience, there is now transformed a young Juliet or an aging Lear. *One sings "I" and one means "I."* The singer is always visible above, below, and around that which he sings. Can it be that we all fear the stripping away of the concealment we cultivate as social animals? Is that what terrifies the actor when he first begins to *sing himself*? Try though he may, the height of any song is always going to be less high than the singer singing it, and will never afford him his accustomed hiding place.

I offer a curious illustration of this phenomenon. Meet an actor whose work you admire, and more likely than not you come away surprised by the disparity between your preconceived image and the genuine article. The differential may even be contradictory. A mouse of a man is recast into a dashing, romantic figure on the stage, and the impersonation is not only acceptable but, for the audience, a truth. A renowned actress who brings the very apotheosis of charm to her roles becomes aloof and forbidding when you are introduced to her after the curtain falls. But meet a singer you esteem, and you are never left bewildered. Garland was and "sang" Garland, Piaf was Piaf, Horne is Horne, Merman is Merman. Everything that is sung is a fingerprint, and never can be a lie. In a *New York Times* interview Harold Pinter has said: "Speech is speaking a language locked beneath it. That is its continual reference. The speech we hear is an indication of what we don't hear. It is a necessary avoidance, a violent, sly, anguished or mocking smokescreen which keeps the other in its place. One way of looking at speech is to say it is a constant strategem to cover nakedness." Song (soliloquy) is that *continual reference* to what we dare not speak but *can sing*. Because there is no explicit cuing, each line must be the verbal/vocal result of thought that is unique to the singer. A well-sung (performed) song gives the illusion that it has never been sung before and, beyond that, that its revelations are witnessed and heard by an audience at the very moment they are self-revealed to the singer.

Another aspect that can contribute to the nonsinger's defeat through song is that he cannot refrain from listening to himself sing. An intolerable friction, in the aesthetic sense, is set into play when he starts hearing sounds that are less musical than he would wish to hear.[1]

[1] In the last quarter of a century the musical theatre has presented to its audiences, and with critical tolerance, everything from caterwauling, bellowing,

It is of no value to assure him that the theatre audience "sees" a song more than it hears it. *He* hears it, and that is enough. His fear and the attention paid to the disagreeable sound replace his concentration on what he knows he knows. It is always a fascination for me to see how knowledge of acting deserts the actor, ability to move forsakes the dancer, and even the singer, splashing through the simplest of subtexts, will fail to use his voice properly, when each of them sings. It is as if what one knows best deserts one first in time of trouble.

SUPPORTIVE ADVICE FOR THE BEGINNER

In the beginning a number of revelations support the actor and enable him somewhat to understand, if not easily endure, this time of torment.

1 It is somehow reassuring to discover that everyone seems to be suffering a similar pain. This is, of course, more discernible in a classroom experience, but I pass it on as fact. Singing in front of any audience is not easy to do if, by that act, one implies a continuous flow of personal revelations superimposed upon a text that illuminates it for those who cannot know its meaning until we do just that.

2 Very little of what the actor and the dancer know is of any value when they first begin to sing. There may be some superimposition of techniques at the end of the learning process, but at the start it is an alien world and ignorance of it triggers the same fear mechanism initiated by ignorance of anything.

3 Unless the actor has had extensive experience with verse in the Elizabethan and the Greek plays, it is unique for him to hear himself speaking in metered rhyme. It makes no difference if you sing "Yankee Doodle Dandy" or the most complicated Sondheim lyric: You are imprisoned in prosody, it is alien, and it is terrifying.

4 The rhyming in a song is sung. It is fractionally true that there is melody in all language. We have heard the sound of "sung" dialogue in the theatre. Sometimes

---

shrieking, and whispering to a sprechgesang less a result of musical need than of the actor's inability to sing in any other manner.

sung dialogue is even at the service of the text (remember
Professor Higgins' xylophone tunes, played for Liza
Doolittle to duplicate while intoning, "How kind of you to
let me come"?). Sometimes it is not, but in either case the
choice is for the actor to make. But when he *sings* the
choice has been fixed by the composer, and the melody
will have a more demanding range than most actors and
dancers are capable of producing. It is recommended that
the actor or dancer study vocal production with a
qualified instructor, so that he is better able to support a
sung sound than the sound he is able to produce when he
speaks on the stage. This element of study in an actor's
preparation is sadly omitted in the United States. At their
best, few American actors have speaking voices of range
or beauty, and at their worst they produce constricted
throat sounds that are a torture for someone who
recognizes the difference between good and poor vocal
production.

5 The rhyming that is sung in a song is also
metered. Again, language has an intrinsic rhythm. That
rhythm, when it is sensitively communicated, helps to
construct the bridge between actor and audience over
which language transmits idea. Bad rhythms of speech
short-circuit that connection and leave confusion and
loss of clarity in their wake. And yet, the actor still can
choose the rhythms of his speech, with consequent good
or bad results; he cannot do so when he sings. If the composer has set the lyric as a march, a march it is; if it is a
waltz or a fast patter, the actor is slave to that time
signature at peril of some nasty notes from his accompanist or the conductor of the orchestra.

6 Nor is the actor cued. From the moment that he
begins to sing, or specifically from the moments before
the moment he begins to sing, he has no reason to do so.
No one is there to oblige him with "And what would you
like me to do for you?" to make saner the singing of "Embrace me, my sweet embraceable you." He must be taught
how to create an *implicit* cue to replace the loss of the *explicit* one.

7 The actor is taught to live on stage behind the
"fourth wall" (the invisible wall between himself and the
audience), and the set gives credibility to his life. It must

be Elsinore for Hamlet if it is to be Elsinore for us. But this does not hold true when the actor sings. A song lives only fractionally behind the fourth wall, and stays there but a moment after its birth. It demands the singer move downstage to sing it into the body of the theatre or, if staged upstage, to create a thrust that will make it *passer la rampe* (go up and over).

8 Last, phrasing and voice production are intimidating factors for the novice. I will not dwell on acoustics here because it is not my domain. I have already suggested that the actor learn to produce sound correctly whether or not he ever sings. As for phrasing, it is discussed elsewhere in this volume (see chapter 3).

Further comments on the singer *singing himself:* The actor, by definition, executes the play. He requires a script in order to function. He reads for the part, ideally gets it, and he will then act in *that* play. The audition is always a reading from the play going into production. The musical theatre audition functions similarly until the inevitable "Would you sing something for us?" The song now sung is *not* from the musical about to be produced, but one the actor has chosen for himself (see chapter 4). By this very act he affiliates himself with the singer, for *all* singers, from the beginning of their careers, choose their repertoire on their own or with the aid of teachers, representatives, or management. The songs you hear sung on records, in nightclubs, on television, in concerts, and, to revert, at that audition for the musical, are the particular choices of the performer, and not the hirer. (First and second callback auditions may require the singer to learn material from the score of the musical for which he is auditioning, but then, of course, the problem is solved, there being no further need to guess what the hirer wants to hear.)

If we accept the idea that singing what you want to say places you where only personally held truths (soliloquy) can be uttered, it follows that it is important to know what essence or essences of ourselves are projected from the stage so that we are not betrayed by what we sing. I am not speaking of the obvious ones of gender that preclude a man from singing "The Man I Love" and a woman "The Girl That I Marry," nor do I allude to characteristic and psychological traits that belong, for discussion's sake, in a doctor's office. But it must be apparent that we cannot all be acceptable singing anything and everything beyond those songs banned by virtue of our sex. An ingenue would confuse if she sang "Silver Threads Among the Gold," as would an aging character actress warbling "Young and Foolish." An effete young man dare not attempt Bernstein's "Pass the Football," any more than the gentleman with a macho self-image would render Coward's "Regency Rakes."

All this may seem manifestly obvious. Nevertheless, before you elect to sing any song, especially for the purpose of gaining employment, it is the better part of wisdom to read it before you risk it. Of further consideration: Stay alert to the possible perils that lie in songs you like to sing, because they are just that, songs you like to sing. The actor/singer misapprehends that "liking" a song is of some aid in performing it well. Remember that what turns *you* on may not generate a similar reaction from the audience. Worse, singing what *you* like to hear sung creates a breeding ground for cheap emotional responses that will rob you of an intelligent control over the material. You may be led into playing "results," the actor's sin of sins, rather than concerning yourself with playing the objective, the *why* you are singing the song.

There is no gainsaying an audience's pleasure in sensing and being affected by that special joy revealed in a singer's vocalism. Garland yearning to fly "Over the Rainbow"; the exquisite religiosity of Mahalia Jackson; the indigenous purity of De Los Angeles' Spain, Piaf's Montmartre and Pigalle, and Chevalier's boulevards; Sinatra, the alchemist who can change the dross of Tin Pan Alley into gold; Streisand's bottomless supply of breath lavished on a single vowel; Astaire, small-voiced, but as elegant as a Fabergé jewelbox; Lena Horne's sensuality; and Tony Bennett's open-throated vigor—the list is, fortunately for all of us, a long one. Unfortunately for the actor, only singers come to mind as prototypical. The point is that singers can *sing*, and when they sing well they take great pleasure in the making of music.

For those who have not been gifted with a superior vocal mechanism, it is wiser to remember that singing is a *doing* and not a *feeling* act, and whatever song you *do* becomes a statement peculiarly your own. It must clothe you and still not hide you. The complex devices the actor employs when he *acts* are denied him when he sings. All his training has been devised to serve him in the role he plays, to construct an image of *another* man in *another* time and place and situation, manipulated by the events of the drama. But now, singing, he stands alone. The song is concerned with what *he* thinks, what *he* feels, and what *he* intends. It follows, then, that *what we are to the audience is what we seem to be;* no matter how we protest this unfairness, the audience, no more than the director and composer/lyricist who hold auditions, cannot be expected to forgive our flaws. Since each of us by virtue of our humanness *is* flawed, that forgiveness must come first from ourselves. By the prudent choice of what you sing, you can present yourself in a particular manner that might never have been evident to the auditor.

Diane Arbus, a photographer who caught images of human beings at the edge where the ordinary becomes extraordinary, said about her work: "It is impossible to get out of your skin into somebody else's. Everybody has this thing where they need to look one way, but they come out looking another way, and this is what people observe. You see someone and essentially what you notice about them is the flaw. Our whole guise is like giving a sign to the world to think of us in a certain way, but *there is a point between what you want people to know about you and what you cannot help people knowing about you* [italics added]." It is at that point where the singing of a particular song, whether you like it (the song) or not, can direct attention to one side or the other of that demarcation.

Emerson's suggestion, "Use what language you will, you can never say anything but what you are," is relevant at the moment we begin to sing and, even if change were advisable, it is too late to effect an alteration beyond the simplest of acting adjustments. The actor/singer must learn to stand on the stage without a role to play, undiminished in his own skin. He must know the extent of his height, his width, and his depth; to sense the ends of himself (hands and feet) and the specific amount of air he displaces. And that displacement of air is as specific as the water he displaces when he lies in his bath.

I have said that singing is an act of doing and not of feeling. For actors trained to codify the spectrum of their emotions, this is not easy to accept. But music is a powerful _sensation_ statement and, upon hearing it, an audience _feels_ without the need for the singer to emphasize the emotional content of the song. Indeed, too much feeling works havoc with one's vocal technique by closing the throat and demolishing breath. To get the listener to react feelingly with his heart, the actor must learn to use his head. This is why I do not consider it important to like the song you sing, any more than it is important for the actor to like the play in which he acts, before either the song or the play can be brought to life. It may be difficult for an actor to play a role for which he has no affection or tolerance, but when he sings (in a study experience) it is better to work on material he does not care for. It is likely that his first professional musical experience will be one in which he is paid to sing a song he does not like in the least. More important is the task of getting the audience to like it.

A GAME: THE YOU NOBODY KNOWS

I like to play a game of "Essence" at the beginning of the classes I teach. Each actor sings the same song[2] and the class and I offer quick subjective adjectives that describe our immediate reactions to the actor in a condition of "singing." No time is allowed for a slow, considered assessment because no time will be given when he is on the stage auditioning or performing. The subjective nature of these reactions is of great importance to the performer because they are, quite simply, evaluations made by strangers, and strangers will be the inevitable assessors of his work. "Essence," of course, cannot be played among friends, for they would know that what one sees need not be so, and are thereby ruled out as

---

[2] I am partial to Rodgers and Hart's "Where or When" for three distinct reasons: (1) everyone knows the melody; (2) the lyric is easily dictated and memorized; and (3) the song is a cool, objective statement that precludes excessive emoting.

valid auditors. No matter how the director and staff who are auditioning performers struggle against this often unjust condition of evaluation and no matter how precisely and objectively they focus their attention on nothing but the performance, they cannot resist making personal judgments that are in error. Auditions often begin and end within a time span of three mintues. How often, when we are on the receiving end of "Thank you very much" or "We'll call you if we need you," would we willingly sell our birthright to know the reasons why. If only we could say, before exiting, "Thank *you*, but I wonder . . . before I go . . . if you would tell me what you saw and why you do not care to buy it? And . . . please . . . do not spare my feelings."

When the class and I have defined for the actor what we saw as he sang and have drawn his profile as constructively as we can, I attempt to find a song that, by its very statement and musical texture, is the *antithesis* of the sum of that actor's essence. The exercises he will perform will be executed on that song.

For those who will be using this book with the help of an accompanist or a coach, the song you choose must be carefully picked to push into the foreground what is recessive about you. Remember, you will not be performing the song, but technical exercises superimposed on the song. The nature of the song's essence will make more primary in color that which is pastel about you, and soften what is too readily apparent. Later, when the actor begins to perform songs he *should* sing, this prosthesis will not be required. What the actor then sings will be himself but, at that point, he will be able to choose acting adjustments that are not redundant to that which he is singing. The effete young man may never sing "Pass the Football," but he will also know enough not to add shades of lavender to "Regency Rakes."

Chapter 6

Alert Warnings

Je commence encore à zéro.

Edith Piaf

Each of the technical exercises described in the chapters 7 to 15 is to be performed on that *wrong song* I have described. Like a student juggler, you will be thrown one ball and then a second, a third, and, finally, a fourth. Each ball is *in addition to* and not a *replacement for* the ones you are already tossing into the air. Similarly, the exercises are to be performed in order, one *on* the other. With practice you will become more facile and execute them with decreasing difficulty. By way of explanation: You cannot say, while learning to drive a car, "I think I'll just practice steering today," or ". . . shifting gears today," or ". . . my hand signals." You must get into the driver's seat, turn on the ignition, depress the clutch, shift into first gear, release the emergency brake, check behind you for oncoming traffic, release the clutch as you step on the accelerator, and, as the car gains speed, shift into second and then high gear. If you are a beginner, this onslaught of activities can be shattering, and everything you do seems to be poor form. Inevitably, what feels awkward will seem less so until a coordinated performance slowly emerges from the mass of discordant acts. Remember, I have said that singing is more an *act,* a thing *done*, than something *felt*. The primary motive behind these first exercises is to bring the actor down to his most simple physical condition, to erase his blackboard before he learns to write on it.

The actor's inventions, born of panic and ignorance, must be redirected first toward an awareness of his physical life while he is singing, and then to a sane control of all four quadrants of his body.[1] Physical statement is an integral element of performing, but in these first technical exercises it will be absent. We are hell-bent, at whatever the cost, to *vocalize* the words and the music while performing disciplines that are, in part, concerned with *doing nothing*: not a twist, not a tremor, not a jerk, not a shake, not a quake, no listing to port or starboard, no twitching fingers that move like worms in a can, no rigid hand, no shoulders and eyebrows duplicating the rise and fall of the melody, no empty or rolling eyes, no tilting head, no bent knees, no slouching—just learning to make do with the you of you when it is at "zero." At this point in your singing a well-shaped nothing is more than enough of a something.[2]

The exercises are to be regarded as elements of a technique and not the performance of the song. Stanislavski has said: "Technique is only of value on the stage when you forget all about it,"[3] but technique must be mastered before one is able to forget it.

The student must accept the demands of technique

[1] In fact, most actors are all too aware of their physical state while they are singing, and admit to a distressing self-consciousness that incapacitates hands, arms, and feet. This malaise does not occur when they are acting, another demonstration that singing what one has to say brings into play a different set of ground rules.

[2] Although we cannot consider physical "zero" an aesthetic aim in itself, the singer may resort to it when a lyric is complicated to project as well as to receive. The song then seeks a minimum of physical expression. "Zero," as used here, relates to a complete lack of physical statement. *It does not connote a death.* The energy that informs interior size is afforded unobstructed space in which to evidence itself. It will be seen, so to speak, on a clean blackboard. Empty gesturing, no matter how beautiful, is disconcerting. An audience can always be relied upon to take the path of least resistance. Why give them something to *see* when it is what you are singing that you want them to *hear*?

[3] Constantin Stanislavski and Pavel Rumyantsev, *Stanislavski on Opera* (New York: Theatre Arts Books, 1975), p. 66.

unequivocally. There is little sense to it in the beginning of a study experience. The "why" of technique has only its correlated "because." A dancer's work at the barre, a pianist's battles with Czerny, a singer's scales, runs, and melismatics, and an actor's improvisations cannot be confused with *Swan Lake,* a Mozart piano concerto, *Norma,* or *Macbeth.* But technique is the imprisoning means to liberating ends.

Don't's

1 Don't seek your comfort in the beginning. Your motor system is learning new coordinations that, in time, will be computerized into habit patterns. There can be no comfort under these circumstances—at least, not yet.

2 Do not seek relaxation if, by that word, you mean a loss or lack of tension. And do not mistake *tension* for *tenseness.*

3 Do not resist the feeling that you are being imprisoned. You are. Move into the cell, hang some pictures on the wall, and make it a home away from home . . . for just a while. The sentence is not for life. You will be astonished, once you give up the resistance, to discover how much freedom there is in that prison cell.

Do's

1 The technical work that follows should be performed with an impelling sense of risk. Learn to dare; do what is asked for and *do it full out,* larger than life. You can always make smaller what is too big, but it is often impossible to make larger what has stiffened into too small.

2 Do ask yourself, "Am I doing this correctly?" If not, be certain you know why, and then fix it. If it is correct, do not be disturbed by how *well* you are doing it. Just: "Pick yourself up, Dust yourself off, And start all over again" ("Pick Yourself Up," music and lyrics by Jerome Kern and Dorothy Fields, from *Swingtime* [film, 1936]).

Chapter 7

The Entrance and the Vamp

"Ready" is the password before Aim. My past is ready not to intervene if I stand out of the way.

Paul Goodman

IN THE WINGS

When I teach, I try to convince the actor/singer that much of the success or failure of an audition rests not only on the quality of his singing and his ability to perform, but on the total impression of him evidenced during the time span beginning with his entrance and ending with his exit. How one *comes on,* in both its literal and idiomatic definitions, registers for or against him in the sum of the reactions to his work.

In the exercises that follow, an audition atmosphere should always be at the core of your thinking as you construct the environment in which to place the work. Anyone who can execute an audition with apparent ease and maintain control over his performance has sung under battle conditions that make all other occasions literal picnics.

Let us consider, then, that you are in the wings or in a room adjacent to the one in which you will audition—and you are waiting. Waiting, by virtue of its importance, could justify a chapter in any book about acting and performing. Waiting by day; waiting by night; waiting in the wings; waiting in the dressing room;

waiting for a cue; waiting for an agent to call—waiting for it all to happen. In no other profession is so much time squandered or mercilessly cut to a minimum for actual work to fill. Time and how to utilize it become a constant confrontation. An audition is a paradigm of this waiting. Few are the times you will appear at the appointed place and assigned hour and find the staff are able to accommodate you.

Don't's

1 Don't fill the waiting time with idle chatter. Should you meet acquaintances and friends in that decompression chamber between the street and the stage, make it clear that conversation is inimical to you. A haphazard backstage meeting must not be interpreted as a social encounter.

2 Don't give credence to gossip about what *they* are looking for. A latrine rumor, as in the Army, belongs in the room that gives it its name.

Do's

1 Put your thinking into what you plan to do, objectivize the time period consciously and you will have rid yourself of a good fraction of nervousness resulting from a concern with self.

2 Go over the lyrics. An interesting revelation: A good audition consists of two (2) performances of the song. The first is a dry run in the wings and internal in execution, while the second is performed before those casting the piece.

3 Quiet yourself.

4 Try to achieve a state of conscious and positive self-control.

5 When you have created this sense of a life force more impacted than your reality, you may enter.[1]

EXERCISE 1: THE ENTRANCE

Move to center or to that space where the audition staff can best see your work. It is a good idea to ascertain that particular location from the wings in order to minimize any wandering and indecision when you come into view.

---

[1] This is a technical exercise. At the audition an entrance is the consequence of hearing your name called.

Keep your attention front. Of major importance here, and in all subsequent technical exercises, is this: Learn to keep your eyes or, more specifically, your focus *off the floor*. Train yourself to think this unconsciously. You will find it an act of uncommon difficulty. Each time ignorance, indecision, self-consciousness, or fear take precedence over your concentration, your eyes will drop and betray you. You must not allow that part of your thinking that creates failure to obtrude here. Only a replacement of a constructive series of tasks can defend you from your own capacity to fail.

You are now standing in and on that optimal spot that affords you the *hottest,* and therefore the most visible, placement. On a stage your choice is more defined than in a room. When there is a choice, be motivated by sound theatre principles. Where lighting is minimal, and often unfriendly, stand where it is brightest and least unflattering. If you are in a room where light is not a problem (daylight is incontestably daylight), stand not too far from and not on top of those who are auditioning you. Often that place will be clearly presented to you. If you are in doubt, be ruled by a desire to position yourself where sight lines can create illusion. Gaston's after-the-fact revelation in "Gigi," "Have I been standing up too close or back too far?"* could well apply here. Finally, if you are still confused, this advice will always obtain: Ask those who are auditioning you where they prefer you stand. Nothing presents you in a more adult light than the intelligent handling of a legitimate ignorance.

You are now facing front. The *given* here is that no one will address you, and you will be without an action. The more sensitive the auditioner, the more aware he will be that a shared moment or two of easy talk (name, history, credits) not only comforts the actor but results in a looser, more honest demonstration of his work. But one cannot expect sensitivity to be a built-in factor at an audition. More often, nothing will be fed you, and in that case I teach the following:

Don't's

1   Don't congeal. In these precious moments, maintain some physical life.

* "Gigi," music and lyrics by Frederick Loewe and Alan Jay Lerner, from *Gigi* (film, 1958).

2   Don't stand at attention. Affect an easy posture by standing *at ease,* your weight on one or the other side of the body. A literal petrification is apt to occur unless you forewarn your motor responses. I even recommend the invention of arm-work here. Study what your hands do under less extraordinary circumstances and attempt to use the information. Straighten clothes, work an earring, adjust a tie or a necklace, perform a hasty scratching (although I suggest preceding this activity with the sense memory of an itch); the essential here is to perpetuate and project a life. Linger on self-physicalization longer than you will have to under battle conditions—out of too much can come the little that will be used. Inevitably your work on stage will find its ownness. For now, invent it.

3   Don't permit any element of the song you are go- ing to sing to be *on* you. There is a subtle distinction to be made between interior preparation and what is apparent to the eye of the beholder. Just as the actor in his dressing room is not Hamlet until the curtain's rise, it is in- contestable that he has already begun his journey into the character. Only a fool would think of intruding upon his privacy. Your demeanor should be *you,* without subtrac- tion and with no addition of amiability. Seeking affection now by employing the eager smile can only have the con- trary effect. Ask people to like you and they reject the of- fer out of sheer perverseness. In the theatre, good work is the legal tender that purchases affection.

Do's

1   Focus into and slightly above those auditioning you. You can relate to them on an eye-to-eye level at this point if, in fact, they are visible to you, but you are not now, or when singing, motivated to sing specifically *to* them. Nothing embarrasses more than having to react to a singer because he is working straight to you. If men are casting, a ballad sung by a man to a man, delivered with eye-to-eye contact becomes a study of a benign but never- theless homosexual proposal; when sung by a woman to a man (or a man to a woman), it seems a proposition. Either way invites misinterpretation. The auditioner's function is not to react to your performance but to cast

the musical, and yours is to demonstrate your work. Their presence is part of your reality, but that presence does not preclude other realities.

2   Focus slightly higher than their heads if you are in a room. On stage, the *trajectory of your eye* should be around the level of the mid-orchestra section. There is a danger that the actor/singer, struggling in the beginning to keep his focus off the floor, will overcompensate and place his line of sight too high. Remember, the higher the focus, the more you will seem to be rejecting the audience by appearing *subjectively* thoughtful. As your focus descends you create the illusion that you are *objectively* concerned with getting that song through the fourth wall and out to the auditioner.[2]

3   Play front so that you can be seen. At this moment, before you sing, your appearance is much of what you sell and much of what they buy. Make this self-merchandising easy for them at the beginning and you can demand that they listen to you later.

4   Do relate into the space *generally* and resist fixing your attention on specific targets. Look everywhere, see nothing.

Before you begin to sing, one mechanical act must be performed, and there is no dissembling or ridding yourself of it. I speak of bringing in your accompanist by the usual procedure: the nod. The nod exists only at an audition. During the performance of a musical, the conductor knows at what moment the orchestra is to play; no cast member ever informs the conductor that he is ready. In nightclub acts, television variety and talk shows, and in all situations where the singer requires the accompaniment to begin (always, by fiat, before the actual vocalizing), adequate rehearsal has taken care of the *when-to-start* moment. At an audition, unfortunately, you will have to notify the pianist and, by the dictate of custom, the nod is the prescribed method of making contact.

Before continuing, I want to decipher further the strange language of the Vamp your nod will introduce.

---

[2] The fourth wall is, of course, the invisible one between the actor and the audience. The other three are the left, right, and rear margins of the stage.

EXERCISE 2: THE VAMP

In chapter 2, on music, the element of "Air" was discussed. All vocal music possesses spaces, or "Air," in and during which the singer is not singing and only the accompaniment is heard. If the "Air" in a song were catalogued in the order of its importance, the Vamp would lead the list. There are justifying reasons for its importance:

1 It is the first music heard after a silence, and signals the arrival of the song.

2 It has, in its containment, extraordinary energy, for it seeks a vocalization from the moment of its birth.

3 It has a built-in inevitability factor. It ends at that exact moment when the singer utters the first vocal note of the song (on the presumption that no singer would ask for a Vamp and, at its conclusion, decide not to sing).

4 Because it represents the prenatal life of the song, the way the singer manipulates the inevitability factor is a demonstration of the grace of his style.

To begin, I suggest a Vamp of four bars of music, a time-span long enough for the actor/singer to experience the specific gradation of mental and physical changes and short enough to prohibit indulgence and slow-motion acting adjustments. In chapter 2 the Vamp's length was determined by the relative personal importance of the script. For now, the four-bar Vamp affords an ideal line of "Air" within which the technical exigencies can be met. The effect of a particular lyric on the length of Vamp is put aside until part 2, "Performance."

The act of singing what you want to say is unquestionably absurd. (We need not speak here of the audience's willingness to translate that absurdity into a sane language that is comprehensible to them.) If language can be labeled a horizontal dialogue, then song must be considered a vertical monologue. When you consider that a song is sung with no cue other than a Vamp to support its ascension from the horizontal to the vertical, you can understand the Vamp's contribution toward the creation of the necessary thrust. The singer, to extend the image further, needs a gantry (the Vamp) to prop up and sustain the missile (the song) before it is launched. The length and the timing of the Vamp is the countdown before the blast-off (the first vocal bar of music).

There is another consideration: In a theatre audition the actor most often is going to sing a song extrapolated from a musical score. Those songs have been carefully created to be sung at specific moments in the script. When a song is surgically removed it still seeks the height it originally possessed. Using *My Fair Lady* as an example, at rise of Act I, Scene 1, Professor Higgins sings:

Look at her, a pris'ner of the gutters:
Condemned by ev'ry syllable she utters.
By right she should be taken out and hung
For the cold-blooded murder of the English
      tongue! . . .
Segue to:
Why can't the English teach their children
      how to speak? . . .

This lyric is expository information and the statement is objective. It is relatively "low" off the floor. In the context of the idea of verticality, it requires a Vamp of minimal length. The eleven o'clock song sung by the same character two and one-half hours later is "I've Grown Accustomed to Her Face":

"Damn!! Damn!! Damn!! Damn!!
I've grown accustomed to her face!
She almost makes the day begin. . .
Segue to:
    "I'm very grateful she'a a woman and
      so easy to forget;
Rather like a habit
One can always break and yet,

I've grown accustomed to the trace of
    something in the air;
Accustomed to her face.

In this perfectly realized lyric Higgins' self-revelation occurs at the same time it is revealed to the audience. The song is possessed of enormous height. In the body of the performance of *My Fair Lady,* it inherits that height from the unreeling of the entire script. In an audition that script has been excised, but the song will still seem to demand its height, even if it must be reached within a mere four, six, or eight bars of Vamp. Aware now of the integral importance of the Vamp, we can return to the mechanical act that will bring that Vamp into being: the nod to the accompanist.

Don't's

1   Don't smile your accompanist in. More often than not the pianist should be considered the enemy (unless he is one of the few great accompanists). But even if he is a friend it is too late to throw yourself on his mercy by adding an amiable nod to the fee you pay for his services. A simple but eminently visible downward curve of the head gets it all started. Subtlety is to be shunned. Two nods, as in the case of two Belltones, are contemptible.

2   Do not signal until you are ready to begin. That pianist is going to play when he sees you nod, because he is so conditioned. Let the nodder beware—a moment too soon may well find the song singing you.

3   If your accompanist cannot see your nod, you must take other action. If a wave must be resorted to, then wave you must. Sometimes he may be behind you, in which case you must turn to cue him in. On rare occasions, the trois coups (the three raps on the stage floor that signal the rise of the curtain in both contemporary and classic French theatre) may be a last resort if he is under the stage and invisible to you.[3]

[3] Often the pianist is in the orchestra pit and is not only hard to see but, worse, harder to hear. I have said an audition is much like running an obstacle

4   Do not register any reaction when your accompanist begins. No surprise (you *did* nod, after all); no rapid acting adjustments that give you the appearance of St. Joan receiving messages from her voices; and no fixating on the pianist in paralyzed fascination with his keyboard artistry. Always remember *he* is accompanying *you*. When the reverse is allowed to occur, something of the amateur is demonstrated—an unpardonable sin at a professional audition. When the work of the pianist takes precedence over that of the performer, your failure is nothing less than total. I have known accompanists who secured employment in the very musical for which the singer was auditioning—total failure cubed.

Do's

1   After nodding, take your attention easily off the accompanist and relate back to the general theatre. The object now is to retain your reality. Were a silent film to be made of you that began before the accompaniment was nodded in and ended immediately after it began, there would be no visible difference in your demeanor. The *arrival* of music must not affect you. You are going to sing but, as in all acting, one proceeds from moment to moment, and the moment for vocalizing, or even the moment *before* that moment, has not arrived yet.

2   You will be hearing a four-bar Vamp to a ballad. I suggest a ballad only because its tempo moves slowly and affords you sufficient time to perform the technical tasks that take place within its time span. The first two bars of the Vamp are to be filled with turning attention away from the accompanist, a return to general focus, and an easy physical behavior. At the top of the third bar the following activities occur: The focus that was general now becomes specific as the eyes move to center (straight front). All songs should begin and end with a *center focus* if only for the reason that it is provocative to begin them elsewhere.

3   As the eyes recognize center, the base (feet) that has been in a sitting posture (weight resting on one side of the body) shifts to weight evenly placed on both legs,

course. In both cases, the winner is the one who copes with and vanquishes the greatest number of barriers.

achieved by the simple act of picking up the leg you are *not* standing on and making an easy base (twelve to fourteen inches wide) in which both feet support the body equally.[4]

4   As the base moves into position, the hands move to the sides, one following the other.

5   As the fourth bar of music ends and you are ready to sing, you should now be, in order from the ground up: weight on both feet, hands at sides, eyes front.

At this point, just as the song is ready to vocalize itself, the first and second technical exercises have been completed. Remember this important element of Exercise 2: The creation of *center as a specific focus or "spot" to which you sing and from which you will create your reactions is always the primary act that* preceeds *the physical tasks that will be assigned to your base and hands.* Later, when you are performing, your body will always respond to what your eye sees. Never sing without someone, or the illusion of someone, to sing to.

Once the Vamp is over and you begin to sing, your hands should remain at your sides. Your hands and feet have much to say during the performance of a song. Until you learn the importance of that specific language, I ask the actor/singer to train the body to say *nothing.* The employment of the *gesture* is merely the advertisement of mindlessness. Again quoting Stanislavski: "Make out of every gesture some act, and in general forget about mere gestures when you are practicing. Action is all that counts, a gesture all by itself is nothing but nonsense."[5] Later, and in greater detail, I will speak of body language (see chapters 12–15). It is the outer manifestation of a subtext, a *second script,* if we consider the primary one the song that is sung.

Review

Before proceeding, I want to reprise the order of the activities beginning with the nod and ending with the fourth bar of the Vamp.

---

[4] Singing seeks solid propping. Too narrow a base provides inadequate support for grounding yourself; too wide a base presents a straddled effect, implying a cowboy at a loss for a horse.

[5] Constantin Stanislavski and Pavel Rumyantsev, *Stanislavski on Opera* (New York: Theatre Arts Books, 1975), p. 6.

1   You are standing on stage or in a room ready to sing. You are resting your weight either on the right or left leg (that is to say, "sitting" on one side or the other of your body), with hands away from your sides, intent on physical activity. The object, of course, is to resist turning into a piece of lumber in these moments before you sing.

2   Nod to the accompanist to signal the beginning of the Intro or Vamp.

3   Remove your focus from the accompanist and return easily to a *general* focus into the theatre or the room in which you are going to sing.

4   Somewhere around the downbeat of the third bar of the Vamp your focus comes to *center* and *specifically sees* what it previously had been *looking at generally.*

5   Upon reacting to the center "spot" or "focus," the base moves from a "seated" position to weight evenly balanced on both legs, with feet twelve to fourteen inches apart.

6   As the base is coming to rest, the hands move, one at a time, to the sides.

If you have timed the Vamp well you should be focused center, base and hands at zero, at the finish of the fourth bar of music. The Vamp is over and you are now ready to sing.

DIALOGUES

There follow now simulated teaching dialogues between myself (herein referred to as DC) and two students, one male and one female. This invention will be employed after each exercise to isolate errors most commonly made and to explain how, like Topsy, these exercises grew.

His Work

Mr. G is thirty-four, of medium height, dark complexioned, with strong masculine features. There is about him a studied muscularity practiced and performed in dead earnest and with broad strokes that are, nevertheless, effective. One imagines rightly that his persona is of his own contrivance, designed to fill archetypal casting requirements. Mr. G's absence of humor induces DC to assign him Cole Porter's "Looking at You" (see chapter 5):

VERSE	I've gone afar collecting objets d'art
	I know the whole game by heart
	Why, Joe Duveen[6] will tell you what I mean
	T'was I who gave him his start.
	But[7]
	Since I looked, dear, in your direction
	I've quite forgotten my art collection
	To be exact, you simply prove the fact
	That nature's greater than art:
1ST "8"	Looking at you
A	While troubles are fleeing
	I'm admiring the view 'cause it's
	you I'm seeing
	And the sweet honey dew of
	well-being settles upon me.
2ND "8"	What is this light
A	That shines when you enter
	Like a star in the night and what's
	to prevent 'er
	From destroying my sight if you center
	all of it on me?
3RD "8"	Looking at you
(BRIDGE)	I'm filled with the essence of
B	The quintessence of joy—
	Looking at you I hear poets tellin' of
	Lovely Helen of Troy
LAST "8"	Darling,
A	Life seemed so grey
	I wanted to end it
	Till that wonderful day you started
	to mend it
	And if you'll only stay.
	Then I'll spend it
	Looking at you.

Here, then, is a good example, to quote Mr. Porter again, of "the wrong song in the wrong style" for Mr. G.

[6] Joseph Duveen was an eminent art dealer.

[7] The ubiquitous "but"; see chapter 1.

The lyric is elegant, the rhymes are witty, and the allusions are less a call of the wild than of Wilde. It will be a perfect prosthesis for Mr. G's assumed self.

While he is waiting in the wings, preparing to enter and demonstrate Exercise 1 as he has worked it at home, DC can use the time to furnish information about the song Mr. G will be singing. "Looking at You" was one of the songs Cole Porter wrote for *Wake Up and Dream* in 1929. Other composers also contributed to the score, including the gifted Arthur Schwartz, the English Ivor Novello, and Philip Charig, a composer who wrote with many lyricists, including one collaborative effort with Ira Gershwin. The 'song is AABA in form.[8] The Verse is scored to be sung easily in ad-lib, and therefore Mr. G, upon nodding to the accompanist, will receive a four-bar *ad-lib Vamp*. All ad-lib Vamps should end with a *sting* (a sustained chord with the melody note given preeminence at the top of the chord) immediately preceding the first sung note of music. There is only this to say about the sting: Never sing on it. It is not a command to sing. Upon hearing it, train yourself to count a heavy three beats before you begin the first words of the Verse. The silence between the sting and the start of the song can be supportive, demanding of attention, and even seem to create its own music. "To everything there is a time to keep silence and a time to sing" (Eccles. 3:7). The space that follows a sting is one of those times.

Mr. G must be ready for his entrance by now. Remember, at an audition or a performance of any kind this entrance is dictated by others, but in the execution of this exercise use your own sense of readiness. But DC cannot continue, for Mr. G is entering, and in the time-honored musical-comedy cue line DC can only mutter: "Ah, here comes Mr. G now. . . ."

It is moments later. Mr. G has reached center stage. DC has stopped him from continuing Exercise 1:

DC: Can you try the entrance again? Your eyes have dropped to the floor more than once, an unpardonable sin that advertises indecision. It also added a somewhat furtive

---

[8] As explained in chapter 2, the first two "8"s and the last "8" are the same musical theme ("A"), while the third "8," more correctly called the Bridge or Release, is a second theme, called "B."

quality onto the adjustment you had already made on yourself as you left the wings. Do not add fractional elements to what is already an integer, namely, you. You are making the false presupposition that if you do not add something to the sum of *you* we will see that it is missing. Just *come on;* leave yourself alone. You cannot sing until you experience yourself on the stage shorn of the inventions you may have employed in social, professional, or personal situations. Get rid of inventions and camouflage. The song you will sing will clothe you. I am trying here to lure you into that country where you will no longer feel the need for invention. Do not be afraid. Once you experience this figurative nakedness you will discover that you have never been more covered. Standing as you are now, clothed in all this machismo, we see how truly naked you are. You are not, therefore, ready to sing. Singing cannot occur under camouflage. I am reminded of a short poem of Samuel Hoffenstein's entitled "Proem":

Wherever I go,
I go, too,
And spoil everything.[9]

In any event, you can only guess what people see you to be and would be the last to know how you appear to others. On the other hand, I am a stranger. I view you honestly and objectively. If there is a *fix* to be made, let me assign the change of color.[10]

Mr. G has taken this criticism with good grace. DC congratulates him for his professionalism. The professional learns to differentiate between criticism directed at him and at his work. Work is what brings us together— only the work, and how to do it with increasing skill.

After a few moments of preparation in the wings, Mr.

---

[9] Samuel Hoffenstein, "Proem," in *Pencil in the Air* (Garden City, N.Y.: Doubleday, 1923; 1947), p. 15. Used by permission.

[10] Another painful experience related to this subject is the first hearing of your voice on tape, record, or sound track. Each of us hears his voice before it is resonated. It is something of a shock to hear what others hear after it has emerged from the mouth.

G reenters and moves center. This time, keeping in mind the directions he received and attempting the suggested change in color, he shows a positive qualitative improvement.

DC: Very good! Don't lose it. Continue the exercise and keep alert. Eyes front and relate generally and easily into the theatre. Not too wide . . . you're working too far to the left and right. Narrow the aperture of your *camera eye.* You do not have to take in the boxes on either side of the house. And watch your eyes! They are going to sleep because *you* are going to sleep. Stay awake! Arm yourself with thought. I cannot dictate that for you. It should be created by you, and molded out of your life, your thinking, your sensibilities, your psychology. It can range from the inanity of a shopping list to the complication of a logarithm table. The important point here is that something we see on you indicates consciousness and not torpor.

Good! Very good! You are catching something here that is eminently attractive. Try to capture it, to feed it into the computer of your mind and memory so that you can call it into play when you need it.

It is a few days later. Mr. G is back on stage. DC, bridging the end of the last session to this new encounter, recalls a story told to him by an eminent actor with whom he had worked many years before:

DC: Mr. K related to me this extraordinary example of the eyewitness factor that is forever at work in the life of an actor. Mr. K had been orphaned as a young boy and had been raised by a maiden aunt whom he had dearly loved. The transition from childhood to manhood worked its inevitable separation between him and the small town in which he had spent his early years. He moved to New York, subsequently married, and began the career that later brought him success on the Broadway stage. On the day a telegram arrived informing him of his aunt's terminal illness, he flew home but arrived too late, her death having occurred before he could reach her. Alone in the clapboard house he had lived in as a child, he surrendered to a grief far greater than any he had ever known. He told me of that day's revelations. His old room, that had once supplied the ample boundaries of his world, seemed to have shrunk, the walls now barely providing adequate space for the long-forgotten and still undisturbed pennants that hung there. He tried to describe the extent of his sorrow, the depth of which was quite beyond any he had ever experienced. And yet . . . and yet, he said to me, even as he wept, a part of his mind whispered, "Take note of all this. You never know when you will be able to use it!" (The class makes sounds of a shared understanding.) An artist has only his life to implement and fulfill his purpose. Impede the collection of memories in the computers of his mind and you short-circuit the very current that powers the lines of communication between his "letter to the world" and those who attend it.

Mr. G has performed that which he reworked at home. The macho excess has been softened, his focus into the theatre is less wide, he is easier with himself, and the tendency to fall asleep has been inverted to an active wakefulness. DC is unstinting in the praise that works an increasing effect on Mr. G, who further surrenders himself to the abandonment of the old invented accretions. As he continues the exercise, seeking to keep his body alive, hands away from sides, base in a seated position with weight on one leg, DC edits further:

DC: May I speak here about your hands? They are, like your feet, extremities, so-called because they are your outer limits, the endings of yourself. Possessed of no mind of their own and cursed with a great distance between them and the mind they must obey, they advertise their pitiable ineptitude. Given half a chance they will flap, flip, fluster, flutter, go up, go down only to go up again, shrug, shake, wave, and waver, intent upon projecting the illusion of a marionette's hands manipulated by an unseen madman (see chapter 17.) In this exercise, before arms come to the sides, and, in general, in the performance of songs, be guided by this simple but wise rule: Whatever your hands want to *say* or *do,* if it can be done lower, tell them—nay, order them—to say or do it as low as it can be done on the body vertical. Hands flapping about the upper portion of your body and your face can and will upstage you. To upstage yourself is self-murder. There will always be others willing and eager to commit that crime against you. Why help them? At an audition you and your work should be accessible to the eye. As the lyric leaves your mouth, it seeks a clear passage without having to be seen through a curtain of dancing fingers attached to witless arms. Decibel count is not the sole factor that enables an audience to hear a song. One unconsciously sees as well as hears the singer. Lip reading becomes a subtle but nevertheless important part of comprehending what we hear in the theatre.

The body has much to say, as we will learn. But now it speaks a garbled language that must be erased before we can construct a clear and sane physical statement on and around what we sing. Before the Vamp begins, Mr. G, you are keeping your hands away from your sides, as instructed, by washing them. That, in itself, is a simple, good choice. But see what happens. Slowly and insidiously they begin to climb. The elbows bend and they rise still higher until you have left yourself and moved into *character,* resembling nothing less than Uriah Heep protesting 'umbleness. Bring those hands down . . . even lower. No, keep washing them, but bring them down. There you are. You see, they are still performing the function you ask of them but they are doing it as low as possible and, as a result, you are again visible to us. Now, of course, you cannot pull at your ear, run your hand through your hair, or straighten your collar and tie without bringing your hand or hands high, but those functions can only *be* performed on specific body levels. The activity you have chosen does not lose meaning when the hands are brought down, and you inherit the added dividend of allowing us to see you clearly.

Your hands and feet wait for your instructions. When those instructions fail to arrive, they go ahead without them. A fortunate few have an innate physical grace. Their motor system is able to sustain elegant moves that, though meaningless, are decorative additions to the singing of a song. The majority of us are not so gifted. Train yourself now to work at *zero,* with no constraint, by giving your hands nothing to say, and they will have no difficulty later, when sanity activates them. Replacing a good nothing with a good something is easier than creating a good something out of a bad something.

Everything seems set for "go" now. Give yourself another moment or two, relate easily into the theatre, and then let us move on and "nod in" the pianist.

Under the circumstances, the complicated coordinations Mr. G has been asked to perform justify DC's confidence in him. Although his efforts are more effortful than they will be tomorrow, we have to recognize again the difference between good and bad contrasted with correct and incorrect work. Mr. G may appear somewhat studied but the technique, as performed, is correct albeit not very good. Until new habits replace them, we cling to old ones. The exercise is being *done* by Mr. G rather than simply *being* him, but it is a beginning.

Mr. G, staying within the demands of Exercise 2, nods to the pianist at his right. The ad-lib Vamp for Cole Porter's "Looking at You" begins. Mr. G brings his eyes to center but, before he can continue, DC stops him and the pianist.

DC: You are going from the pianist to the center focus with no local life between these two express stops. Leave the pianist without jerking your attention away from him and move back into the theatre but *not* to center. Remember, that specific focus on center does not occur until the third bar (the middle) of the Vamp. If the pianist is on your right, as in this case, linger for a moment somewhere to the right of center, in that area of the theatre between the pianist's location and the center destination. In that short moment you will have thwarted the look of an eyes-left military maneuver.

Timing your arrival at center to the third bar of the Vamp must be executed with grace. No jerk, no snap of the head, no sudden arrival. When it is time, gently put your eyes center and then follow with your head. Under less self-conscious conditions it is what you would do as a matter of course. Now we are imitating life as artfully as

we can.[11] After arrival at center, I want to believe you are
seeing what you went there to see. Blink! It is neither Dr.
Mesmer nor a twirling twinkling trinket that catches your
eye. You are not under hypnosis. No need here to indulge
in profound thinking. Merely say "hello," figuratively, to
that which or to whom you are reacting. What is essential
is that there be recognition. Energize the focus by
ideating. The creation of ideas in endless series can be
likened to the production of energy. Energy, in turn, connotes the concept of "heat." And heat, unfortunately,
cools unless it is reheated. Focus into the theatre requires
this kind of reheating (reideating) or it, too, will cool, and
you will be staring with blank eyes that press on the
center "spot." The more you press, the more you seem to
be insisting (unnecessarily) upon the presence of the
theatre. But the theatre *is* there. Seeing it merely cor-
roborates the fact. It is not "more" there when you "see it
harder" or, worse, play at seeing it.

Mr. G, relating to DC, has regained his ability to
focus, since DC is alive and need not be imagined. DC
points this out, and even suggests that Mr. G put DC in
that center focus by an act of anthropomorphosis. Mr. G
moves his attention from DC to the center focus, without
pressing on it when he arrives there. The class can now
discern the difference between the aspect of *seeing* as opposed to the nonsense of *acting* seeing.

DC: The pianist on your right was exerting some kind of effect
on you before you nodded to him. It was as if you knew
he was there and that knowledge influenced you in this
way: You played into the theatre almost exclusively to
the right side of the house and seemed unaware that there
was a left side to be taken in. But you see, there is no
pianist until you need him. And even the *need* of a
pianist must be dissembled. *You need nothing and no*

[11] Breaking down the act of seeing into two counts will illustrate the sense of
eyes first, head second. One recognizes by a follow-through of the head what
one first sees with the eyes. Only the blind reverse the action. Deprived of
sight, the head moves first as the ear seeks the sound source. The eyes, unsee-
ing, follow, but only to join the head in establishing a general location for
what has been heard.

one. *During the moments preceding the nod to your accompanist you do not even need a song.*

Finally, before you try the entire Exercises 1 and 2 for their final fixing, remember this: Focus, like your hands, wants to rise. You are on the threshold of singing. This is an act that you, as an actor, unconsciously consider unbearable. Too late to avoid it, your focus, seeking to reject the presence of the theatre, rises. It is another failure invention you must police. When you feel your focus climbing, become your own editor and bring it down. You must create a life, a recognition of a reality to which you will sing, or you run the risk of singing to yourself. There is nothing wrong with that when you are alone. In a crowd, however, it passes as eccentric behavior, a religious dialogue with the deity. There is enough eccentricity at an audition without further coal deliveries to Newcastle. And as for religious dialogues, keep them in *Fiddler on the Roof*.[12]

Mr. G exits for the last time and reenters to perform Exercises 1 and 2 in their entirety. All the work is performed as if by the numbers but DC approves of this as a transitional moment in the learning process. The Vamp is well played and at its finish Mr. G is focused center, at attention, his weight on both legs, with his hands at his sides. When next we meet him he will be singing. Ça commence.

Her Work

Miss B is in her twenties. She is gifted and attractive but there is about her a benign belligerence that DC intends to conceal behind the wrong song he will assign to her. During her first interview with him, and on numerous later occasions, she proclaims an unconcealed involvement in the women's rights movement. DC applauds her sociopolitical commitment but not her conviction that all men are the enemy. She is overarmed in the battle of the sexes. DC, determined to soft-pedal her bent for disputation, chooses Rodgers and Hart's "He Was Too Good to Me."

[12] "If I Were a Rich Man" (music and lyrics by Jerry Bock and Sheldon Harnick, from *Fiddler on the Roof* [1964]) is sung into the theatre, the subjective lyric requiring an objective delivery. The focus can then rise when, in the course of the song's development, Tevye speaks to God. The charm of this section of the lyric is, to a large degree, the result of the change from low to high focus.

      The song was written for *Simple Simon,* a 1930 show that starred Ed Wynn and Ruth Etting. There were nineteen songs in a score that included "Don't Tell Your Folks," "I Still Believe in You," and "Ten Cents a Dance." Dropped from the New York production were "Dancing on the Ceiling" and "He Was Too Good to Me" because the producer, Florenz Ziegfeld, was convinced Rodgers and Hart's songs were "too highbrow."[13] Today the caliber of these two songs would insure their presence among the minimum number of songs published in the first printing of any score in which they appeared. "Dancing on the Ceiling" surfaced again that same year in *Ever Green,* a successful revue produced in London with Jessie Matthews and Sonny Hale. "He Was Too Good to Me" was not heard in a later production, at least not to my knowledge, but one can ascribe its long and healthy life to the old saw, paraphrased somewhat, that you can't keep a good song down.

VERSE	There goes my young intended.
	The thing is ended.
	Regrets are vain.
	I'll never find another half so sweet
	And we'll never meet again.
	I was a good sport
	Told him goodbye
	Eyes dim, but why complain?
1ST "8"	He was too good to me
A	How can I get along now?
	So close he stood to me
	Everything seems all wrong now!
2ND "8"	He would have brought be the sun.
	Making me smile
	That was his fun!
3RD "8"	When I was mean to him,
A	He'd never say, "Go 'way now."
	I was a queen to him.
	Who's goin' to make me gay now?
LAST "8"	It's only natural I'm blue.
B	He was too good to be true.

[13] Samuel Marx and Jan Clayton, *Rodgers and Hart: Bewitched, Bothered and Bedeviled* (New York: Putnam, 1976), p. 135.

Miss B's acceptance of the Rodgers and Hart tune was not without struggle. It is relevant to comment here about the resistance women today bring to the singing of the sex-object songs Tin Pan Alley and the theatre churned out by the thousands during the first half of this century. Female dependency on the unfeeling male, the benign or blatant subject matter of almost all the songs we call "standard," is repugnant to women today. In my own teaching experience I have unhappily laid aside countless songs whose melodies are written on the memories of our minds because the words are insupportable to women at a time when they are demanding and winning equal status with men. Not only are the sentiments of the "My Man" genre of song:

What's the difference if I say
    I'll go away
When I know I'll come back on
    my knees someday. . . .[14]

"My Man," music and lyrics by Maurice Yvain and Channing Pollock, from *Ziegfeld Follies* (1921).

intolerable, but it is a further irritant that the words were written by men for women to sing. Only now are we hearing blues created by women for women to perform, a listening experience that is at the same time valid and novel. A vast culture gap displaces Rodgers and Hart's "He Was Too Good to Me" with Holly Near's "Get Off Me, Baby":

Get off me, baby
Get off and leave me alone [repeat]
I'm lonely when you're gone but
    I'm lonelier when you're home.
Get off me, baby
You're weighin' my body down [repeat]
Your lovin' don't make me tingle,
It only rolls me aroun'
I'd tell ya to go find another woman
But I'd hate to pass you on

[14] This was a signature song of the late Fanny Brice, reprised by Barbra Streisand four decades later in *Funny Girl*, the film based on Miss Brice's life.

That would be like passin' on to a sister
A pretty packaged bomb.

Miss B's resistance to the Lorenz Hart lyric, with its pandering to the superiority of the male (the "young intended"), is a stumbling block. In the specific case of Rodgers and Hart, however, a substantial brief can be made that would place them, historically, on Miss B's side of the progress fence. In 1936, six years after they wrote "He Was Too Good to Me," they conceived three musicals, writing not only the scores but, for the first time, their own librettos. The first of the three, *On Your Toes*, included a ballet created by Mr. Rodgers and choreographed by George Balanchine, entitled "Slaughter on Tenth Avenue." Danced by Ray Bolger and Tamara Geva, it can be said not only to have introduced a "serious" dance statement to the Broadway scene, but to have fathered the gangster-cum-moll ballets we have seen so often in the movies and on television. Mr. Balanchine made similar contributions to the remaining two musicals fashioned solely by the writers—*Babes in Arms* and *I Married an Angel*—and choreographed a fourth, *The Boys from Syracuse*, with a score by Rodgers and Hart and a book by George Abbott out of William Shakespeare. In all four instances, the presence of so eminent a dance director can be considered a radical departure from the norm of the time. As for Lorenz Hart, he may well have been the first lyricist to strike a blow for women's and gay rights, forty years before their currency, in the Bridge and last "8" of "Too Good for the Average Man":

Lots of kids for a poor wife are dandy
Girls of fashion can be choosy.
Birth control and the modus operandi
Are much too good for the average floozy!
Psychoanalysts are all the whirl
Rich men pay them all they can.

Waking up to find that he's a girl
Is too good for the average man.

DC may sympathize, then, with Miss B's unwillingness to sing a script sung by a self-proclaimed "discarded sex object," but he also admires the song and, not being a woman, finds no difficulty disregarding those sociological changes that can invalidate many of the songs he grew up hearing in the theatre.

Noel Coward claimed to have been born in a generation that still took light music seriously. That generation, the one that preceded mine, passed on to us this same regard for theatre songs and, by extension, the Tin Pan Alley product. The music of Gershwin, Kern, Rodgers, Porter, Berlin, Arlen, Schwartz, Youmans, and the other contributors to the marketplace was collectively prized, afforded respect, and given the ultimate reward—sung, whistled, and danced to everywhere. That conditioning, and the concomitant osmosis that educated our sensibilities to pure melody, are denied those born in the last twenty-odd years. There is much to praise in the contemporary music scene, but it has not contributed any significant melodic material to the collective American unconscious. I am convinced that the nostalgia craze among the younger audiences is, at its base, a yearning to hear sheer music, melody for its own sake, and straightforward *vocal* songs.

In the case of "He Was Too Good to Me," Miss B is finally won over by Richard Rodgers' music. The song is, after all, a beautiful example of his art. Simple in line but sumptuously singable, it is irresistible. The sixth and seventh bars of the Verse include a shifting of keys assigned daringly to the melody that, once learned, can never be forgotten. The music of the second and fourth "8"s of the Chorus is not only vaulted in its vocal arc, but the vowels are carefully chosen to allow the singer to be at her most open-throated as that arc reaches its apogee. Miss B, as thousands of audiences before her, falls prey to the power of the music and agrees to accept DC's choice of material. Score one for Noel Coward who first recognized and labeled (in *Private Lives*) the potency of cheap music.

Before beginning Exercise 1, DC explains the structure of "He Was Too Good to Me":

DC: The Verse is in ad-lib, and will be introduced by an ad-lib four-bar Vamp. The length of the Chorus is thirty-two bars and it is in the ABAB song form. The first and third "8"s are identical musical themes and the second and fourth "8"s approximate. In the ABAB song there is no Bridge or Release, the third "8," as described, is an identical reprise of the first eight bars.

Miss B has witnessed the work of Mr. G and does not require a recapitulation of Exercise 1. DC waits for her entrance, but not for long. Her natural rhythms propel her out of the wings and into center stage as though pushed from behind.

DC: There is no need to make your entrance in a rhythm faster or, for that matter, slower than can be defined as normal. It may be *your* tempo but to my eye it is hurried. Also, from the moment you cleared the wings, your eyes went to a center focus and waited for you to join them there. Proceed in this entrance as in all your work, from moment to moment. When you enter, a valid task for your eyes to perform would be to take in the section of the theatre to the right of you as you are moving from right stage to center stage. In that way you can see the part of the house you are leaving and, as you cross the stage, pan[15] the theatre. By the time you reach center stage your eye will have taken in the margins of the theatre or the room you are going to work in. You should be aware of the space you will have to fill. Here is a perfect time to measure its lateral limits.

Miss B exits to enter again. This time her pace is slower and her eyes have taken in the width of the theatre. DC instructs her to continue the exercise in center

[15] The word "pan" (from "panorama") is employed in film to describe the movement of the camera along the horizontal plane to achieve a panoramic effect.

stage, keeping her arms away from her sides and maintaining a seated position in her base.

DC: Let us take a moment here to talk about your feet. They, like your hands, are extremities, but they are even further away from your mind. If your mind can be considered the sun, your feet are as remote from it as Pluto. Again, as in the case of one's hands, feet must be considered prime offenders. They can put the lie to what you are thinking, or what you think you are thinking. One of the reasons why, in Exercise 2, I ask the actor to move his base immediately *after* focusing center is to insure that, in subsequent performances of songs, he *acts* from the base up. The audience's attention should be directed in such a manner as to leave it no recourse but to concentrate on the singer's face in the final moments before he sings. If the actor does not control this *base on up* physicalization, the audience's attention may well be directed to one end of the singer, the feet, at the point when the other end is beginning to sing the song.

Another point of order: Be sure, when you are in the sitting position before and just after you bring in the pianist, that you do not short-circuit the ankle of the leg that is not sustaining your weight. Your feet look false, prettied, behaved. You are not a model demonstrating a product or a gown. Police all parts of the body where fear can be detected. Chief among them are ankles, knees, hips, elbows, and wrists—those joints through which must pass the current that carries the dictates of the mind to the motor system. Short circuiting at those points betrays the density of your thinking. Thin out your concentration and I will see a wrist go limp, an elbow break the line of an arm, a hip drop when you are singing that which should demand a pull-up onto both legs, or, in your case, the pretty pose of the *broken* ankle. Learn to experience the feeling of the space you displace—the air you preempt. That ankle's behavior is taking space that does not belong to it. Lock the joint and you prohibit the theft.

Finally, your shoes. We discuss choice of clothes here only as it pertains to the theatre and its imperatives. You are wearing white shoes. They are most attractive. Were you modeling shoes, the color would be an ideal choice. Because they are white I cannot take my eyes from them. But for this very reason I would not advise white shoes for the stage, under audition or other circumstances. You want the audience to hook in to the other end of you, and your feet, unless you danced (tap-danced, preferably) are the least interesting element of your singing. Shoes are dictators, too, or your performance. For example, in my classes, as you know, the wearing of sneakers is proscribed. Wear them and you sing them. Footwear affects one's sense of self and you are powerless to resist. When you are standing before your closet, choose your shoes and your clothes with this in mind: What you wear on the street and on the stage is chosen with different motives and from different closets.

Miss B is eager to try the exercise again. This time, having been made aware of her entrance tempo, her focus right and left into the theatre, and the behavior patterns of her feet, she improves her performance. DC points this out to her: "The more sense of detail you bring to your work, the richer its texture and the less prone you are to the dangers implicit in thoughtlessness."

DC summarizes the lessons to be learned from Exercises 1 and 2 before outlining the next step, the singing of the song:

DC: Both Mr. G and Miss B have accepted the peremptory dictates asked of them. Actors, beginning with the new experience of singing what previously was only spoken, may resist the arbitrary staging called for in sections of this volume. It behooves the actor to learn to create content within the arbitrary shaping of the staging device. What is alien to the straight play is inherent to the musical theatre. Direction often consists of autocratic instructions, and "staging" or "form" may even decree content. The direction and rehearsals of a play comprise countless moments of discussion of character and psychology of intent, and this accretion of detail enriches the final texture of the piece. Musicals are more mechanical in structure. Time in rehearsals is the enemy. Choreography must be created, music scored, and scenes excised of all expendable writing. There is no time for discussion. Externalized staging, considered the bane of the serious actor's professional life, is not only routine but an effective method for achieving the results we see on stage. Learn to live within the demands made on you by the director and choreographer. Even when the direction seems awkward or, worse, false, do it. You cannot know what the director sees out front.[16]

Interesting and often serendipitous results can be found in the journey the actor/singer takes during the rehearsal period in the life of a musical. Exercises 1 and 2 and the tasks you are asked to perform in the following chapters afford a small hint of that dictatorial climate. Go with it. You are gaining fractional experience that will get you through the raised voice, the hysteria, and the self-directed rages directors of musicals are prone to send your way. Fear not—on opening night, with the arrival of glowing notices, everyone becomes an instant lifetime friend.

[16] Of parallel interest, relating as it does to comedy (a major element in the musical theatre), is this extract from the essay "Chaplin on the Set," by Penelope Gilliatt (in *Unholy Fools: Wits, Comics, Disturbers of the Peace* [New York: Viking, 1973]): "Eventually the moves harden and become mechanical, which is what he wants. Once the routine is fixed and has started to bore the actors, the comedy begins to emerge. He works from the outside inward: first the mechanics, then familiarity and physical skill, and after that the right emotions will come. It is the diametric opposite of the Stanislavskian style that has become accepted modern dogma."

Chapter 8

"Air": The Space between the Lines

Don't just do something, stand there!

Perversion of an intramural show-biz admonition

I have said that the actor/singer must be taller than anything he sings; he must be more important than the song. No song may appear as *more* interesting than the singer who is singing it. If, at any moment, an inversion occurs, either the performer has chosen the wrong song or, as he was singing it, he was losing altitude in the "Air." The work in this chapter and in chapters 11–15 concerns the basic concepts that will guard against these *drops*. These concepts are essential to all the technique and performance classes in my studio.

To do battle with "Air" and to maintain buoyancy while singing through it, it is necessary to separate the three *how-to* divisions that are the parts of its sum:

1   How to identify it.

2   How to time it.

3   How to fill it.

WHAT IS "AIR"?

Identification is a simple equation. "Air" = music *not* sung within the body of the song. As previously defined, this music is found in the Vamp, in the spaces between the lines of the lyric (music "fills"), and in the Rideout.

This chapter (Exercise 3) is devoted to a simple device, the sole purpose of which is to instruct the actor in the *timing* of the "Air" pockets in the song. Exercise 2 in the preceding chapter isolated the Vamp from the song proper and formulated an activity to physicalize the Vamp and bring the actor, at its conclusion, down to a state of "zero." The exercise ended the moment before the vocal song was born. The first word sung can be said to have proclaimed and induced the death of the Vamp. Before I describe Exercise 3, let us investigate the subject of "Air."

It must be apparent to the actor/singer that he has no previous knowledge of "Air" as an integral placement in vocal music because it does not occur in acting. In his natural habitat, he speaks, and the end of the speech contains the cue words for someone else's speech. The mechanics of dialogue obviate the need for "Air." The actor employs pauses to create spaces around the language flow, but these choices are his to make and are subject to argument. "Air" in song is a fact of music. Choice is not allowed, nor is debate for or against the space. The "Air" occurs as a result of the mathematical base of the music and has nothing to do with the actor's decision to stop (or not to stop) the movement of the song. The "Air," then, is part of the game, and when the actor/singer sings, he often betrays his amateur standing. Deprived of the verbal reaction at the end of one lyric line that justifies the start of the next line, he stands with nothing on his mind but the weight of waiting through the composer's *music fills* until he can continue his sung monologue.

Before we concern ourselves with the creative aspects of filling the "Air," we must learn the amount of it that must be filled. Exercise 3 shows the actor how to move within the exact space afforded him by the *arc of "Air"* he inherits without forfeiting, for the present, the physical zero he was in at the end of the Vamp. Not until chapters 11–15 will we begin to define and execute through body language the role played by the hands and feet, and indeed all quadrants of the body, during the act of singing what the actor wants to say. For now, in Exercises 1, 2, 3, and 4, "Do nothing till you hear from me."

EXERCISE 3: HOW TO TIME IT AND FILL IT

If you are working on a stage you will have to shift *up* (back) at the end of the Vamp to allow yourself room enough to *cheat* downstage during the song. In a room, move to an area that will permit you to come forward without encountering obstacles in your path. In each case, however, stay as much as you can within your tonal life at the end of the Vamp.

The Vamp has ended, your focus is center, your weight is evenly planted on a base not too narrow and not too wide, and your hands are at your sides. You have begun to sing, using the center *spot* or *focus* as the specific to whom you address yourself. As the first *music fill* in the Verse arrives, you will define the length of the *arc of "Air"* by moving downstage *one step*. It is of no importance whether the stride is made with the right or left foot. The step ends with the second foot joining the stride leg and making a new base similar to the one you held before the step was begun.

I shall attempt to describe the timing of this move. These are the important factors:

1 When does the step begin?

2 How long does it live?

3 When does it end in the new base?

"Air" can generally be expected in the seventh and eighth bars and in the fifteenth and sixteenth bars of the Verse, and always between "8"s in the Chorus. More "Air" can occur if the song is longer than the customary sixteen-bar Verse and thirty-two-bar Chorus. But you can recognize the *music fills* at those key places and acknowledge their presence when they appear more frequently.

The step is born as the last word of the line begins its verbal life. This moment is generally on a downbeat and the music that is the "Air" or *fill* starts its life with the arrival of that downbeat. The leadoff or stride-step begins then and is kept alive, moving downstage, with the second foot making the new base. However, that base must *not* be made the instant the actor/singer starts to sing the beginning of the new line (a natural tendency), but be timed to occur somewhere within the middle of the new verbal line. The following lyric ("America") is one we all know. I have chosen it for no other reason but to indicate the duration of the one "Air" in it:

My country, 'tis of thee,
Sweet land of liberty,
Of thee I sing. [Air]
Land where my fathers died,
Land of the Pilgrim's pride,
From ev'ry mountainside,
Let freedom ring.

The step would occur and define the air between the words "sing" and "where my" in the following line. Here the step ends in the new base.

Don't's

1 In your eagerness to move, do not anticipate the arrival of the "Air" by leaving too soon. In "America" that would be illustrated by starting the step down on the words "thee I" instead of on the "s" of "sing."

2 Resist the temptation to bring down your second foot (the one following the stride leg) to make the base simultaneously with the start of the new lyric line. Again, in "America" do not end the step on "land" but continue its physical life so that the new base occurs on "where my." You should be at zero, in the same base as you began, but downstage one step, by the time you are singing "fathers died."

Do's

1 Try to time the move downstage smoothly. If there is a long fill, the step will be slower. If the duration of "Air" is short, the step will mirror that by being more compact, and not in slow motion. The intention of Exercise 3 is to keep the step moving as long as the arc of "Air" lives.

2 Take yourself with you as you go. Resist the tendency to tilt back or lunge forward while moving. It is an easy step down that should not be decorated with any frills. The *move's* the thing wherein you'll catch your consciousness when you sing.

The actor/singer translating his comprehension of "Air" into a move downstage indicates that he is in control of both the concept (mental) and the execution (physical) of the technique. In recent years I have discovered a further value in exercises that use the feet to define expertise and, further, to reveal the clarity of one's thoughts. Television and film have bred a truncated actor who, as a result of too many close-ups and head shots, may remain unaware that he possesses a lower half. Along with the dance, singing brings this lower half to the actor/singer's attention with stunning impact because all four quadrants of the body are used and seen. No film editor or television director decides what will or will not be seen; what the hands and feet do is eminently visible. There is, then, good reason for the performer to feel a physical self-consciousness when he sings. In many cases this is an original experience. All of him is on stage and he is only too certain that all of him is not carrying an equal share of the burden. Exercise 3 and the work in chapters 11–15 are not only valuable as an introduction to this totality, but will help the actor make a much-needed adjustment after being too long in television and film.

DIALOGUES

The Character Actor

Mr. M, despite his years, presents himself as a younger man by dressing modishly to effect a youth he can no longer claim. DC is unwilling to tamper with personal motives, but he assigns "Alone Too Long" to make more obvious the poignancy of Mr. M's evident Faustian inclination:

VERSE	If I seem to be shy and slow to hold your hand,
	It's because we're face to face this way,
	And there's so much I'm afraid to say. [Air]
	Could I tell if I try the hundred things I'd planned?
	Could I somehow feel you'd really understand? [Air]
1ST "8"	I'd kiss you if I dared,
A	I want to but I'm scared,
	I should have known I've been alone too long. [Air]
2ND "8"	My lips are much too still,
A	My arms have lost their skill,
	My charm has flown, I've been alone too long. [Air]
3RD "8"	It's been years since I have whispered
(BRIDGE)	a foolish love-word,
B	And I'd be afraid I'd sing you a faded song. [Air]
LAST "8"	But if you smile and then
A	Say, "Darling, try again,"
	I'll know you've known
	I've been alone too long.

Mr. M has witnessed the work of Mr. G and Miss B. There is no need to reprise the requirements of Exercises 1 and 2, but while he waits in the wings in preparation for his entrance DC speaks about "Alone Too Long" and his choice of it for Mr. M.

DC: In the case of the character actor, the wrong song has less value than it offers the younger, more flexible actor. At an audition, the given is that the character actor/singer is there to read and sing for the character role. Categorical casting, so much a part of the musical theatre, does not permit too radical a *fix* on what the *eye sees*. The song chosen here is a subtler adjustment aimed at the ear of the auditor, coloring his judgment of the actor/singer less by what he sees than what his *ear hears*.

Mr. M is unaware of DC's motive behind the particular selection of "Alone Too Long." It is a lovely song and he is more than willing to sing it. The fact that it announces what his choice of clothes prefers to mask is not evident to him and can be considered DC's good fortune.

The Verse is, again, to be sung in ad-lib, further validating the discussion in chapter 1.

The Chorus is AABA and the "Air" is marked in order for the reader to know, in advance, where Mr. M's moves downstage will occur. The lyric is an example of Miss Fields' ability to capture romance without recourse to sentimental cliché. "Close as Pages In a Book," "The Way You Look Tonight," "I'll Buy You a Star," "Lovely to Look At," and "You Couldn't be Cuter," to name only a few of her lyrics, bear witness to man's eternal delight in women. And the music Arthur Schwartz has composed is as lyrical as her words. The A theme is reprised in the second and last "8"s except on the final title in the penultimate bars of the Chorus, when the melody rises on *"alone* too long" a major second higher than it is scored in the first two "8"s. By this simple highlighting of the title, the surge that occurs surprises and beguiles the ear.

Mr. M enters. His nod and subsequent activity during the first two bars of the Vamp require no comment from DC. But he is stopped before the third bar will bring him to a center focus.

DC: Very good. See if you can keep hold of that vitality as you shift upstage.

Mr. M, still playing into the theatre, moves back, nods again, and this time finishes the Vamp and begins to sing. His focus is center, weight on both legs, and arms at his sides. He accomplishes the first downstage move in the "Air" between "I'm afraid to say" and "Could I tell if I try". DC interrupts:

DC: I would like you to try the step again, keeping in mind these adjustments. Do not think of the move as a change in geography but as a *pull up* as you proceed downstage. The "Air" must be considered the element in the music that supports its continual escalation. You do not need to cover ground (a horizontal sensation) so much as to stay in a moving state as long as the vertical escalation demands it of you. Seven-league boots are not required here. You can achieve this sense of climbing as you step forward by placing one foot almost directly in front of the other. It is the tension contained within the body and not a flabby step forward I want you to experience.

The semantics that distinguish "tension" from "tenseness" is often confusing. Tension, as utilized here, is a positive force achieved by the control of the energy produced within the body and the expension of it to sustain movement. Tenseness is a negative and, therefore, an impeding condition. Many words the actor uses in his work are dangerous when applied to singing. "Comfortable," "improvisational," and "relaxed" may have their value in creating a constructive environment in acting but, although one cannot sing when the body is tense, singing is by no means a *comfortable* act. Today improvisation is recognized as a valid approach to play and cinema acting (although I doubt if the affection for it is as universal among writers as it is within the ranks of actors and directors). In singing it is of no value at all. A lyric, the music to which it is allied, and the accompaniment that supports the song are all finely wrought pieces of work. No singer can possibly improvise the complicated configurations of rhyme, meter, melody, and harmony.

If "relaxation" connotes a state in which constriction cannot occur, I embrace the word. But with little effort (no pun intended) relaxation mutates into dangerous cognates like "ease," "repose," and "leisure." Do not permit yourself the luxury of *comfort* and do away with whatever makes you *tense*. Tension, as opposed to tenseness, is the practical gray that teeters between the white and the black.

Mr. M tries the Vamp and Verse again, but this time without his entrance. Once the actor/singer has mastered the technique of making the journey from the wings to center stage without inventions of false behavior, with an energizing walk, and with a *general front* focus into the theatre or room, there is no reason to execute it each time he gets up to sing. All subsequent performances of his material will begin with Exercise 2, where all of us take up residence in our dreams: center stage.

The moves downstage are more controlled and DC permits Mr. M to sing the entire Verse and continue into

the second "8" of the Chorus. He is stopped and con-
gratulated. DC explains that there is little need now to
sing further since the mechanics of the step stay the same.
If it is correctly performed three times, as in the case of
Mr. M, it is evident the actor/singer is aware of the feel of
it. Mr. M, who possesses a felicity for language, describes
the sensation of the move.

Mr. M: I felt as if I was meeting with a resistance in the *air* in
front of me. It was like . . . like moving through
black jello" [a reference to the blackout and the front
lighting in the studio].

DC knows better than to fight him for the curtain line.

The Leading Lady

Miss H presents to the world at large a ceaseless optimism in partnership with a toothsome smile. At an age
closer to the forty wherein not life but prevarication
begins, her relentless good spirits must be dampened with
the choice of a wrong song. Unwilling to make the change
too drastic, DC chooses the soft self-recrimination of Irving Berlin's "Fools Fall In Love."

VERSE	Why do I allow my heart to make decisions for me?
	Why do I keep list'ning to my heart? [Air]
	Why do I get so involved when I would rather be free?
	Maybe it's because I'm not so smart— [Air]
1ST "8"	Fools fall in love
A	Only lunatics fall in love
	And I'm a fool— [Air]
2ND "8"	Fools seek romance
A	Only idiots take a chance
	And I'm a fool— [Air]
3RD "8"	I should be able to put all my feelings aside,
(BRIDGE)	I should be able to take one free ride–
B	In my stride– [Air]
LAST "8"	But fools cannot play
(A) WITH	They get serious right away
CODA	And break the rule— [Air]
EXTENSION	My heart's on fire when I know I ought to keep cool,

Fools fall in love
And I'm such a fool.

Miss H embraces the Berlin tune with her customary ebullience, which exhausts more than it elates. As in the case of the others, she goes into the wings to make her entrance. DC uses the time to speak about Irving Berlin and "Fools Fall in Love."

DC: Irving Berlin is assuredly the foremost creator of popular music for the world, for the theatre, for Tin Pan Alley, for film, and for all of us who are his benefactors. His professional modesty[1] and low public profile may be the factors responsible for his name and work being less in the forefront of today's consciousness, but he has been creating minor masterpieces for seventy years. (His first published work, for which he wrote only the words, was "Marie from Sunny Italy," written in 1907.) Alec Wilder, in his fascinating work *American Popular Song: The Great Innovators 1900–1950* (New York: Oxford University Press, 1972), said: "Admirers of the music of Jerome Kern, Richard Rodgers and Cole Porter are, in my experience, unlikely to consider Berlin's work in the same category. I believe that out of forgetfulness and confusion, they are inclined to minimize his talents." He goes on to list some of Berlin's most lovely songs, and to it would have to be added "Fools Fall in Love." The song is somewhat eclipsed in the *Louisiana Purchase* score by the more often heard standards: "You're Lonely and I'm Lonely" (an enchanting duet sung by Vera Zorina and Victor Moore), "You Can't Brush Me Off" and the show's title tune, made famous in the memorable act put together by Kay Thompson for herself and the Williams Brothers.

The Verse, again, is in ad-lib, and the Chorus is AABA, as marked. Of some interest: The A theme,

---

[1] He generally withholds permission to use his music or lyrics in any published form other than the sheet music that is its original home.

although called by its generic name "8" is only six bars long. The Bridge is the usual eight bars in length, but the A reprise in the last "8," due to the added Coda, is fourteen bars long. The last words of the first "8," "And I'm a fool," are scored on the third of the key. When the same lyric line reappears in the second "8" it has surged up to the fifth of the key and achieves an impelling and elegant change of key into the Bridge. The same phrase in the last "8," on the words "And break the rule," rises still higher to the sixth of the key and further swells the Coda. All in all, the setting of the lyric is one of Berlin's most sensitive creations. The actor/singer receives the direction he needs from the composer. The pain of self-reproach is vocalized.

Miss H's entrance requires much adjustment before she is permitted to move upstage center and begin Exercises 2 and 3.

DC: I have nothing against unbridled good humor, but we are working for an entrance in which particular color characteristics are sacrificed to the larger goal of a *general personality complex.* Unattractive demeanor is no more or less to be excused than the selection here of the more acceptable but nevertheless unjustified and excessive elation.

Miss H is confused. No one has found her natural vivacity cause for adverse criticism. DC must continue.

DC: It is important to understand the purpose of the entrance I am asking the actor/singer to make. To say that one is *naturally* behaved is not to say that one behaves ideally. I speak only of the time you will live on the stage *before* you sing and without the protective cover of a scene to be read or a song to sing. It is only *you* who enters and I, as witness, must tell you what I see. It is not significant to me that what you are is an ancient or an ad hoc self-invention. I point out, like the mirror in Snow White, what is there. You must try to separate yourself from the defense mechanism we all invent to withstand criticism, particularly, as in this case, when it is constructive. A mirror reflects; it is not an adversary. Do not fear! No matter how far I move you away from what you are (or what you project), you will never be read as melancholic. We are speaking of degree only.

Quite apart from this, it can be of some value to hear what *we* see when *you* enter. Auditions, like fleeting social encounters, may induce us to alter somewhat those surface characteristics we presume require accommodation. In neither cases are witnesses called upon to register their impressions of you. But at an audition you not only *want* to know, you *must* know. You can take arms against any opponent when you are in total possession of the computed data he possesses on you. You are both the spy and the superior to whom you report. Sometimes it is beneficial to think of yourself in the third person singular. A most crass image comes to mind: You are packaging a product for the buyer. If you consider yourself as *he* or *she,* you can achieve the objectivity to comprehend and edit what you are and what you do to tamper with *his* or *her* conduct.

Miss H attempts the entrance many times. DC is supportive. This is the most difficult objective to grasp: to understand that one enters into a world where there is no need to create subtle protections against a presupposed enemy. Miss H, as all actors must learn, is not required to be charming, to be likable, to be angry, to be haughty, to be defensive, to be gay, to be humble, to be aggressive, to be macho, to be feminized—to be anything but who and what she is, presented at its most genuine, natural, and unstudied.

When Miss H, after many tries, begins to project the outer margins of a realer sense of herself, DC suggests she work on it at home and, for the present, move upstage and go on with the introduction of the Vamp and Exercise 3. At the completion of the first downstage step she is stopped.

DC: The arrival of the step was well executed but the base came to rest on the downbeat of the next line. Let me show you.

DC joins her on stage. They sing together:

Why do I allow my heart to make decisions for me?
Why do I keep list'ning to my heart?   [Air]
Why do I get so involved when I would rather be free?

He makes his base, with her, on the downbeat of the third
"Why."

DC: The arc of "Air" must be continued and defined by the
move downstage beyond that downbeat and into the middle of the line.

He moves up to sing the first three lines of the Verse,
and this time the new base is made around the words "get
so."

Why do I allow my heart to make decisions for me?
Why do I keep list'ning to my heart?   [Air]
Why do I get so involved when I would rather be free?

Miss H tries it alone and corrects the timing of the step.
She sings further, moving down at the end of the Verse
and at the end of the first "8." Each time the mechanics
of the footwork correctly defines the "Air" as it escalates
the song. DC praises the work and sums up Exercise 3:

DC: There is a definite contradiction you must understand before you are free of the tyranny of the music. The *musical
phrase*, when you hear, read, and/or sing it, includes not
only the melodic line but the music fill/"Air" that finishes
it. To take recourse again in "America":

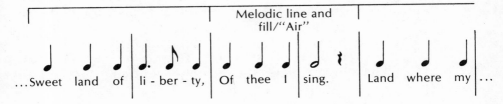

The performer, while *vocally* engaged in the "hold" on
the word "sing," must learn to pull away from the sense
of music and become *intellectually* aware of that "Air"
as the space in which the thinking that creates the next

lyric statement must live. The arc of "Air" is now to be considered as:

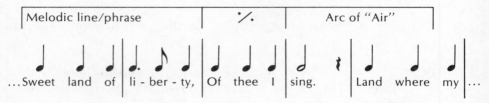

A good picture to keep in mind is this: The "Air" in the song is like the roof of a house. It extends to, and overhangs further than, the vertical walls in order to make the eaves. Similarly, the beginning of "Air" is preceded by *the start,* not the end, *of the last word of the line.* It *finishes beyond the birth of the new line* and not at its beginning.

The moves we have discussed in this chapter are inevitably going to be replaced with specific acting beats that will live in the exact time now filled by the step. My purpose is to restrain the actor/singer from *acting* the song before he knows the difference between *what* he is singing and what he is singing *about.* The nature of all text (in this sense, the lyric) is that it is the child of subtext (the *inner* monologue that creates the text and gives it its reference). This is, for the actor, an unchallengeable fact. But we cannot deal with subtext until the spaces that contain it are defined.

Exercise 3 educates the actor/singer to the specific shape of the spaces within the music of the song. When he is cognizant of their form (here defined by the move downstage that matches the length of the arc of "Air") he is ready to concern himself with content.

Exercise 4, in chapter 9, returns to the subject of focus and completes the technique section.

Chapter 9

Focus

All I see is my reflected eye.

Elder Olson

EXERCISE 4: SPOTTING

We have been singing to one focus, center, but it must be evident that there are an infinity of *spots* into which one can play. The actor/singer can sing to any focus out front: high, low, left, right, and the ever-widening lateral shifts to the left of left and to the right of right. Short of singing into the wings, you are permitted to sing anywhere, specifically or generally, you choose. This allowance of choice will be detailed when we are concerned with the *performance* of sung material (see chapter 17, under "Focus"), but for now there is no constructive merit in a technique that wanders between unifocus and infinity. We must define what is limitless down to a manageable circumscription. It is for that reason that Exercise 4 consists of only three spots to be focused upon: the center (C) (always the most powerful choice), left (L) of center, and right (R) of center. (In this section the words "lateral focus" will be used to define right and/or left spots.) But the actor/singer must remember I am speaking of the *technique of spotting* when I refer to C, L, and R. It will never be so rigidly employed when the performance of a song is the primary goal. We are engaged in the mastering of a technique which for now, but never again, will be visible. (Technique is made evident to the audience when it is improperly executed.)

All songs, whether sung for technical study work or in performance, should begin C and, generally speaking, be C at all pivotal lines in the lyric:

1   First line of the Verse.

2   Last line of the Verse.

3   First line of the Chorus.

4   First line of the Bridge or Release.

5   Last line of the Chorus.

This is no ironclad rule, but I find the more it is ignored, the more provocative its replacement becomes. Questions arise:

1   Why did he begin singing way to the left? Unless there is cause, it seems a mindless act.

2   Why did she start the Chorus working far to the right? Is her husband there in the audience?

3   Why was the song's Rideout delivered to a box seat? Is his agent in town?

The truth is that only whim dictated the artless choice. Too often the actor/singer, unless regimented, sings laterally to evade coping head-on with the potency of a center focus. One does not take command when one is unsure of the tactics to use. You can convince the actor to sing, especially if he needs the job, but you cannot expect him to do it well for the same reason. Fear repels him from C focus, for that would be, so to speak, looking the audience straight in the eye. The shifting, *shifty* spotting to the left and right advertises not so much his unwillingness to sing but his guilt in the knowledge that he does not know how and to whom to do it. It is for this reason that I ask him to recognize the power of center and to use it where it is most effective: at key points in the lyric.

We know the lines that will be delivered C. With that knowledge, we know, too, that the lines *preceding* those center choices can have a lateral focus. You have already performed this at the top of the Vamp before coming to center at the Vamp's third bar. The arrival at center at the top of the second half of the Vamp is given its power because we *come* to it rather than having been there all along. This will be true, then, of all the lines that precede those given to the C focus, as noted on the above list of five key lines. It is not important whether you go left or right on a line before coming center, except that it is wise to alternate them or you may bounce back and forth from L to C to L to C or from R to C to R to C and be unaware of your lateral yo-yoing.

We know now *where* we will change focus. Let me speak about *when* we will do it. The step downstage in Exercise 3 defined the musical fill or "Air." The change of spot has *nothing to do with the music and all to do with the words.* You change focus because you have something further to say to another part of the house. It becomes imperative to switch your spot before the new line is born. If you were moving downstage on the "Air," the *spot change must occur a moment before the step is born! First spot, then move!* Can you change focus without "Air?" Yes, of course. As a practice device, change it whenever you can, and you can whenever you have completed what you were saying to the "old" spot.

Don't's

    1   Never leave arbitrarily in the middle of a sentence. A change of focus is more sensible after the sentence has concluded its predicate.

    2   Beware, on a lateral focus, that you do not go too far to the left or right. Narrow the aperture of your camera eye. You are the point at which those spots converge. In the reverse, as they leave you, they move away from each other with increasing distance between them:

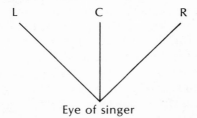

Eye of singer

When in doubt, tighten the spots:

Eye of singer

As you can see, a minimum switch to the R or L still creates a line that moves further and further away from C. Correctly aimed (narrow in adjustment), the spot figuratively should hit the middle of either side of the orchestra section of the theatre. When in doubt about how wide to go, take one step to the L or R and focus straight ahead to your new center spot. Leave your eyes there and return your feet to the old center position. You are now focusing to a lateral no wider than it should be. Too wide a change and you will be singing/working to the side wall, unaware that the entire theatre has been ignored. Were you to do this on a punch line, you would lose the laugh simply because the theatre would not have seen/heard the joke.

3 Don't wait to change focus until the last word is dead on your lips. As soon as it begins, go L, R, or C, although you are still singing the word.

Do's

1 Try as many spot changes as the song permits. This is an exercise in technique. Whether you would employ that many changes in a performance of the song is not valid now.

2 If the song is objective (*you* appears throughout the lyric) or subjective (*I* or *me* is the recurring pronoun), practice the focus changes regardless of their relevancy to the lyric. Remember, if you were singing a presentational song whose sentiment is intended for the entire audience or "house" in Exercise 3, the single center spot would have been constrictive. Now, in Exercise 4, the use of C, L, and R will be a liberation, since you will be singing the song to more of the audience. Conversely, if you were singing an intimate love lyric that focused on an ex-

clusive center spot, C, L, and R spots will seem to make of you something of a Casanova. Ignore all of this. We are practicing *spot changes*. What is important is that you cannot perfect them "without a song."

3   For another curb on the tendency to ping-pong from L to R, use C to pass through, as in C-L-C-R-C-L-C-R (see following lyric of "Boy! What Love Has Done to Me!").

4   Should you *freeze* your focus choices? Yes. Again, this is only a technique, and that is the determinant now for singing this song. For performance purposes I do not suggest a frozen spot plan, although you will always know where you must be at significant lines in the lyric: center.

DIALOGUE: THE INGENUE

Miss R is archetypal and, as in the case of the character actor, DC cannot create a major prosthesis with the choice of a wrong song. He can only attempt to "age" her by the assignment of a lyric that sings, with irony, of experience. Whereas most actor/singers resist the wrong song, it is of some interest to note that both the ingenue and the juvenile embrace it. I present this as probable evidence of their discomfort with the insipidity of the roles they are relegated to play. For Miss R, George and Ira Gershwin's "Boy! What Love Has Done to Me!":

(C)[1]
1ST "8"
A

I fetch his slippers:
                                   [L]
    fill up the pipe he smokes.
I cook the kippers:
                       [C]
    laugh at his oldest jokes:
Yet here I anchor—
                     [stay C][2]
    I might have had a banker,
                   [R]
Boy! What love has done to me!   [Air]

[1] The Vamp, from the third bar, is focused to center (C), as pr
sequent spots are marked when and where they should o

[2] Stay C because the title of the song first appears here a
to C, where it will receive the most attention.

2ND "8"   My life he's wrecking,
A
                     [stay R]³
    Bet you could find him now
Out, somewhere necking
         [C]
    Somebody else's frau!
You get to know life
            [L]⁴
    When married to a low-life,
           [C]
Boy! What love has done me!   [Air]

BRIDGE   I can't hold my head up.
B
    The butcher, the baker,
         [R]
All know he's a faker!
         [C]
    Brother! I am fed up!
            [L]
But if I left him I'd be all at sea.   [Air]

LAST "8" I'm just a slavey:
A
              [C]
    Life is a funny thing.
       [R]
He's got the gravy,
          [C]
    I got a wedding ring.
But I have grown so,⁵
I love the dirty so 'n so!
Boy! What love has done to me!⁶

e here because the sentence is not finished.
le after the first time it appears in the lyric.
al spot change on "grown so" for "I love the dirty so
enter for the last line—the title. I chose to stay center
the end of the song because the revelation is so stun-
es, the long derogative list of the lady's unhappiness
er surprise in the confession of her love for him (she
he would say that when she began the song) but her
e seemed to me to demand the intensity of remaining

r" and the spot choices in order to help the actor/
f Exercises 2 and 3. Once he fully understands spots,

Miss R is in the wings preparing to enter. DC again uses the time to speak of the song and the Gershwins.

DC: "Boy! What Love Has Done to Me!" is from the George and Ira Gershwin score for *Girl Crazy,* produced in 1930. The lyric I have used omits the Verse for reasons of length and limited value as a preface to the Chorus. The Refrain here is compounded of two complete lyrics that I have blended to gain the best of each. (Although the song must have demanded recapitulation because of its humor and rhyme as well as the wit of both the melody and its harmonic support, two choruses at an audition do not guarantee double enjoyment; the operative phrase should be, "Leave them wanting more!") *Girl Crazy* is significant as the show that introduced Ginger Rogers and Ethel Merman, and in which Miss Merman first sang the song under discussion and also offered her historic renditions of "I Got Rhythm" and "Sam and Delilah." Further, the musical enjoyed the distinction of a pit orchestra led by Red Nichols, including among its personnel Benny Goodman, Gene Krupa, Glen Miller, Jack Teagarden, and Jimmy Dorsey! If these were not riches enough, the band applied their skills to a score that included not only Merman's three hits, but also "Embraceable You," "Bidin' My Time," and the ravishing "But Not for Me."

The song is AABA. The Release (Bridge) is not an easy one to sing. There are octave jumps and syncopated, quasi-instrumental phrases that require a cozy familiarity with jazz. However, as in the case of all Gershwin's songs (with, of course, the exception of *Porgy and Bess*), the singing actor can cheat around vocal corners without doing dire damage to the vocal line. I confess that I prefer a more stylistic vocalism of Gershwin to the purer singing required of Jerome Kern's songs. An Ella Fitzgerald would be the consummate proponent. However, in the theatre, the actor and the dancer often are more able than the singer to interpret the musical and verbal lanuguage the Gershwins employ. As justification for this opinion, many of their greatest songs were first introduced by Fred and Adele Astaire, Gertrude Lawrence, William Gaxton and Victor Moore, Walter Catlett, Clifton Webb, John W.

I suggest that he choose his placements on songs he knows, in order to acquire a familiarity with the technique.

Bubbles, Avon Long, Gracie Allen, Ginger Rogers, George Murphy, Lyda Roberti, Florenz Ames, Jack Buchanan, and hosts of others whose names would sadly have little or no significance for today's younger actors. The common denominator for these eminent performers is their secondary vocal talents. Dancers, comedians, and actors, take heart. The Gershwins will not only not let you down but may very well supply the musical magic that transforms the crow into a reasonable facsimile of the nightingale.

Miss R's entrance and Vamp have been commented upon at a previous class session. DC is eager to see her perform the physicalization of the "Air" in the Gershwin song and her mastery of the technique of focus changes. She is permitted to sing the first two "8"s and the first half of the Release before DC interrupts.

DC: Considered in the light of a first try it is quite passable. Before I edit your work, let me say how pleased I am with your evident delight in singing the song. We are not here to perform or to discuss performance. There is none to discuss as yet. But the lyric is giving you a larger palette on which your manifest youth can find older and wiser colors. The one dimension required of the ingenue in a musical rarely offers a challenge to the actor/singer. Later, however, when you sing songs chosen to gain employment, it will be of value for you to remember the wit and the wisdom explicit in this song and to use it to give texture to your implicit thinking.

In your eagerness to move where the "Air" begins (as practiced correctly in Exercise 3), you are moving *before* the new spot change is executed. True, you are not stepping, but there is a visible listing of your body from a position of weight on both legs to weight on one leg as a preparation for the move. But, you see, the step will later be replaced with an acting beat related to what you are going to say (sing). You must in no way telegraph that adjustment until you have achieved the new focus to whom you will be singing it. The new spot will inevitably receive, first, your attention, and then both the ideated space ("Air") and the new sung line. Before I go further, try just that sequence on, say, the last line ("Boy! What love has done to me!") of the first "8." You were center for its delivery and then, on the downbeat "me," you changed to a lateral (R) focus, followed by a step down that defined the arc of "Air" between the first and second "8"s. Do you recall the specific place in the song?

Miss R nods. DC instructs the accompanist to play only the Belltone for the first word. Miss R, focusing C, sings the title line. Again there is a muddying of the spot change and the step.

DC: Try to change only the spot and cut the move so that you can distinguish between the two separate acts of focus and "Air."

Miss R again sings the line C and on "me" makes a narrow focus change to the R but does not move. DC asks her to do this more than once until the technique is secure. Then he continues:

DC: Now, out of the context of the rhythm of the song, do the line again, and when you have changed focus from C to R, and only then, shift your weight and move downstage.

DC instructs the pianist to go out of tempo on the downbeat of "me" to allow Miss R time to spot and move without the demands of rhythm. Miss R sings the line to C, spots R on the "m" of "me," and then, indulging in the permissiveness of a rhythmless fill, waits a moment, then shifts her weight and moves down, spotting throughout the life of the step to the narrow R focus. After consolidating this sequence by repetition, DC speaks:

DC: All right. Now, of course, what is difficult is to do it within the strict rhythm of the musical fill. Again, as you refine the technique, uppermost in your mind and your motor responses must be: to whom am I *now* singing (spot change), then the ideating that will sire the new verbal line (the step downstage), and last the sung line, in this case "My life he's wrecking. . . ."

I am somewhat pained to speak of changing your focus on the downbeat that begins the verbal life of the last word of a line. To begin with, direction such as this is so mechanical that the actor/singer may feel like a Rockette performing close-order drill. It is true that were you to take a stop-action film of spot change it would fall fairly close on the bar line of the downbeat, but we are in the country called *timing* and its borders are not as unequivocal as those on a map. What I suggest you use, to achieve less rigidity in the spot change, is the image: When you are convinced the start of the last word has left your mouth and is on its flight through the fourth wall and into the theatre, then and only then change to the new focus. Feel this as relevant to the *birth of "Air"* rather than to the *birth of the downbeat*. As I have said, you will always *need someone*, or the illusion of someone, *to whom you sing before you have something to sing about.*

An interesting marginal fact about focus and its changes: As you become more facile you will feel the last word go dead while you are singing (holding) it. At the same time you will be aware that you are still working to the old spot. Be eager to get on with it without cutting too short what you have just said (the end of the line). The word "me" in the line "Boy! What love has done to me" is still directed, in the first "8," to the center focus, just as are the preceding words of the line. It would be confusing to sing "Boy! What love has done to" to a C focus and then jump to R for "me!" That R focus is not born until C has received the complete line.

Another sidelight: In the performance of songs, one can spot change *on time, too early,* or *too late.* Beyond the obvious preference of *on time, too early* is better than *too late.* And, considering the speed at which light travels, by the time an audience *sees* what it sees, the original action, as in the case of a conductor's downbeat, has already occurred.

The following steps in the technique of executing a song have been covered in Exercises 1–4:

1   The entrance.

2   The time spent in center stage before the song begins.

3   The nod to the accompanist.

4   The performance of the Vamp.

5   The steps downstage that delimit the time span of the musical fills or "Air."

6   The execution of the three spots chosen from the infinity of focus.

In my studio this work is contained in the First Class and requires eight weeks to perfect. Before continuing with the technical device or invention contained in chapters 10–15, there are some observations to be made.

WHEN THE WRONG SONG SEEMS RIGHT

Before the fact (in this case, personal knowledge of the actor/singer), selection of the wrong song for the actor to sing is not a difficult task for me. In the calendar of the class, I assign that first piece of material early in the period of the First Class, before the particular tonality of the group has been sounded and shaped. Most students are unknown to one another, and even when an actor of repute is involved, the real person is usually disparate from the unreal public personality. However, as the weeks elapse the class chemistry changes. Outlanders become insiders and even foes become friends. It is then that the profile of the class finds its definition. This metamorphosis from a formless group to one possessed of specific color, character, and achievement quotient never fails to fascinate me. I do not choose the parts that make up the whole with any preconception of what a class should be. The selection is predicated on the professional background of each actor/member and not on the chemistry of the aggregate group. But each class takes on a distinct personality.

As this conversion progresses, interesting factors are set into motion. Among them is the astonishing demonstration of the rightness of the wrong song. By the end of the First Class, everyone who has been singing what was, at the beginning, agreed upon by the class and myself as an unwise (for an audition) choice of song seems to be singing material chosen expressly *for* the actor/singer.

Does this alteration nullify the original selection and

the assessment of what we saw? Not at all. That music was designed to dress the performer in a costume chosen by and for a stranger. A similar cast of characters will people an audition. Seldom will the actor have a relationship with those for whom he is singing. Knowledge of what and what not to sing for those who do *not* know us is of great importance. But it is of some interest to note that when we sing what is recessive in our presentation of ourselves, the song, laminated onto that which is dominant about us, presents a full and rounded portrait for the eye to see. Therefore, what we call the wrong song would appear to be the perfect choice for an audition.

Unfortunately, casting from type exists in the musical theatre more than in any other division of our profession. The wrong song at an audition or in a performance is a disservice to the actor/singer. He must sing what he appears to be. The purpose of an audition is not to perplex but to present you with the least confusion to the eye. A song that protests that what we see is *not* so is ill-chosen. As I have said, the valuable lesson to be learned is this: Always sing what is proper to the circumstances,[7] but the choice of the thinking that establishes what you are singing is for you to elect. It is there, in *your song*, that the wrong song is indirectly sung.

DOING NOTHING IS NOT SOMETHING

I am always despondent when an actor I have taught for a short period of time tells me, with great pleasure, that he gained employment in a musical by "doing nothing" at the audition. Not having been with me long enough to learn to *perform* anything, he was forced to sing the song he worked on to perfect the technique of the First Class. I assume the steps downstage have been cut, only because at an audition they would be inexplicable. By "doing nothing," I imagine he refers to standing still, spotting C, L, and R, and risking nothing else. Achievement of that limited goal is certain to have value at any audition, if only because too much ventured might result in less than nothing gained. Most auditions come packaged with

[7] The ingenue should sing an ingenue song; the juvenile, a juvenile song; the character man or woman, a pertinent song in character. In other words, everyone should choose songs corresponding to roles on the casting sheet.

greater objectives and so suffer greater failures. A good nothing is to be preferred to a bad something or, as elegantly phrased by Jean-Paul Richter: "A variety of nothing is better than a monotony of something." However, that performer who might have thought he fooled the world may have fooled only himself. Epigrams aside, a good something is indisputably better than a good nothing.

We have been dealing with the concept of zero physical language while learning to time the "Air" in the song and to focus through the fourth wall. Now the technique of moving becomes our primary purpose. Chapters 11–15 are concerned with the hows, whys, wheres, and whens of body language and its function in singing.

The work of Exercises 1–4 should be left to rest for a while, since it is in no way concerned with the subject matter contained in the following chapters. We are leaving one part of the forest for another.

Chapter 10

Introduction to Five Technique Exercises on a Lyric

Don't just stand there, do something!

Corrected version of an intramural
show-biz admonition

A recurring question plagues the actor/singer when he begins to marry his music to his words. "What do I do with my hands?" becomes an accompanying leitmotiv that disturbs and vexes, and the search for an answer lingers as a poignant desideratum throughout his singing life. Hands are the primary enemy. Feet are no less a harassment, but hands, being closer to the actor/singer's field of vision, are more observable in their distress. In his own work the actor is never impelled to say to a director: "I understand my action in this scene but I wonder if you could suggest something for me to do with my hands?" But when they sing, both the beginner and the player of renown suffer an acute physical self-consciousness.

Only the degree of discomfort justifies posing the question of hands and what to do with them, since the actor (now an actor/singer), confused by his confusion, is oblivious to the foolishness of the question he asks.

Physical comfort while singing seems to be enjoyed more by those who are better described as *entertainers* than by actors who cannot, by definition, be included under that rubric. When singing is a natural act, as in the case of the born performer, the entire mechanism supports the very art itself.[1] No psychological barriers exist. Joy is compounded by a spiritual and emotional release. The great gospel singers, epitomized by the late Mahalia Jackson, seem to incandesce when they sing, further illustrating my point.[2] But when singing must be learned, not as a natural but as a mechanical expression, one may expect a veritable Pandora's box of hang-ups that will unleash their destructive forces. Jaws tighten, throats close, tongues swell and rise to meet the soft palate, shoulders lift, breath vanishes and reappears in short pants, arms stiffen, and the whole experience becomes the antithesis of an act supposed to be free and, if not easy, certainly unconstrained.

To compound the physical barriers invented by the actor/singer to impede vocalism, breach of technical know-how is called into play. Indicating, or acting both the words and on the words, may be a crime the actor eschews as a primary sin, but it is one he commits with little or no conscience when he sings. This crime is more grievous in singing than in acting. Bad acting advertises the amateur, the banality of his thinking, and the absence of craft, but it may often pass muster with audiences, critics, and, sadly, the actor himself. Indicated singing is apparent to everyone exposed to it, for it unveils the singer who does not know what to do with himself. And worse, the offender suffers from self-awareness of the gaucherie. The empty gesture and the meaningless charade superimposed on the lyric afford him no pleasure and act as a continual irritant to his aesthetic.

I have demonstrated that when thoughtlessness lies behind language (when the singer's "thinking" is con-

---

[1] Throughout this volume I have attempted to keep the actor/singer clear and separate from the actor and the singer. Jolson, Piaf, Garland, Streisand, Sinatra, and Horne may be considered actors, but there can be no doubt that they were born to sing, and their professional lives began and continue by verifying this.

[2] I never refer to singers of the classic and operatic repertory only because there is little to no resemblance between the actor and that vocal breed.

cerned only with the text he sings), a unique condition arises in which the mind becomes a blank. Body language is not an echo of what we say but the result of a shadowy kaleidoscope of thought impulses that feed what we are thinking into our motor system. It, in turn, responds with limitless physical language before, above, and around what we speak, to give that speech its totality of expression. This flow of thought-language is infinite in its variety.

We are all confined in our verbal lives to the restrictive range of our vocabulary. Most of us get through our three score and ten with a minimum of words and phrases, whereas each of us is Oscar Wilde in the richness of the subtexts we create to decorate what we say with the physical and emotional language of *what we mean by what we say.* When that element is absent in the language we speak (sing), the bewilderment of the body is easy to understand. Pathetic attempts to define with our hands what we hear ourselves sing are artlessly superimposed on the song. It is a well-recognized range of gesture the singer resorts to: hands up, hands down, hands out, hands in and down, one hand up, one hand down, the other hand up and then down—and if a number from one to ten appears in the lyric, it will be digitally represented. Only the limits set by ten fingers, two hands, and two arms define physicality, until a bizarre inversion occurs: Speech, deprived of its rightful association with thought, is surgically cut off from the very element that gives it its birth. In essence, instead of the singer singing the song, what we see is the song singing the singer. Because of its prevalence, this cannot be considered a heinous crime. Beyond demonstrating a simplistic innocence, however, there exists the glaring possibility, nay, the probability that someone can *sing* the song better than he. With the significance of the text disregarded, body language must go either for nothing or for the eccentric arm calisthenics described above.

As soon as the actor/singer recognizes the need of a continual wellspring of *speech we do not hear* but nevertheless acknowledge behind the song we *do hear,* he has begun to isolate the answer to the nagging question, "What do I do with my hands?"

I have said that when you deal with the subject of

"Air" in a song, you must be able to identify it, time it, and fill it. We identified it in chapter 2 and we learned to time it in chapter 8. We are now ready to fill it by replacing the steps downstage that defined the arc of "Air" with our own created content. Once the performer has perfected this technique he will have liberated his body and returned to it the task it is, by nature, accustomed to perform. If physical self-consciousness is the result of having only one script in mind (the lyric of the song), we are now prepared to create the *unheard script* that will accompany the lyric and *explicate for the eye to see what the ear will hear.*

The following five chapters concentrate on *subtext* and its application to singing. Each chapter will present a new exercise to be performed on a lyric.[3] The exercises will be identified numerically as the **One,** the **Two,** and so on. Chapters 11, 12, and 13 do not require an accompanist. If music has been something of an enemy, you can now relax. The pianist is gone and once again you are back in the land where words are spoken and not sung. Hallelujah and Amen!

---

[3] The technical work in these chapters is of extreme difficulty. In my studio it is confined to a special class experience of eight weeks.

Chapter  11

The One

And bad thinking do not wrest true speaking.

William Shakespeare

We have dispensed with music in these exercises so that we can see the words of the song that will be our script. As before, I will assign one lyric to a man and one to a woman for the sake of neutrality, and because it is somehow easier to relate to a technical device used by someone of your own gender. However, gender has nothing to do with the execution of the technique. Before beginning, let me reassert that we are not yet performing. Continue to maintain strict control over your emotions and carry out the demands of the work with a dedication to the mastering of craft.

Mr. T is a character actor, a probable thirtyish, who finds employment in middle to low farce. DC chooses a song that attempts an adjustment away from the baggy pants and closer to the pinstripe:

1ST "8" If I had a cow and a plough and a Frau,
A   How good my life would be.
           I'd make a home where I know my heart would
               rest.
2ND "8" I could hitch the cow to the plough
A   While my Frau looked on and smiled at me.

Smiled as she dreamed of the dreams we love the
best.

BRIDGE Dreams about a meadow rolling in the sunlight
B   And a field of clover for the pretty cow.
Dreams about a baby laughing at a raindrop.
          How do you suppose
          A new world grows?

LAST "8" Starting with a cow and a plough and a Frau
A   It's simply A–B–C.
I'd plough more land if the cow had children
We would expand if my Frau had children
Things must be planned for my children's children
          Now!

CODA   All I need is a cow and a plough
          and a beautiful Frau.

Miss W is a young actress of exceeding range, but is rarely permitted to vent her humor on anything more comic than television's police melodramas. To lighten her heavy professional load, DC suggests a heaping tablespoon of the meringue of Cole Porter:

VERSE   Since I went on the wagon, I'm
          certain drink is a major crime;
For when you lay off the liquor
          you feel so much slicker,
Well, that is, most of the time.
But[1] there are moments sooner or later,
When it's tough, I've got to say,
Not to say: "Waiter,

1ST "8" Make it another Old-Fashioned, please,
A   Make it another double Old-Fashioned, please,
2ND "8"   Make it for one who's due
B   To join the disillusioned crew,
Make it for one of love's new refugees.
3RD "8" Once, high in my castle, I reigned supreme.
A   And oh! What a castle! Built on a heavenly
          dream.
LAST "8" Then, quick as light'ning flash

[1] The ubiquitous "But,"

B   That castle began to crash.
         So, make it another Old-Fashioned, please!
CODA   Leave out the cherry,
         Leave out the orange,
         Leave out the bitters—
         Just make it a straight rye!

THE ONE: **THE FACTS OF THE LYRIC**

You are now in possession of your scripts and we can begin with a description of the first exercise to be performed on the lyric.

I want you to come on stage and, in *your own words,* tell us what the *script says.* Your physical demeanor while performing the **One** is of no importance. You may sit, stand, or lie down. The exercise is verbal. It will be revealed to you how little time you have spent in the past reading a lyric with any degree of perception away from and uninfluenced by the melodic line—and how much information, story point, and character data are to be read *in* a lyric without reading *into* it.

1   Start the **One** with the sentence: "This is a story about . . . ." Is it a man who narrates the tale? A woman? A boy? A girl? Could it be either gender? You will be surprised to learn that many songs are not denied you, although custom may have established the precedent that a man or a woman sing a song that need not have been so channeled. The **One,** then, begins with: "This is a story about a man," "a woman," or, if you can so demonstrate, "a man or a woman."

2   Give me the age of the narrator. The lyric seldom presents you with this information, but we can set it within these three categories: The maximal age (late thirties, forties, fifties, or up to the eighties if nothing in the lyric forbids the limits); the minimal age (teens, twenties, and so on); and the optimal age (that which best serves the writer's intentions). Never cite a specific number. Twenty-three, twenty-four, twenty-six, and twenty-seven are no less valid than twenty-five—mid-twenties is the apt designation.

3 Where does the lyric take place? If there is a place-name, so much the better. Porter's "I Happen to Like New York," Rodgers and Hart's "Manhattan," and the Gershwins' "A Foggy Day (in London Town)" leave no room for conjecture. When there is no geographic definition, we can still, *with objectivity,* define the setting as rural, urban, suburban, or even exurban.

4 If you can, give me the general economic bracket within which the narrator can be placed. Slot him in a sort of Mitfordian manner: lower-lower, middle-lower, lower-upper, middle-upper, or upper-upper, or a range that may include a combination of more than one. If you cannot do so from the information provided in the lyric, then do not.

6 What education has the narrator experienced? Certainly Porter's people are either well-educated or self-educated. Their language evidences this, whereas Berlin's Annie in *Annie Get Your Gun,* with all possible restraint on subjective interpretation, never passed through primary school. Often it will be impossible to isolate this element of information in the **One,** but you can sometimes gain an indication from the character's particular sensibility for words, choice of phrase, and sophistication of insight.

7 *Use your own language.* Make every effort not to employ the words of the text. Tell me the story of the lyric without decoration, omit nothing, and speak as you do in your own manner.

8 It is imperative to keep an objective distance from the lyric in the preparation of the **One.** You will find that it will not be easy to do. We all read too soon with our hearts, emotions, and, worse, moral judgments. Inferences are to be shunned. To make certain you stem the tide of your own personal assessment of the situation and the narrator's recounting of it, resist using the word "I" anywhere in the **One.** No "I think," "I would say," "I would guess that. . . ." Approach the **One** as a piece of reportage. Be prepared to defend it if challenged, and know that the defense must rest in the stated lyric and not in what you have imagined or assumed it to say.

Why a **One**? I have tried to lead the actor toward the realization that he cannot *sing* the song. The motive behind all singing is not what a song *says* but what it *means* by what it says.[2] We have excised the music in this exercise because it weakens our power to see what the words are telling us. A pretty song is sung prettily, a gay song gaily, and all sad songs sadly. It is not as easy to remove *ourselves* from the song as it is to remove the melody, but the effort must be made. Although technique is never more than the means to an end, and most of what this volume teaches will be relegated to that place in our minds where it will function without conscious application, I suggest that there is value in doing a **One** on every song you sing before you go on to perform it. We cannot be concerned with what a lyric means (the cornerstone of all performance) until we know what it says. And that is why a **One.**

DIALOGUES

Her Work

Miss W is ready to do her **One.** Since it has been made clear that stage demeanor has no relevance to the exercise, she moves a chair from the wings to C and sits. DC, somewhat amused by her metamorphosis from the terrified lady of the First Class to this paradigm of stage ease, fills the time, again, with background intelligence regarding Cole Porter's "Make It Another Old-Fashioned, Please."

DC: This lyric is from *Panama Hattie,* a Porter musical of late 1940. The musical, along with *Let's Face It* (1941) and *Something for the Boys* (1943), was concerned with or colored by World War II. If one were to add to these three scores those of *Mexican Hayride* (1943), *Seven Lively Arts* (1944), and *Around the World* (1946), this period of Porter's creative flow has been described as less than top-drawer. The ballads are not as fresh, although among the total group can be found "I Love You," "Ev'ry Time We Say Goodbye," and "Ev'rything I Love." The general level of excellence, however, was judged by Broadway professionals as having dipped. The price of genius is made

[2] The idea of subtext and the complicated structure of an inner monologue is not a new one to the actor. An interesting discussion of it and its application to a particular scene can be found in Nikolai M. Gorchakov's *Stanislavsky Directs,* trans. Miriam Gololna (New York: Minerva Books, 1968), chap. 4.

heavy indeed by this kind of critical sophism, and I imagine that it brought Porter great unhappiness. Whole scores were wrapped up and tossed away as a result of the Porter-is-written-out whisper campaign. I make no plea for the librettos of the musicals that were often the reason for the calumny, but certainly the composer-lyricist of *Kiss Me, Kate* (not to be written until 1948) cannot be considered as counted out. As a teacher, I am indebted to him. Many songs from these failed scores are Porter at his best. Among my favorites I list: "Ace in the Hole" and "You Irritate Me So" from *Let's Face It;* "He's a Right Guy" and "Could It Be You?" from *Something for the Boys;* "Girls" from *Mexican Hayride;* "Should I Tell You I Love You?," "Look What I Found," and "Pipe Dreaming" from *Around the World;* and "Only Another Boy and Girl" and "When I Was a Little Cuckoo" from *Seven Lively Arts.*

Panama Hattie boasts "I've Still Got My Health" (the only song I know that lists vitamins to gain a Roxy Rideout), "Fresh As a Daisy," "Let's Be Buddies," "All I've Got to Get Now Is My Man" (possessed of a stunning rhythmic verse that recalls the pithy and fresh-rhymed lines in "Ridin' High" from *Red, Hot and Blue!*), and the song Miss W will be working, "Make It Another Old-Fashioned, Please." The Coda of this song, and the intricacy of the interior rhymes in the Verse and second "8," are added sweeteners to a luscious melody.

(To Miss W) We can begin. I will be interrupting you as you proceed. My purpose is to achieve closer attention from the class by representing myself as an interlocutor-cum-interrogator. Remember, they do not know the lyric and both you and I share the same goal: to make certain they receive the **One** as uneditorialized fact. Be assured that my intention is to keep your rendition as true as you can maintain it. When I find exception to anything you say, our ensuing dialogue is motivated solely toward that end.

Miss W: This is a story about a woman who . . . .

DC: Is there anything in the lyric that would prevent a man from singing this song? (The reader at this point is advised to keep the lyric of "Make It Another Old-Fashioned, Please" in front of him.)

Miss W: Well, I think . . . .

DC: Please, I have asked that the pronoun "I" be cut from the **One.**

Miss W: The lyric is about a woman.

DC: I suggest you take a moment to reread it. (The class waits as Miss W, a bit less sure of herself, checks the lyric and finds nothing that would preclude a man singing it.)

Miss W: Isn't that strange? I could have sworn it was exclusively a woman's script.

DC: In a way, you were correct. There are no *specific* words a man could not safely speak, but one can go further and remark that the tonality of the language has a distinct feminine cast, a tendency toward a softer lyricism in the descriptive exposition of the lyric:

Once, high in my castle, I reigned supreme.
And oh! What a castle! Built on a heavenly dream.

A man, unless of royal caste, would not be easy with this imagery, whereas an audience could never construe the couplet, when uttered by a woman, to be part of a queen's narrative. But to guard against generality, the **One** should be corrected, at the top, to: "This is a story about a woman or a man, with the evidence more in favor of the woman." (In its original context, the song was sung by a woman [Ethel Merman].)[3]

Miss W: Well, as we said, this is a story about a man or a woman, but more probably a woman, whose minimal age, I would say . . . oops, sorry . . . cut that. . . .

[3] A recent English revue employing words and music by Stephen Sondheim has enjoyed success in London and the United States. One song in particular is sung by a man in total disregard of the gender for which the material was intended. My own sensibilities reject this as self-conscious androgyny. A woman who spits out these rageful revelations to her husband:

Could I live through the pain
On a terrace in Spain? Would it pass?
It would pass.
Could I bury my rage
With a boy half your age in the grass?

DC: Good.

Miss W: She is minimally eighteen or twenty-one, depending upon what state in the Union we find her.

DC: Why do you say that?

Miss W: Because she is in a bar drinking hard liquor.

DC: Do we know the particular kind she favors?

Miss W: Yes, rye Old-Fashioneds.

DC: Very good. Continue. . . .

Miss W: Some states have a minimum age of eighteen, others set it at twenty-one. In either case, she cannot be younger and be served.

DC: First rate! How old dare she be?

Miss W: I think . . . .

DC: (Interrupting) Never mind what you think . . . . Tell us how old she can be and still sing this lyric.

Miss W: (Chastened) Late forties, or early fifties.

DC: Are you saying that if she is in her late fifties, the song is denied her?

Bet your ass!
But I've done that already,
Or didn't you know, love?

is given vocal material that deepens our knowledge of her and adds complexity to her history. A man who sings it opens up an entirely irrelevant (to the song's intention) can of proverbial peas.

Miss W: Well, I . . . no . . . probably not.

DC: How about early sixties?

Miss W: That would be stretching it.

DC: Only to someone your age. (DC turns to the class to involve them in an explanation of the disagreement.) Here is a woman who, we will find out, is suddenly left by the man with whom she was living. By the way, Miss W, were they married?

Miss W: The lyric does not say. They could have been, but then again, they need not have been.

DC: Correct. And this . . . relationship . . ., she tells us, came to an abrupt end. Nothing in the lyric discloses how long they were together. It could have been a long-term association. From a dramatic point of view the lady's distress would be greater in direct ratio to the intimacy's perdurance.

Miss W: If I'm allowed a moment in the first person singular, I'd like to say that I felt that, too. In fact, the optimal age I chose for the woman was early forties.

DC: I will excuse the "I" because, to a degree, we must think subjectively when we choose the optimal age. But here we have demonstrated the dramatic values that lie on the side of *older* rather than *younger* by searching the lyric for justification. I only want you and the class to agree that the maximal age, in this case, has only the ceiling of improbable senility to limit us. Nothing in the lyric explicitly describes the woman as geriatric, but today a woman in her sixties may still be physically, mentally, and sexually alluring.

As in the case of gender, age brackets have their own coloration. A woman of eighteen (the minimal age) singing this song brings to the eye of the listener her unique impress. Certainly in this case, pain though she may be in, her youth affords her the promise of healing and new adventures in a life still ahead. For a woman in her sixties (the maximal age) the loss is more affecting because her future is more finite. The decade of her forties, as Miss W has observed, is a perfect optimal choice. Mr. Porter is well served, and the actress singing the song, with this simple age factor impelling its choice as, for example, audition material, inherits a quite special script/song. (To Miss W) Let us move on.

Miss W: The song takes place in a city. There is none named and it doesn't even have to be a large one, but Cole Porter people don't sit in bars drinking Old-Fashioneds in the middle of Oklahoma or North Dakota.

DC: I buy that. (The class reacts. The pressure is off Miss W, and there is an easing of tension.)

Miss W: The lady's economic bracket is anywhere from lower-middle to middle-upper.

DC: Defend that for us, please.

Miss W: The lower-class group is not found drinking cocktails in bars. Beer, maybe, but not cocktails. The upper-upper class? Well, it's doubtful it would be in a bar recounting its love lives to a bartender. That is not to say that this kind of experience doesn't occur to them. But they probably would drink it out at home in a room equipped with all the trimmings that obviate going out to a bar.

DC: Splendid. (To the class) This may seem inferential but it is relevant to and rooted in the lyric. The economic status of the narrator of a song, when it is sung out of context, may seem a trivial matter, but as actors we must collect all the information that will affect the way we sing the song: the manner in which we dress, stand, and even think. Lyrics, like one-act plays, are impacted full-length dramas, and the techniques the actor employs are no less valid in one than in the other. Of course, I refer here to the kind of material I have chosen for these exercises—songs that possess a strong narrative/subjective lyric. You cannot use this device on songs without some narrative element, although a fraction of this particular technique can be applied to almost all material. "I Got Rhythm," however, would gain nothing; it relies on other bags of tricks.

Miss W: May I add a factor that dates this lyric? The cocktail the lady orders is an Old-Fashioned. I think its name is appropriate. I had to look it up in Webster's Unabridged Dictionary and it wasn't even in it. Only after I asked friends did I find out what it was. How do you suggest the actor handle this?

DC: When we construct the **Two** (chapter 12) we will discover that this lyric has nothing to do with Old-Fashioneds or, for that matter, liquor of any kind. Here is the beginning of your understanding of the two elements with which we will be working: The verbal content (what the words say) and the significance of that content (the subtext). Macbeth may drink his pot of ale, Falstaff may quaff his burnt sack, and Stephano and Trinculo be besotted on grog, but their scenes are no less playable today because their tastes do not run to Bloody Marys, Vodka Sours, or straight-up Martinis. What *is* of importance is the sobriety of the lady in question. Can you tell me, at rise, if she has already been drinking or if, as the Verse affirms, she plans to jump off the wagon?

Miss W: (Answering too quickly) She is cold sober at the top of the song.

DC: She may be sober, but cold? No. The title of the script tells us otherwise. She has been drinking rye Old-Fashioneds and at the rise of curtain is ready to order "another, please." How many drinks have been consumed depends on an objective rendering of capacity loads. You can safely say she has had, minimally, one, and maximally three. Above that number, "sober" ceases to define her condition.

Miss W: I see. I never thought of the title as a story point. But it is important for the class to know that she has, in the recent past, had a "drink problem." She speaks of having "gone on the wagon."

DC: How heavy a problem?

Miss W: To give the lady her due, not a major one. I have myself to use here. When I diet I stop all social drinking, not because alcohol is my enemy, but because it is plain fattening. Since the lady in question never mentions the subject again, "going on the wagon," I mean, one can assume we are not dealing with a problem drinker.

DC: Absolutely.

Miss W: Like all of us who do something good to and for ourselves, the woman, right from the start, indulges in self-satisfied proselytizing.

DC: I know what you mean, but the class is not familiar with the lyric. Can you explain yourself, in your own words, of course.

Miss W: (To the class) Well, we all know, for instance, how tiresome we can be when a diet has enabled us to lose the fifteen pounds we wanted to be rid of. We go around telling everyone how *they* ought to stop overeating and how marvelous they'll feel if they do. It's all very much a turn-off. Well, this lady does that. She takes time out, before the actual narrative begins, to tell the audience how great you feel when you're not drinking . . . what it does for the figure, and that sort of thing.

DC: Yes, that's true. Not drinking at all has everything to say for it, save one. There comes a time when you need a drink, and when you need a drink you need a drink. (To Miss W) Has that time come for the lady in question?

Miss W: Most definitely. As we said earlier, an extraordinary relationship has come to an end.

DC: Was she aware of any problem in that relationship?

Miss W: No. It happened, as she says, as quickly as a flash of lightning, with no previous warning.

DC: Where is she? Is she in her home?

Miss W: No, she's in a bar, drinking Old-Fashioneds.

DC: A point of inference, not so much subjective as experiential, can be made here. The lady is on her way toward a massive falling off that wagon she told us about. But her grief is large enough to have pushed her, unfeeling, into the outside world rather than remaining within her own four walls. This is not an effete agony. It's size precipitates a public act of lamentation.

Miss W: Yes, I felt that, too, but I thought it was too personal for the **One.**

DC: Perhaps, but again, we can find justification for it in the words and our knowledge of human behavior under stress. We now possess enough information about the lady in question. You can move quickly through the Chorus since we have already touched on the main exposition of the narrative.

Miss W: Well, there she is, in a bar, calling the waiter for another Old-Fashioned, but, having ordered it, she changes her mind *and* the order to a double. She tells the waiter, who we assume is near at hand, why she's there, what has happened, and where she's headed.

DC: Where she's headed?

Miss W: Yes, to become a part of that loveless crowd who have loved before and, as the saying goes, lost.

DC: Ah . . . and the bartender? Does he speak?

Miss W: No, there is no indication. But I've always thought bartenders suffer an occupational disease from having always to be on the listening end of somebody's troubles. Silence is a probable defense. (The class laughs)

DC: That is purely parenthetic. But I imagine in certain kinds of bars you may be right. Here, however, it is not the bartender but a waiter who hears her tale. That rather destroys your occupational disease theory, at least in this Cole Porter lyric.

Miss W: Yes, it does. But the place must be having a light night if the waiter is free to stand around and hear about her sorrows . . . this perfect relationship that turned out to be a good deal less perfect than the lady assumed it to be.

DC: Who left whom?

Miss W: Why, naturally, he left her.

DC: No politicking, please. (Laughter, again, from the class)

Miss W: He left her quickly, and with no hint of why. She tells us her life is now in ruins. Relating the story to the waiter has been so painful for her that she changes the order, this time, to a simpler one. Never mind the cocktail fixings—the cherry, the orange, and the bitters—she tells him. She'll have a "straight rye."

DC: Very good, Miss W. (To the class) That gives us a comprehensive **One.** We know who is telling the story, where it is being told, why it needs to be told, and the major story points. There are two elements in a **One** I have waited until now to discuss. (To Miss W) You may sit. Both the class and I are grateful to you for the work and your good humor. (To the class again) We have omitted in the list of who, where, and why the most important: when.

The "when" in all singing is *now.* I am inclined to think that even *now* is too flabby a concept. It would be better to consider that every song you sing takes place in the *now of now.* Nothing is duller in a theatre than the past or imperfect tense. Even if the lyric is written as a past statement, flash back and sing it *now.* I will go further into this when we are speaking of the **Two.** But remember, a song gains interest *when it is revealed to the audience at the same time that the revelations occur to the singer of the song.*

Another factor in singing that I want to bring to your attention at this time: Remember that songs are soliloquies, unspoken reflections that have found a voice. Since none of us soliloquizes lies, *all songs must be considered absolute truths.* Dialogue may confuse and even tamper with the facts, but when we are alone we sing the unvarnished truth. Because this is so you can never, in a **One,** say of the person who is singing the song: "He thinks" or "She says that. . . ." If he or she says it, it is true. We can never be wiser than we are. In Miss W's lyric, if the lady says she *is* on the wagon and *feels* (notice I do not say "was" and "felt") good for not drinking, then we must believe her. If she says the relationship with the man was comparable to a heavenly dream, she wasn't mistaken—deluded, perhaps, although that, too, is judgmental, but not mistaken. Remember: All songs are sung in the present tense by those who are, by virtue of being alone, no longer in need of self-deceit or held silence.

His Work

    Mr. T, emboldened by Miss W's **One** and DC's running aid, is on stage and eager to begin. (Again the reader is advised to keep the lyric in front of him as the **One** is delivered.)

Mr. T: May I hold my notes?

DC: I don't think that should be necessary. You must know the lyric by now and, as you have seen, I will help you.

Mr. T: (Deprived of his security, puts his notes away) This is a story about a man.

DC: In this case there is no question of the gender of the narrator?

Mr. T: None at all. Only a man can sing this song. His age is minimally upper teens, maximally, well . . . (to DC) I had some trouble setting this, especially hearing you set the age limits with Miss W in her song.

DC: I can't see why. (To the class) We are dealing in this lyric with a man who fantasizes a wife, children, and grandchildren, somewhere in his future. (To Mr. T) How old dare he be?

Mr. T: I thought . . . I mean . . . fifties would be the outside age.

DC: No, you can go higher. Even without a Charlie Chaplin in mind, it is possible that we could find him still virile enough in his late sixties or even a little older than that. I see you rejecting the idea of this, but you must remember that we are not speaking of an ideal age, only one the songs permits. The minimal limit of upper teens is no less hard to accept even though it appears seemlier.

Mr. T: I guess I was too concerned with how he looks. . . .

DC: You mean his optimal age?

Mr. T: Yes. I set that at anywhere in the decade of his thirties. So late sixties is a bit of a stretch for me.

DC: We are attempting to banish subjective attitudes toward the lyric. What seems too old to you is of no consequence whatever. All we want to know is this: Can a man in his late sixties marry, father children, and still be alive to see his grandchildren? The answer has to be yes.

Mr. T: I see.

DC: As in Miss W's lyric, the two polar age limits are never ideal. Not only do they color the lyric one way or another but, in the case of extreme age brackets, psychological overtones crowd in on the eye of the listener. When the class is in possession of the entire **One** I will explain this further. For now, the optimal choice of "his thirties" is a good one, and later we will see how it best illuminates Dorothy Fields' lyric. Where does the story take place?

Mr. T: (Proudly) Anywhere *but* on a farm.

DC: Very good. The man says at the very top of the script, "If I had a cow and a plough and a Frau." We can rightly assume he does not have all three. About that title, class. It does get in the way when we first hear it: "If I had a cow and a plough and a Frau" seems to promise a comedy lyric because of the rhymes and their juxtaposition. Early on we discover that the song is in no way amusing, and by the time those three words have appeared in their final context, we will have recovered from that first shock to our ears. In actual fact the song is from the musical adaption of *The Pursuit of Happiness* (by Lawrence Langner and Armina Marshall) and the character who sang this Morton Gould–Dorothy Fields song was a Hessian in eighteenth-century Colonial America. It must have intrigued Miss Fields to inherit the word "Frau" as part of his rightful language, thereby allowing her its legitimate use in this rhyme series. When the song is removed from the score, we do have that first line to get over. (To Mr. T) I assure you the composer's melody for these words is quite lovely and of distinct aid in squelching any impulse the audience might have to laugh. Let us go back to your correct placement of where he lives. You said anywhere but on a farm. Another way to say that would be. . . .

Mr. T: In a city or any place where one does not enjoy those values that are native to a close-to-the-earth life style.

DC: Very well put. We know how old he is and where he is. We can even add when it is.

Mr. T: It is now. Right now.

DC: Bravo! Can you place the man economically and may we also be given an idea of his educational background?

Mr. T: There was no hint I could find in his lyric to help pin down his financial worth. A poor man, a middle-class man, even a rich man could sing this song.

DC: I congratulate you. That is correct. And his education?

Mr. T: I'm afraid I couldn't come up with anything there, either.

DC: Perhaps. But he is certainly not uneducated. And he also has a pronounced gift for words. Let us agree then that he is neither under- or overeducated and possesses an ability to describe with sensibility how he feels.

Mr. T: I'm sorry, but can you give me an example of that?

DC: Surely. To define a place that would diminish the anxiety in his life he tells us that, if he had a farm and a wife, he knows he could make a home where his heart would rest. A healthy baby is characterized as "Laughing at a raindrop." I think it is safe to say that these are not the images of someone lacking in a certain feeling for language.

Mr. T: I see.

DC: A particular adjective describes the man, or a description of a major propensity, or, if you will, a tendency, a bias—can you help me?

Mr. T: I think so. He is a man given to wishful dreaming, a Walter Mitty sort.

DC: Exactly. (To the class) This lyric begins with "If I had a . . ." and it ends with the same fantasy. The lyric is nothing more than a pile-up of "ifs," each one taking the man further into that world of his reveries until he has built fantasies on top of fantasies. The sudden revelation of this wakes him and he reprises the first "if" with a small editorial addition. (To Mr. T) Will you tell the class the specifics of this point I have made?

Mr. T: Yes. The man dreams of having a farm. . . .

DC: What sort of farm?

Mr. T: A small one. One cow, one piece of machinery, and, oh yes, a wife. And as we said before, if he had these three . . . uh . . . items (the Class responds) he would be at peace with himself.

DC: Then we may add that, along with the habit of daydreaming and fantasizing, he is also restless and uneasy in his reality life.

Mr. T: Yes, I concede that. But about that editorial addition at the end of the lyric. At the top he wishes for the cow, the farming equipment, and a wife. At the finish he still has the same three wishes except that he wants a wife who is beautiful. I suppose he feels as long as he's wishing he might as well raise his standards.

DC: We had better stop there before the ladies begin to see a man more chauvinist than dreamer.

Mr. T: Shall I go on?

DC: Yes, quickly, please.

Mr. T: Well, if he had that one cow, one piece of farm equipment, and a wife, he says he'd put the cow and the equipment together and work the land.

DC: And his wife? Where is she?

Mr. T: She's on the sidelines smiling and sharing the same fantasies.

DC: So we can add that he wishes not only a wife but one who is in full accord with his dreams. No bickering, no dissension. Tell me, what further dreams do they . . . we can now say "they" . . . indulge in?

Mr. T: The kind of farm they want. . . .

DC: How do you mean that?

Mr. T: They don't care to own a flat Kansas kind of farm, but one that has hills and dales that seem to roll beneath the sun.

DC: (To the class) Mr. T is almost quoting the lyric, but we will let it pass. Here, then, a further example of our narrator's skill with words and the images they evoke.

Mr. T: I like the next fantasy because it concerns that cow and how it will have its own field in which to graze on its favorite fodder.

DC: Yes. When we daydream we usually wish for what we alone want and seldom bother with wishful thinking for others.

Mr. T: Yes, and of course, the next dream is a baby.

DC: What kind of baby?

Mr. T: Very happy, a healthy baby.

DC: At this moment our man leaves the world of fantasy to address the audience. What motivates him to do that?

Mr. T: I think. . . .

DC: (Interrupts) No, it's what *he* thinks we're interested in.

Mr. T: That slipped out. He thinks there is nothing over-complicated or oversophisticated about his dreams—that new worlds always begin this way.

DC: What way? Which way?

Mr. T: You start with a cow, one piece of farm equipment, and a wife and then a baby, and with these elements a whole new world can begin. And, as he points out, it is very simple from there on. He would work hard and, as time went by, where there was only one cow there'd soon be a herd.

DC: And one baby would have siblings.

Mr. T: And they would grow up and have their own children. . . .

DC: And this final fantasy brings him back to reality, doesn't it?

Mr. T: Yes, because you see (to the Class) he realizes he has, right now, nothing at all like these dreams and if he wants them he has to get started.

DC: When?

Mr. T: Immediately.

DC: Is there more script?

Mr. T: Only what was mentioned earlier. He reprises the first three "ifs": the cow, the minimal amount of farm machinery, and, as we said before, not *just* a wife but a beautiful one.

DC: You may sit. The **One** is splendid. (To the class) All that is left is a short clarification of the minimal and maximal ages we left open for discussion until you were in possession of all the facts. It is evident that these age brackets are, by definition, not optimal. In this script a teenage boy who would speak of a "restless heart" knows little of the meaning of those words. He may indulge in fantasies but, in fact, that is what all of us are prone to do during those painful years when we are too old to be children and too young to be taken seriously. Yes, we may fantasize, but we cannot act on our fantasies, not because of neurotic paralysis but as a result of societal restrictions. Because this is so, the minimal age is less than dramatic, suffering, as it does, from normalcy. At the other end of the age scale we see something quite different in tone. If we allow that a man in his late sixties can still sing this script, then questions crowd in—questions born not from the facts of the lyric but from the connotative problems we see *on* the singer. Why has a man of such advanced age waited so long to make a reality of his fantasies? What inhibits him? Is this loss of serenity of the heart he speaks about of a protracted history? Neurosis appears as a possible motivating force and the ellipses in the lyric assume a suggestive significance. We can see that minimal and maximal age brackets are permissible. But although the lyric tolerates them, it is not well served by them.

As I have pointed out, optimal age choice is always somewhat subjective. We must choose an age at which the lyric is best sung and balance that choice with an objective rendering of the narrative coupled with our own knowledge of human behavior. Mr. T elected the decade of the man's thirties, and I seconded the selection. At that age the man in question can have accumulated enough history to know not only the restless state of his spirit but what would bring it peace. There is, too, no hint of a neurotic implication. Many of us take longer rather than less time to find out who and what we are without incurring the label "neurotic." Finally, the planning of a marriage and a subsequent family need not be considered tardy at this age level. The man seeks a major change in his life style. In his thirties there is still enough time to translate the dream into reality. Does he, Mr. T?

Mr. T: We do not know.

DC: That is correct. The script is left unresolved. It speaks only of the man's fantasies and not of any action he takes.

The **One** is performed to afford the actor/singer the utmost information to be found in the words of the lyric. It is an exercise that deals with facts. Once we are in possession of that data, or story, we can proceed to seek out its significance—the creation of the **Two**.

Chapter **12** The Two

Heard melodies are sweet, but those unheard are sweeter.

John Keats

It is reasonable to maintain that if one, two, ten, or even a hundred actors were asked to do a **One** or to tell you the story of, for example, *Hamlet,* you would hear the same tale. These same actors, if asked to tell you what *Hamlet* is *about,* would splinter into personally held conclusions of as many variations. *Hamlet* is about an infinity of things. That is both its abiding mystery and its promise. Its very fathomlessness is the source of each actor's and director's compulsion to fathom it. As in all art, the eye of the beholder is both witness to and assessor of the work. For every production of *Hamlet* there will be someone who will *see* it differently, direct it dissimilarly, and act it in yet another variance. When we construct a **Two**, then, it will be a highly subjective choice arrived at not so much by *reading* the lyric (a **One**) as by reading *into* it what each of us *thinks* it is about.

THE TWO: **THE SIGNIFICANCE OF THE LYRIC**

The primary function of the **Two** *is to make you move.* Whatever you choose to write must emerge as prose that will physicalize itself. If you find you are standing still, with all four quadrants of your body at rest, you will know you are *not* in a **Two**.

Begin the text, as before, with "This is a story about . . .," but replace the object—man, woman, boy, or girl—with the pronoun "me." All **Two's** start with the sentence: "This is a story about me. . . ."

The **Two** begins at zero, hands at sides and a base with weight on both legs. Focus center and begin the sentence. You will find it contains a built-in energy increase. The first word, "This," announces a targeting-in, "story" is what all listeners want to hear, and "about me" is what all storytellers warm to.

Following this opening, we will create a subjective narrative/dialogue with these inclusions:

1   *To whom* are you speaking? I want you to name the person, as, for instance: Fred, Mary, Dr. Smith, Mrs. Jones. This name will appear immediately after the opening sentence: "This is a story about me, Mary." Choose a vis-à-vis who, by his very invention, will be an active adversary. Do not elect to speak to someone who wants to hear the tale, or doesn't care whether he hears it or not. There is no value, for example, in working to a psychiatrist. He is paid to listen and is not the devil's advocate by virtue of his professional role. *Whom* you speak to determines, at the very top of the **Two**, not only the subject matter but how you choose to tell it. If *infidelity* is the revelation in a **Two**, you boast of it to someone in the locker room; you repent of it to the man in the confessional; you resist revealing it to your wife; and you are shamed by the telling of it to your son or daughter. The importance of the *whom* or the *feed* is evident. Choose your focus to achieve maximum energy through conflict. That center focus we have been using is now named.

2   *When is it?* We have already chosen the time. It is *now*. Of added interest to the time factor: Know that *now* affords you the urgency that impels the **Two** to be told.

In English we do not have a present narrative tense without resorting to improper grammar. We say, when telling someone what happened to us the night before: "I had (past pluperfect) the strangest experience last night. I've been having (past perfect) the darndest things happen to me lately. I was walking (past imperfect) down the street and I meet (present) this man and I says (vulgarized present) to him. . . ." When relating an adventure, our need to gain and maintain the interest of the listener is so great that we continue to pull up into the present what occurred in the past, even if we must resort to solecism ("I *says* to him"). It is as if we do not trust the power of the narrative to hold and keep attention unless it unwinds in the present. If this is true in our lives, it is more so in the theatre. On the stage the hour is now, and even when we flash back from the present to the past we return to that time in order to live it, once again, in the present.

These dramatic verities are no less valid in singing. The actor/singer must use the song to reveal incident, or character, or even tedious exposition as it exists for him *now*. Although it may not appear in the verbal performance of the **Two**, there is the knowledge of what just happened, what may happen, and what possibly will happen. Without *time* (the *now*) there is no reason to feel the urgency to speak or sing of anything.

3   *Where are you?* Do not construct the **Two** without knowing where you are delivering it. Often the choice of location can make a contribution to the physical life that is the primary purpose of the **Two**. Are you in a library where one must whisper? In a crowded room where you are jostled? In a hot or cold place that results in your being over- or underheated? In the texture of your thinking you must be aware of the totality of your environment. As in the case of *when*, *where* gains by a knowledge of where you have just come from and where, *after* the **Two**, you will be going.

4   *Why* are you telling the **Two**? Do not create a subjective narrative that is devoid of all provocation. The *need to tell it* must be absolute.

Don't's

The following are designed to keep you from skating too close to the red flags:

1   Don't waste time on exposition. A **Two** is active. It is a dialogue, if you will, with all the lines given to you. You may allow the vis-à-vis a word or two that will reenergize what you are saying. But do not permit an in-

dulgence on his or her side that forces you to stand listening and reacting. Here is the actor's dream come true— the script is all yours. A **Two** that busies itself with expository detail, not germane to the "conflict" that is unraveling throughout its presentation, is passive and of no value. For example,

This is a story about me, John. I'm working in that new photography shop on Main and Broadway; you know, the one with the window full of camera equipment. Well, there's this guy there who's a pain in the neck. He's running for crown prince of the place. Always getting on the boss's good side while I'm coming off all the time like some kind of fool. It's a good job, though. When I'm there a full year I'll be eligible for benefits and then Mary and I can get away for a two-week trip to Yosemite. Boy! That's a vacation I'd sure like to take!

This sort of banter is not a **Two**. It can and probably will be delivered with nothing moving but the mouth. Can it be altered and made to work? Yes. The first change would be to make John the other chap who works in the photography store and who is, from what the inert and undramatic exposition has told us, a perfect antagonist. We can then cut all the information about the shop since John knows it as well as the man doing the **Two**. Simply by changing the "to whom am I speaking?" and adding "why am I speaking thusly?" we achieve an active **Two** between two men vying for position and security in their jobs. The handle (or subject matter) of the **Two** may have been altered and rendered unusable, but the actor has discovered what is or isn't a **Two** by what does or doesn't create movement.

2   Do not move arbitrarily in order to make a physical life for yourself. All body language must be organic. No superimposition of movement for movement's sake can be tolerated.

3   Do not lose your center focus. Every once in a while repeat the name of your vis-à-vis to rediscover its reality for you. Talking to yourself is only of value when you remember to put your alter ego out front.

4   A **Two** has no literary function. There is no need to hone your prose as you build the **Two**. It will never be published, and once it is united with the lyric (the **Three**) it will not even be heard. It can be regarded as the small

talk (catalytic agent) that activates body language. The impulse to make the **Two** a splendid aural experience for the watcher/listener is to be vigilantly monitored. I have seen admirable **Two's** that verge on the nonverbal and others that become mute as the actor/singer mimes the burden of the subject matter. This is not to say that the classic vocabulary of the mime is what we are after—indeed, keep all body language as true to reality as you are able—only that words do not, by virtue of their elegance, make a **Two**. In this regard, shun jokes. You may get your laugh as you speak and play the **Two**, but remember that this is subtext and it will very soon never be audible again. That laugh, so precious to you now, may be the least relevant one you will ever go for.

5   The nature of the **Two**, as I have said, is a subtext to the lyric/text. What you are doing (the physical appearance of the **Two**) should describe exactly to the beholder's eye that which his ear is hearing. If you are commenting on the heat in a room I should *see* you uncomfortably hot. If you say you were running to get here, I should *see* you out of breath. If you are doing a **Two** I do not hear, then you are indulging in a subtext on a subtext. This road leads to madness when the **Three** is performed. The inner monologue (the **Two**) will create the text of the lyric. Do not invent a third voicing.

6   Stay away from props. None may be used. Don't call your vis-à-vis on the telephone; have him over. No mimicry of toasting the New Year with invisible goblets; no eating of unseen food. Body language is based on the moment-to-moment *action* of the **Two** and not on superimposed *activities* better employed in a social game of charades.

7   Do not conceive a *someone* to do the **Two** for you; resist characterization; come out from behind the artful dodger. Actors/singers who find it difficult to be themselves often fashion a character persona that allows hiding. But singing cannot exist behind camouflage.

8   Do not "stage" yourself. A **Two** is not a choreographed solo. It is imperative that the moment-to-moment action of the **Two** be frozen, but its external appearance should remain loose and fresh each time the **Two** is performed. Don't concern yourself with *what* you are doing, only that you are playing the inner monologue

to effect body language. If you say, wiping your brow, "Dammit, it's hot in here," it is only important that it *be* hot. Which hand wipes the brow doesn't matter; in fact, you may not wipe the brow at all, and instead find yourself loosening your collar, fanning the air, or performing any number of activities that are supported by the line. If it is hot enough for you, move you will. It is good to keep in mind that body language has its own statute of limitations. Were you to do the **Two** ten times you would soon exhaust the physical vocabulary that defines being overwarm and repetition of activity would be inevitable. Freeze the monologue—not its aspect.

Of further importance: I have cautioned against the use of literary language in the verbal statement, since the **Two** is only valuable to the degree that it can be "read" by the beholder as the physical manifestation that mirrors what is being said. Everybody can comprehend a **Two.** An Englishman, a Frenchman, a Czech, an Australian aborigine—each of them will understand what you are saying by what they see. In this sense the universal language of the **Two** is preeminent. Staging it will falsify it and, in turn, blur the clarity of what you are thinking/saying/doing.

How far from the lyric may you go when you are seeking the handle or subject matter of the **Two**? Of all the questions asked of me this must be the most common. The answer is not easy. I have seen **Two's** constructed along lines almost the same as those of the lyric. And I have seen variations that go wide of that mark and are still useful. The best response, then, is this: Remember, the lyric and the **Two** will come together in the **Three** (see chapter 13). One need not go far afield of the text unless *what it is about* fires your creative imagination in such a way that, although the **Two** *seems* distant from the lyric, the acting beats that bind it together and are the source of its physical expression are, *in actual fact*, almost directly equivalent to the words.

Do's

1 In the early stages, when you are still fumbling for a handle upon which to build your **Two**, keep the lyric always in mind. The more you read it, the closer you will get to understanding what it is about. *What it is*

about is the beginning of the end of your search. In "Make It Another Old-Fashioned, Please," one can select from any number of significances. Among them, e.g.:

a) This is a script about self-punishment. When we are badly off we are sometimes impelled to do damage to ourselves in order to anesthetize the pain of failure, loss, or guilt. If that is your inference, examine your history or your knowledge of witnessed behavioral patterns and ascertain when you have had or observed a similar self-punitive episode. Isolate that event, apply the "to whom," "where," "why," and "when" rules of construction, and you will be well on your way to creating a viable **Two**.

b) Are there other inferences to be drawn from "Make It Another Old-Fashioned, Please"? Of course. I have said that there is an infinity of significance subject only to the particular beholder's line of sight. This lyric could be about loss—how it occurs, and our ability to fight it, withstand it, and come through it. There is no one who cannot find a personalized experience relative to loss; we have all suffered its pain.

c) Is "Make It Another Old-Fashioned, Please" about drinking? No. You could as well be going off a diet as the wagon. Substitution is a valuable factor to keep in mind. Just as you do not have to have murdered a king to play Macbeth, you do not have to experience the effects of alcohol to experience self-punishment.

2   Keep the lyric in front of you as you create your **Two**. Better still, write the lyric on a tablet and skip three or four lines between each line, using that space in which to weave the **Two**. In this way you will be assured that the lyric always initiates its significance (the **Two**). The **Two** cannot be permitted to tell its story in any way it chooses. It must be kept in line with the progress of the lyric. Resist the tendency of the **Two** to fight for its own life and not that of the script it sires.

3   If you need a moment at the top of the **Two** that is expository but acts as an aid in setting your course, allow it. But know that it will be cut when you are working the **Three**. Better still, choose exposition that gives you an activity to "do" while you are verbalizing it, e.g.:

This is a story about me, Helen. (Looking around with contempt) Why did you insist upon meeting in a dreary place like this? Oh, all right. I don't mean to find fault, but really it *is* depressing. We'll just have to get past it, I suppose. (Squinting) The lighting isn't very friendly, or is it? (Laughing at her own joke) One could really get away with murder in here, and no one would ever know. Well, I mean, no one would ever *see* it to know.

Here is exposition, but the actor has *activity* before the action between the speaker and Helen begins.

    4   As in the case with all technical work in these chapters, execute the **Two** full out. Body language that remains overcontrolled and underdelivered is of no value. The actor/singer must experience the maximum physical statement. Train yourself to experience too much while you are still in rehearsal; it can and will be pared down later. There is today a kind of revulsion for the large silhouette. The word "ham" is considered opprobrious and, although I do not espouse the notion of flagrant decoration that passes for theatrical style, I do mourn the loss of *size* in the new actor. Again, film and television support the small by enlarging it cinemascopically. The stage, particularly the musical sector of it, has no technology to magnify the image. I do not want to imply that a **Two** is better for being bigger in its external appearance. But if the action of the **Two** is powerful enough and the dramatic verities are there to make it play, then the interior size the actor/singer experiences will result in body language of similar daring. By learning the outer limits of your physical life you will have explored the maximum displacement of space. In theatres that seat three thousand people you may find you do not want to pare down what those in the rear of a second balcony are, for once, able to see.[1]

    5   May you employ more than one vis-à-vis? Yes. If you are talking to a center focus called, for example, Barbara, there can be others to the left and right whom you see and to whom you relate. What is important is that you are aware who it is you are addressing. For example:

(To center) This is a story about me, Barbara. There's so much I have to get up the courage to say to you, but that moon. . . .

---

[1] In summer theatres the number of available seats is sometimes awesome. St. Louis Municipal Opera has a capacity of 10,117; Kansas City Starlight, 7,858; Indianapolis Starlight Musicals, 4,400; Dallas State Fair Music Hall; 3,420.

(Spotting R or L and on a higher plane)
It's so damned beautiful I . . .
(Back to center)
can't keep my mind on what I have to tell you about.

6   You will have to write a short coda to the **Two** designed to bring you back to zero. These moments will sustain your physical life, even as it is dying, throughout the Rideout. If you remember, the **Two** ideates an inner monologue that sets up the line of the lyric that follows in its wake. When we reach the *last line* of the lyric there should be no need to extend the **Two**, for there is nothing further to be *said*. However, the Rideout is a musical addendum set apart from the text. It is there to shape the song's *musical* resolution. If we do not have a life to live while it unwinds we drop out of the song too precipitately. A good rule of thumb to apply in that part of the **Two** that follows after the last line of the lyric is this: Try to create a simple physical life that cools you, finds you at zero by the Rideout's end (four bars of music), and allows you to reach that state with grace and ease. For example (picking up the imaginary closing moments of a **Two**):

Well, that's how it goes, Harry. One minute I was high up there, had the world right in the palm of this hand, and then—pffft—I lost it all. The money, the job, and, worse, she walked out and I haven't seen her since!
(Rideout)
    Oh well, you live and you learn. Next time I won't be such a sucker for an easy buck. You know what I mean, Harry?
(A carefree shrug and . . . out)

Another way to describe this would be to say that if a **Two**, in order to activate the lyric into the vertical, begins with "This is a story about me," then, as the lyric ends, the **Two** slowly returns to the horizontal with a *fictive* "me about story a is this."

7   When you are still in that gray time when the handle and subsequent writing of the **Two** are not yet chosen and executed on paper, keep in mind that the tonality of the lyric and of the **Two** you create should be consonant. A lyric of Cole Porter's will not find any comfort in a subtext that is leaden and witless, whereas the words of Irving Berlin can find no rest under a canopy of elegant

humor. Subtext best informs text when they share a common genre.

Must a **Two** make narrative sense? No, but it is preferable that it does. I have on rare occasions applauded the performance of a **Two** that had no story continuity (or, for that matter, no story points at all) or consistent focus and that changed course in midstream with kaleidoscopic speed. For example, this extrapolation:

(Center)
This is a story about me, Dr. Fardel.
(In a growing rage)
I've been sitting out there . . .
(indicating office location in the R wings)
. . . in your office for over an hour. Why the hell does your nurse give out appointments that no one takes seriously?
(R *focus*: warming and affectionate)
I was only kidding Mary, I *like* your dress . . .
(L focus—growing puzzlement)
. . . that car, well, it's just not *me*, Mr. Jordan. I can't figure it. Why should I buy a gas-guzzler like that in these times? It's sinful!
(Center—deep pleasure)
Hey Ma! You made my favorite! Coconut cream pie! I sure hope you didn't invite a lotta people. I'd hate to have to share this with . . .
(Center focus, sudden interest)
Liz said she was *coming*? But she would have let me know . . .
(Mounting anger)
Wait a minute! You haven't been opening my mail?! Now, you promised!

This **Two** will physicalize without difficulty, but it requires great skill in slithering in and out of each acting beat as it moves through the shoals of a subtext with no development, continuity, or narrative line. Furthermore, it makes heavy demands on the ability of the actor/singer to achieve graceful transitions, since each element is unrelated to that which precedes and follows it. The task of executing a **Two** is a good deal easier when it unwinds with related story points revealed by the teller to the antagonist out front. Concentration is thus facilitated. Once the **Two** is played and not heard (the **Three**), an inner monologue with a coherent sequence makes fewer demands on the retentive power of your memory. The mind, in consequence, is more able to send ungarbled messages to the motor system. However, I am reminded of the moral fable of the parents who, as they are leaving their house for the evening, admonish their two children not to put peas up their noses. Of course, as soon as they are gone, the children, who have never heard of such a seductive activity, race to try it. To guard against forbidding the actor/singer this kind of spasmodic **Two** I say: Try it if you care to. Those who are not disturbed by its sudden shiftings may find it useful. Those who cannot sustain an even flow will return to the safer waters of the who, when, where, why, and to whom.

DIALOGUES

In my classes I have found that an infertile time lag of almost two weeks follows the assignment and explication of the lyric and the **Two**. This period is the natural result of confusion, anxiety, and a bemused search for a handle that is viable and, more to the point, physically actable. Inevitably, the first intrepid actor/singer will agree to show me the opening moments of his **Two**, preferring to test the water with a toe rather than a dive. I do not object to the student's bringing in only the opening moments of his **Two**. Often I may be able, once I *see* the handle, to help find a clearer course. Also, there is nothing as comforting to the timid as approbation. This opening up is followed by others. Once a **Two** is witnessed, we are out of the mire of description and into seeing and hearing the subtext.

Her Work

Miss W volunteers to show us her **Two**, and DC bids her to go to stage center. Once there, she is eager to begin.

DC: Before you start, let me use you to illustrate for the class the correct opening procedure. I want you to focus center and, as I have instructed, begin with the zero position—hands at sides and an easy base with your weight on both legs. It is exactly the physical appearance we perfected at the end of the Vamp before we began to sing.

DC offers some don't's and do's for the class to keep in mind.

Don't's

1 Do not take this position until you are ready to start. Once in it, a moment or two is all you should permit yourself before beginning: "This is a story about me." The time spent in preparation should not be in this zero position but in a comfortable and easy behavior. Be at ease and unfocused but, most important, do not allow the song to be visibly on you straining to be performed. When, in time (reasonable in duration), you find this state of self-possession, move into the prescribed positioning, focus center, and begin "This is. . . ."

2 Do not *act* on these first two words. They have been carefully chosen to give you a sense of the *general* moving toward the *specific*. Begin, then, with an *unacted* committment to the center focus.

3 Do not speak the sentence too quickly. If anything, start its verbalization under tempo. Correctly executed, you should have the feeling of the white of "This is" changing to the pink of "a story" and ending with the scarlet of "about me." Said too rapidly, these color transitions, which should construct a moment-to-moment entry into the stratosphere of the **Two**, will be rushed and, as in the case of a jumped cue, make for a jerky elision. Another image to describe the sensation: Think of yourself as the stage manager who calls "curtain going up" as well as the man who takes it up. Too jumpy a rise results in a jolting; too rapid a rise forces the play to start before it is ready. Do not tamper with the rhythm that produces the artful beginning of a life.

Do's

1 As the sentence begins its verbalization, with its subsequent successive transitions, I must see the physical appearance of the first "beats" of the **Two** as they make their passage from zero to a fully involved body language. On the words "about me" you should be fully into the **Two** and I should know it by your arrival at a total physicality.

2   I teach the concept of singing from the base up, rather than the reverse, from the mouth down to the floor. Train yourself to begin the physical life of the **Two** somewhere around "a story about" by reacting first with your feet (base) and then continuing that first physical beat on up until all four quadrants of the body are involved.[2] I have always mistrusted actors who play only with the upper portion of their bodies (face, arms, and hands) while their feet put the lie to what I am asked to believe is real. This unintentional betrayal of total interior experience is discerned more in singing than in straight speech. We must remember that there is only the singer to see. Distraction away from him to other actors, sets, and props is denied him. If the singer is all there is to see, make certain *what* we see is what you *intended* we see. Experience the **Two** entirely.

In December 1976, distinguished actress Eva Le Gallienne gave an interview to the *Los Angeles Times.* Among her many insightful observations were these words:

I always say to actors, don't put corks on your fingers. So many of them stop here," she said, indicating her hands, "instead of letting it go on like a ray. An actor should be bigger than his body.

I am equally concerned with those "corks" the actor/singer plugs into his midriff that inhibit his hips, legs, and feet. Uncorking occurs when you think: *feet first.*

3   A valuable trick that eases you into the **Two** with a controlled efflorescence is this: Give your vis-a-vis, not yet named, a cue (unheard by us, of course) that gives you a reaction to play. It need not be a line he or she says, but an appearance, or even a word:

This is	a story	about me, John	
[zero]	[the beginning of a cue from John]	[physicalizing reaction to John's cue]	[and into the **TWO**]

[2] This is a further investigation of what we have done before, as described in chapter 7. However, in the earlier exercises we went from *something to nothing*; now the reverse is our intention. We want to achieve the beginning of the **Two** by proceeding from *nothing to something.*

Later, in performing, we will see how elements of this device can be employed to get a song off the floor, especially when it has to begin with no more of a cue than the director's or casting agent's "Can you sing something for us?"

DC: (To Miss W) Can you try that opening sentence for me? (Miss W gets into a zero position)

DC: No, stay easy. You are not ready to begin. If you go right into position now you will be forced either to prepare in that preposterous stance or, worse, to start before you are ready.

Miss W: It's so difficult to stand up here doing nothing.

DC: For one thing, there is a big difference between *doing nothing* and striking the arbitrary posture of zero that I have asked for. And, second, if you permit yourself to think, "This is where I *do* nothing," you will end up *doing* something, badly. Simply be you. Whatever your life is in these moments before you begin should continue without any self-consciousness. You are going to be up there, inevitably, to sing a song. How to do that is not one whit more important than learning how *not* to sing a song before you have one to sing. Am I clear?

Miss W: How strange. This is the first time I understand what you mean about not *doing* anything specific before you have to *do* the song. Let me try again.

DC: Of course!

Miss W takes a deep breath[3] and begins to experience herself on the stage, without any stiffening, adjusting, rearranging, ingratiating, or any of the other inventions we contrive to make our lives tolerable during these difficult moments before we begin to sing.

DC is enthusiastic, and does not object when Miss W,

[3] The first and most important practical tip for the beginning actor was voiced by Dr. Tyrone Guthrie: "Before you say anything on the stage *take a breath*." *Tyrone Guthrie on Acting* (New York: Viking, 1971), p. 13

spotting center, slowly gets into the zero position for the opening sentences of her **Two**.

Miss W: This is a story about me, Max.

DC: Try it again. I thought you were into the color of the **Two** too early. You have to give the start to the life out front, in this case, to Max. See how artfully you can begin by manipulating his gestation.

Miss W tries again, but this time the focus comes to life too late in the sentence. A third attempt hits the mark.

Miss W: (elated) I really felt that! It was the smoothest transition I've ever achieved. Going from nothing into the end of that silly sentence!

DC: Try it again. We are still working with technique as the means to our ends. The mechanics of a good beginning never change. What you can do once, you should be able to do over and over again by employing the same thinking.

Miss W does as suggested and demonstrates that whatever interior process she used was not only valid but capable of reprise. She has conquered the rising arc of "This is a story about me, Max."

Because a **Two** is a visual exercise it is impossible for the reader to experience the seeing of it. I have, therefore, written Miss W's **Two** as it *moves, always ahead* of the lyric. It can be assessed in this way and even employed by the reader who may want to use it as her own script in order to apprehend it personally. It is necessary to parenthesize the acting "beats" with adverbs and descriptive phrases. What any good director would delete from the writer's script, I have resorted to as much as I think necessary for the actor to visualize the physical (exterior) appearance of the **Two**. Beware of playing results. Keep the **Two** alive by recognizing its action. Cause and effect are referred to in that order, for without the first, there is no second.

The TWO	The LYRIC
This is a story about [Zero] [Max mentions Miss W's weight] me, Max. . . . (She reacts with amused placation) All right . . . all right . . . so I put on a little weight. Ok, Ok. Maybe more than a little but smoking . . . smoking, Max, is worse! You listen to me . . . (Watching him light a cigarette—with dire warning)	Since I went on the wagon, I'm certain drink
. . . that weed'll kill you . . . I know!	is a major crime;
But look at me, Max. Three months without a cigarette and I'm Miss America. A little heavier, but a winner!	For when you lay off the liquor
(She takes a deep breath—running her hands down the sides of her chest) Clear lungs, no headaches, no throat aches —and food . . . Max! You can't believe what it really tastes like!	You feel so much slicker,
(Her hands have arrived at hip level—she looks down and then back to Max) So all right—what's fifteen pounds? I put 'em on, I can take 'em off.	Well, that is, most of the time.
(A bit nervous—fixes her hair in an effort to appear casual) But never mind that, Max. The audition. I want to hear what they thought about my reading. No, tell me all of it. (A timorous shrug) Frankly, I thought it went quite well.	But there are moments sooner or later,

Of course (a bit edgy) I was a little shaky. You know, the added weight and all. God! How I hate those cold readings! But, Max . . .	When it's tough, I've got to say,
. . . be a friend for once and not an agent. Please! Tell me! The truth, Max. . . .	Not to say: "Waiter,
(Supplicating) Stop the hemming and hawing and come out with it.	Make it another Old-Fashioned, please,"
This job's so important, Max. I mean, all this self-improvement—shaking the weed and all, it's . . . well, I need the work, Max. You can see that,	Make it another Double Old-Fashioned,
can't you	please,
(Growing indignation) That's what irritates me—*really* irritates me. There you sit like some complacent, smug little. . . .	Make it for one who's due To join the disillusioned crew,
Oh, I can't . . . I just can't face this endless rejection. (Surrenders to a complete exhaustion) Is this what my life's to be about, Max? No thank you's, maybe next time's? Too olds, too youngs, and unemployment insurance?	Make it for one of love's new refugees.
(With glowing recollection) Lord! What I'd give to have just a little of it back! It's always so full of light at the beginning!	Once, high in my castle, I reigned supreme.

(Reaching up with joy) That feeling of infinite possibilities with no limits! Anything can happen and you know . . .	And oh! What a castle!
(She touches her breast gently) . . . you know right here that it will.	Built on a heavenly dream.
(Exhausted again, she sags) All right (resigned) tell me, right now . . . where I stand. . . .	Then, quick as a light'ning flash
(Hands up as if to shield the blow) I didn't get it, did I? (She shakes her head in imitation of his silent "No")	That castle began to crash
(Quick change) Oh, forget it! The lousy part was only twelve lines . . .	So, make it another Old-Fashioned,
and no good to begin with!	Please!
(She pivots and starts to leave, then turns) Max, how about my buying us both a dinner, tonight?	Leave out the cherry,
We'll start with drinks and not count one damn calorie!	Leave out the orange,
and end in a blaze of soufflé!	Leave out the bitters—
(Second thought) Oh, and Max . . . can I bum one of your cigarettes?	Just make it a straight rye!

Rideout
(She smiles, weakly puts out her hand for the
cigarette and—out)

DC: (To Miss W) A most interesting **Two**. Can you tell me and
the class how you built it so that others still adrift in confusion may hear it from one of their own?

Miss W: There isn't much to say. I did what was suggested, and if
it has been passed by you, all I can add would only
underline what has been said before. (To the class) I do
think reading the lyric more than once and having it there
in front of you while you create the **Two** is important. I
was surprised to find how eager the **Two** was to go its
own way unless the lyric reined it in, so to speak.

DC: Why don't you tell us about your handle? How you came
to choose it?

Miss W: Well, again, I read and reread the lyric and finally came
to think of it as a story about failure. Maybe that and the
narrative I chose to dress it in were due to my own personal life at the moment. (The class laughs) Agent problems, television interviews, and all that barbarism, and
then, suddenly, I found the hook in my giving up smoking
recently. Who can figure out how the creative juices
flow? I only know one minute I had nothing and then it
all fell into place.

DC: The class may not think this helpful but I can assure you
that you will experience the same sudden awareness of
the significance of the lyric, followed by the idea of how
to dramatize it by means of an inner monologue, much as
Miss W has described. Using the suggested implements, it
somehow does get done, although the actor/singer up, until the moment of conception, remains in the dark. (To
Miss W) I want to make a few suggestions that will help
sharpen the inner emotional life of the **Two** and thereby
effect a larger physical statement, which is, after all, the
primary purpose of the **Two**: namely, to reintroduce you
to the extraordinary range of body language.

To begin with: I feel certain you will gain added size if you heat further the elements of the **Two**. For instance, the "to whom" in this case: Max. We understand him to be an agent, your agent, but he lacks profile. Perhaps, purely as the *writer* of the **Two** and not the performer of it, if you knew he was disinterested in your career, or planning to get rid of you by ending your contract with the agency, more grist for your (the *actor's*) mill might result.

"When is it?" Could you have just done the audition that very day—forcing him to call to find out how well or poorly you did? And this need for you to know *right now* is due to the fact that a payment on your car is due and you have planned on this particular job for the money. This last fact can sharpen the why of the **Two**.

Finally, again, concerning only the technique of the performance and having nothing to do with performing as we will discuss it later (chapters 16–17), try to rise higher from the simple or comparative rendering of the **Two** to the superlative in order to achieve the most, rather than the least, awareness of the extent of your size on stage. End every physical response (most important) to the verbal statement (least important) of the **Two** with "-est." Do I make myself clear?

Miss W: I understand. Angry and angrier are not as valuable as angriest. Joyous and more joyous are less worthwhile than most joyous.

DC: Exactly.

Miss W: It is very difficult not to go for these points, like a Rockette kicking for a hand. I'm always terrified I'm doing a Shirley Temple routine.

DC: We have said a **Two** is a physical indication of what you are saying. This is not synonymous with indicating. Flapping your hands around may be moving but we all agree it is not an organic physical act, nor is it art. I would hope that you (to the class), all of you, will bring your total craft as actors to the performance of the **Two**. I do not want any of you to surrender what you already know. What does concern me is how best to utilize that body of expertise when you sing.

His Work

A week later Mr. T is ready to perform his **Two** on the lyric of "A Cow and a Plough and a Frau."

Mr. T: I don't think you'll have to help me with the first sentence. I took all my notes as Miss W worked it and I feel fairly sure I have it down.

DC: Nothing would please me more. Shall we see?

Mr. T is correctly *at ease* prior to beginning and then moves into the position of zero and starts.

Mr. T: This is a story about me, Captain.

DC: "Very good. Try it again because it *was* very good. (The class responds) No, I'm quite serious. One learns only from mistakes. When you do something well it can be terrifying. Was it an accident? What, in fact, did I do? Study is of value only as the act itself stumbles toward those hazy goals where you know not why something works, but why it doesn't.

Mr. T begins his **Two** without further interference from DC.

The TWO	The LYRIC
This is a story about me, Captain. [Zero] [The Captain looks up from his desk, unhappy with the interruption, an inquiring "Yes?"]	
(Sheepish) Sir, Sgt. Blackstone said . . .	If I had a cow
(He kicks his foot, "Skippy" fashion) . . . that this would be a good time for me . . .	and a plough

(A rush of courage) . . . to make my request to be in Special Services. . . .	and a Frau,
(Warming up) Why, Captain, when I heard I was drafted, I said to myself, Freddie, I said, the place for you is in Special Services!	How good my life would be.
Hell! You could do what you know and be making a real contribution while you're doing it!	I'd make a home where I know my heart would rest.
(Growing excitement) Ya' know that old movie house near Camp Funston . . .?	I could hitch the cow to the plough
(Losing himself and all military demeanor) Boy! What a theatre that'd make!	While my Frau looked on and smiled at me.
Oh! Just close your eyes, sir. (Doing the same . . . really "in" it) I can see it now!	Smiled as she dreamed of the dreams we love the best.
(Bends down, arms spread, as though raising the curtain himself) The curtain goes up . . .	Dreams about a meadow
(In ecstasy—rising) . . . the lights . . . come up . . .	rolling in the sunlight

(Sweeps his arm R to L) . . . and the entire First Infantry Division Band marches on playing "Everything's Coming Up Roses!"	And a field of clover for the pretty cow.
(Stops . . . sees the Captain's consternation; quickly changes to mend his fences) No good, huh? (A moment) I know what I could do! I could read some poetry . . . maybe . . .	Dreams about a baby
(Off in his own world, awed) . . . like . . . Edna St. Vincent Millay!	laughing at a raindrop.
(Sees Captain shaking his head, "No"; joins him in the negative head-shake) Well, maybe it's not such a good idea.	How do you suppose
("No" shake changes to a "yes" nod) It doesn't *have* to be a theatre.	a new world grows?
(He walks away, fighting for his life as he tries desperately to come up with another idea)	Starting with a cow and a plough and a Frau
(Snaps his fingers at the birth of a new idea and races back to C) I got it! A traveling mobile unit!	It's simply A–B–C
It's all so simple! We could do a morality play.	I'd plough more land if the cow had children
(Off on a creative binge again) Better yet! We could do *Macbeth!*	We would expand if my Frau had children

(Victorious exaltation) "Birnham Wood" . . .	Things must be planned
. . . comes to Dunsinane between the tanks!	for my children's children
(Sees the Captain looking at him as though he thought him raving mad; joy slowly turns to weak fear)	now!
(Picking up the pieces) All you'd have to do, sir, is sign . . .	All I need is a cow
(Points to paper in front of Captain on his desk) . . . so I could get . . .	and a plough
. . . into Special Services . . .	and a beautiful Frau.

Rideout

. . . please. . . .
(Destroyed by his obvious failure
with the Captain, he waits a moment in
embarrassment and then turns to leave)

The Class responds to the emotional pull of the parochial subject matter. Then, silence, as DC waits for the applause to end.

DC: The class has spoken, it seems. But I agree. It is most affecting, not in its verbal statement, which I fear still holds first place in the class's consideration of its worth, but in the highly original physical appearance of the man. I can only assume you have used some poignant memory of a moment in your army life that is feeding a special language to your motor system.

Mr. T: I have to be honest. I fought like the devil to keep away from anything autobiographical but I found that with every invented **Two** I fell into the same trap over and over again of inventing my body language. Then I remembered you said at one point that the purpose of the **Two** is not only to make me *move*, but to make me move in the way *I* move. (The class laughs at his choice of phrase.)

    DC: Yes. Later, when we are speaking only about performance and not technique, you will often hear me suggest that your body is moving in an imitation of life rather than in its customary manner. (To the class) This is the last time I will ever know what you are thinking as you move. The **Two** corroborates the physical life and the **Two** is audible. But it will never be so again. How often in the theatre do we catch ourselves wondering what was on the actor's mind when he did something we liked or even something we objected to? But we are destined never to know. A famous singer once said to me, "I have many imitators but no one knows what I'm thinking." How right she is. I am only intent here in cautioning you to make certain that your thinking is always your *own* thinking, clear and ungarbled and of a pattern consonant with the script we *do* hear—namely, the song."

           Mr. T's **Two** is purely his own. We could imitate what it looks like as we see it but, had we not heard it, we would never know the complexity of the thought process that achieves such rich body language. (To Mr. T) Not the least of your success is this: I assigned the lyric to you to edge you further from the comedic work you are called upon to do professionally. You have attained an effective amalgam of that comedy that is born of truth and reality and that is, finally, *not funny.* Because your imagination moves along comic lines the blend of that gift—the painful **Two** of a malassigned soldier fighting for his life as well as a transfer into a military environment that will secure his sanity—with Dorothy Field's lyric makes a stunning comic invention. To dramatize the significance of the lyric you have used a valuable substitute adventure. On the face of it there would appear to be little congruity were we to read your **Two** and the lyric. When it is played, however, they will be in perfect harmony.

The Two is now ready to assume its proper function as the fulcrum of the text from which the *emotional and physical statement* emerge and furnish support for the lyric. We have torn the veneer from the wood, the facing from that which it covered. The two elements must now be brought back together: the physicalized thought process (the **Two**) that creates the verbal statement and the spoken/sung language thus created—the **Three**.

A note of irony: Because the **Two** is a monologue with no music assigned to it, it is natural to presume that the actor will be more comfortable now that his words are separated, once again, from the need to sing them. Taken a step further, "the better the actor, the better the **Two**" would be an obvious presumption. But this is not the case. Of the thousands of **Two's** I have witnessed, it is often the beginning actor with less training who delivers a truer and more interesting statement. The *locking* that results in partial paralysis afflicts the student in undefinable ways, none of which appears to have much to do with the actor's technical brilliance. It is true that the experienced actor may display more ability to find the handle of a **Two** and to execute its *verbal* construction. But the *physical* performance of the **Two** has no categorical rule of thumb. Actors, singers, and dancers share the same psychological blocks that are at the root of the awkwardness in physical self-consciousness. The dancer may be on intimate terms with his motor responses and find no obstacle to dancing what he feels, but a **Two** moves in realistic body language and not from plié to arabesque to pirouette. The singer, robbed of song, is the most guilty only because he spends too much time securing a sound vocal technique (no pun implied), and usually very little in the bailiwick of the dancer and the actor. I speak in general terms only to clarify that, on empirical evidence alone, the **Two** will be performed to the best of each individual's ability to delineate a limitless variety of body language. Be assured that the actor's technique, the dancer's technique, and the singer's technique, each by itself, is not necessarily, a panacea for what ails you when you are asked to move.

Chapter 13

The Three

Suit the action to the word, the word to the action.

W. Shakespeare

THE THREE: THE LYRIC AND ITS SIGNIFICANCE COME TOGETHER

If I were to plot a diagram to indicate the relative difficulty of the technical work as it is fed to the actor/singer in my studio, I would have to graph a continual curve rising to its apex with the performance of the **Three**. But lacquering the **Two** onto the lyric (the **Three**) with proficiency is not easy. Conquest of it and its function, in a much simplified adaptation, sets into motion my credo of what singing is all about. I speak of this here to assure the reader/student that once the **Three** is mastered, what follows is increasingly *less* demanding.

I have said that the **Three** is the coming together of the **Two** and the lyric. The **Two** is now to be played, *silently* acted out, while you are speaking the lyric. This union of the subtext played and the text (lyric) spoken is difficult only in the sense that they must, like gears, mesh and not collide. I think of the timing of the **Three** as *arcs* of thought and speech (the lyric) that intersect, the speech *following* the thought so as to give the distinct impression that the **Two** is always precipitating the lyric. One thinks the **Two** and speaks the lyric. Remember that your adherence to the **Two** remains as dedicated, now that it is silent, as it was when it was heard. The following don't's and do's are designed to make possible the most effective achievement of the meld. I enumerate both as before, even though, in the case of the **Three**, a well-monitored don't often results in an automatic manifesting of a do.

Don't's

1   Do not yet discard "This is a story about me." It is to be *thought of* as the first moments of your **Two**. We need a starting line and this one is still usable. You will find that once the gradations of a graceful beginning have become more or less second nature to you, the line will fade away of its own accord. Until that time, the **Three** evolves from a C focus, hands at side, with weight on both legs. Just as the **Two** was born from this zero body language, so will the **Three** find its life beginning.

2   Don't speak too soon. Better late than early or even on time. Let the arc of the **Two** (its physical appearance), as it effects the lyric line to which it relates, be well *on* you before you speak.[1] When in doubt, play the **Two** a moment longer before you verbalize the start of the new lyric arc/line. Nothing aborts body language faster than the mouth.

3   I am most often asked whether one *cuts* or shortens the **Two** when it becomes the silent element of the **Three**. I always cross my fingers and say: "Never!" It is an obvious lie but if the student is told "yes" he will cut it to shreds and remain unaware that he may be removing important information that mortars one brick of the **Two** to its neighbor. Don't destroy your transitional moments by overcutting what you may have underestimated. In my own case I try not to think I am cutting something so much as compressing it. The actual physical appearance may have been altered, but I remain aware of where A must go to C without giving up my commitment to B.

4   Relative to *cuts*: Do not stand miming away your **Two** until it has the appearance of a silent movie. Overdedication to every single move the **Two** created when it was spoken is as destructive to sense as cutting

[1] The placement of the lyric during and after the beats of the **Two**'s in the preceding chapter attempts to illustrate this for the reader.

may have been to transitions. What you want in the arc of the **Two** is its *essence*, its essential reason for being there—and not a blow-by-blow rendition of what is now shorn of words, a redundancy of physical expression. If in your **Two** you were busy defining the physical appearance of being overheated as you complained to the Superintendent about the breakdown of air conditioning, in a **Three** the essence of being warm does not require the full alphabet of a dumb-show reference to heat. Is this synonymous with cutting? Not at all. If I see you hot, it is time to speak the lyric; don't keep showing me you are hot with activities that are only variations on the same theme.

5   Do not orate or recite the lyric. As soon as you hear yourself elocuting the light verse you will kill the **Two**. This is not an audition for a poetry reading. A good rule: Do not project the lyric. Play the **Two** fully. It is of no great importance that we even *hear* the lyric clearly. A monotone, a whisper, a colorless expression of the text are ways to keep the **Three** from turning into a recital.

Do's

1   A **Three**, a **Four** (chapter 14), and even a **Five** (chapter 15) are, in their playing, to be considered a **Two**. *Think and play the* **Two**. Lose the subtext and you will be committed all too soon to the lyric. In this regard, memorize the words so well that there is no possibility of your forgetting them. I am always saddened to see how quickly the actor/singer, so eager to be with text (the lyric), will murder the inner monologue, whereas I am cheered when a **Three** is so committed to an observance of the physical life of the **Two** that the actor may forget a line of the lyric. Remember, a **Three** *is a* **Two** with the lyric in its wake.

2   Keep your focus alive. Silent renaming of the vis-à-vis is of great aid in making certain your eyes are not rolling in your head. It must be clear to you now that Mary, Dad, John, Dr. Fardel—all of the names we have named in our **Two's**—are merely nominal labels to define the presence of the audience. The **Two** belongs to them (in this case, C focus). The **Three, Four, Five,** and finally every song you will ever sing is in need of listeners.

3   The pianist is still not present. Remember that the

ultimate moments (the Rideout) are played out *after you have spoken the last line of the lyric.* When music returns in the **Five** it will make its sense apparent. Despite the sensation of nonsense, for now—*do* it.

4   Pay particular attention to the transitions that take you from the end of one arc to the beginning of a new one. There is a tendency to jerk from one physical statement, as it wanes, into the beginning of the new arc of body language. What separates the good actor/singer from the bad is not only how fully he lives *in* each moment, but how well he gets *out of* one moment and *into* the next. That silent-movie appearance evinced by some **Three**'s is due to this absence of transitional grace.

5   Until the motor system becomes accustomed to the **Two** and the lyric having to work *out-of-sync* with each other, the student may have the sensation of rubbing his stomach with one hand while at the same time patting his head with the other. It is the flow of the **Three**, or rather the lack of it, that is responsible for this impression. It is like driving that car we have spoken about. At the start you are convinced you will never find an easy coordination of eyes, feet, and hands, but somehow we all learn it. One moment the **Three** stops and starts and jerks and jumps; then suddenly the mystery of its synchronization is solved and the silent movie now proceeds at a realistic pace. A **Three** moves with the flow that is the consequence of knowing at every moment where you are in your **Two**. Lose your place in the **Two** and the body goes dumb. The mouth will continue speaking the lyric, but the body will have no idea of what to do until it is told. A **Three** is, as I have said, 99.9 percent a **Two**. In this exercise, a commitment of one-tenth of a percent to the lyric is all the lyric merits.

6   I have allowed the actor/singer, if he felt the need, the indulgence of a short expositional reference at the start of his **Two** before confrontation began. Now it must be cut. For example:

This is a story about me, Dan. What do you think you're doing? Climbing up a fire escape, opening my bedroom window, and coming in like some thief in the night! You've got to get out of here! The cops'll be here any minute.

In a **Two** this lengthy description of what Dan has done may have aided the actor to achieve a growing outrage. In a **Three**, as exposition, it is expendable. The **Two** now must be amended to read:

This is a story about me, Dan. You've got to get out of here! The cops'll be here any minute.

The outrage remains, compressed now, and in no further need of the excess verbal crutch.

I have forgone the dialogues with Miss W and Mr. T with good reason. Performance of the **Three** is the most difficult of all the technical exercises performed in the studio. No one can be expected to deliver a full performance the first time—proceeding from the top of the **Two**, with the lyric in close sequence, and ending with the final moments of the Rideout. Coordination is achieved in the relative time it takes the new information to be fed into the computer of the mind. There is a seduction (which must be resisted) to speak the lyric at the same time that the **Two** is born, *in* as against *out* of sync. The **Three** becomes fluent over weeks of practice, even though its accomplishment mirrors what we do all through our lives (move and then speak). Art imitates life, but not without a struggle.

I have been known to pass the work of a student if he can give me only the equivalent of eight bars of his **Three**, thereby convincing both himself and me that the sensation of the **Three** is not only *understood* (if not sustained) but *experienced*. I recommend a constant reference to the don't's and do's as the best gauge for perfecting the exercise. Make yourself aware of what you are doing incorrectly. *Feeling* less will permit you more room to proctor your work, so resist any excess of emotion that disengages you from a strict control of the technique of the **Three**.

Chapter 14
The Four

> *Do not commit your poems to pages alone—Sing them, I pray you.*
>
> Virgil

THE FOUR: SINGING THE THREE IN FREE METER

The **Four** is a slow change of course away from speech and aimed toward music. But if that musical door were opened wide the **Two** would suffer a quick death by suffocation as the melody and its rhythms asphyxiated it with song. To allow the **Two** a longer life, the pianist—who now, and forevermore, reenters your singing life—will not play an accompaniment but just the Belltones of the lyric's melody, supplying the starting notes you need to continue the **Four**.

Don't's

    1   These Belltones are not an order to sing. They are played, and often played again, to afford you the proper pitch *when you need it*. Again, the **Two** is the element that must remain in your consciousness when you sing.

    2   Don't sing out. This is an exercise in retaining the life of the **Two** ahead of the lyric. It is not a vocalized performance of the melody. There are no quarter notes, eighth notes, half notes, rests, or bar signs—all the trappings that adorn melody and transform it into song.

In a **Three** you may have employed a monotone or a whisper to prohibit elocution. The **Four** matches the **Three** exactly except that what was droned is now given its proper pitch level. A film of a **Four** would superimpose accurately on one of a **Three**. Only the soundtrack would differ.

3   Don't sustain notes. Just as you spoke the lyric, softly sing it. Shun the making of music.

Do's

1   Learn the melody so well that your need to lean on the Belltones is minimal. The pianist is there to keep you from losing all semblance of pitch, but if the **Four** is playing correctly, a missed note here or there is of no particular importance.

2   Again, as in the **Three**, we are fighting to keep the **Two** alive. It is the **Two** that the lyric, and now the lyric plus its melodic dressing, is about. Do not derive an emotional charge out of hearing the melody. Know that music is the murderer of the **Two** and that we are, in the **Four**, allowing only its minimal death-dealing power to enter the life of the **Two**.

3   Remember to play out the Rideout, as in the **Two** and **Three**, despite the fact that, in this exercise, the last note of the song will not be held.

A note of interest: In the metamorphosis of these exercises based on subtext as the thrust element of singing, the **Four** was a late arrival. For many years it did not exist at all. The **Three** was followed by what is now called the **Five** (chapter 15). Addition of the present exercise was suggested by many actors who felt the jump from the **Two** played while *speaking* the lyric was self-defeating when followed by the singing of the song with full accompaniment. This massive transition from no music to full-throated vocalism worked too much damage to the student's concentration on his **Two**. The validity of these objections led to the **Four**, as described in this chapter. I mention this to add further caution against the singing, as such, of the **Four**. As before, it is the **Two** that is on both our minds and our bodies.

Chapter 15
The Five

A translation is no translation, he said, unless it will
give you the music of a poem along with the words of
it.

John Millington Synge

THE FIVE: **THE SONG AND THE** TWO
COME TOGETHER

The **Five** is the last of the technical exercises taught in my
studio. It brings into play the remaining elements that
have, until now, been refused entry. Again, the **Two** is
primary, but now it has as its accompaniment the full
trappings of the song. The pianist plays what is scored to
be played. That simple series of Belltones in the **Four**
blossoms into melody in a **Five**, along with rhythm, bar
signs, and harmonic complement.

Before the fact, the actor/singer is convinced his **Two**
cannot move fast enough to stay ahead of the lyric and
still remain organic. But it can and it will.

Before the fact, the actor/singer is convinced the arrival of 4/4 time will wrench his **Two** into 4/4 acting. But
it won't and it doesn't.[1]

[1] All songs used in these exercises are ballads. One can appreciate, while doing the **Two** and singing the **Five,** that the slowest of ballads can seem like a
song running wild. A **Five** combines the natural sedate tempo of a ballad with
the kind accommodation of the accompanist.

And before the fact, the actor/singer is convinced he will be forced to cut the **Two** down to skeletal size in order to squeeze even a fraction of its life into the spaces ("Air") of the song. But he needn't and he won't.

How, then, does the **Two** survive? When the actor was the creater of the rhythms in which the lyric was spoken (the **Three**) and/or sung (the **Four**), the **Two** was given the time it demanded. Nothing forbade making each beat of the **Two** (the subtext) a country in which one could stay—or at the very least, linger—if there was the aesthetic justification for making the **Two** truer. Now the rhythms of the text are created by the composer. The actor/singer can no longer sing when he wants to, as he does when he speaks on the nonmusical stage, for the demands of the composer must be met. There is, after all, an orchestra playing the same song that you are singing, and there would be anarchy if both of you didn't do it together. Therefore, the desire to stay on in the country of the **Two**, for whatever reason, is no longer vouchsafed you.

The **Two,** in a **Five**, is better thought of as a series of motel stopovers you will check into and immediately check out of in order to hit the road. The operative phrase in a **Five** that governs the relative speed of the **Two** becomes: "It's later than you think." Don't allow yourself to get too comfortable at any point in the **Two**. That song is hell-bent to be sung and it will sing itself as the composer intended. However, the speed with which the **Two** will now move does not mean you must abdicate your commitment to that subtext you have fought so hard to retain. Singing deprives the actor/singer of those sometimes indulgent reactions to what he has *said/sung*. What he is *going to say/sing* is always a moment away and, if it is so near at hand (mouth), what he is *thinking* has to be even closer to the conjuring of it in his mind.

Finally, practice makes for perfection. One learns where the "Air" in the song permits a shorter or longer time to stay or move ahead with the **Two**. With each try coordination becomes more facile. What seems impossible to synchronize soon acquires an ease that astonishes.

DIALOGUES

Her Work

After a week of preparation at home, using a tape of the accompaniment, Miss W is ready.

DC: Before you begin let me tell you, and the class, about the Vamp. The **Five** begins where we left off in the First Class (chapter 9). We are still working in a technical country. The song began with a Vamp employed in the following manner: Coming from an *at ease* position, we nodded to the accompanist to signal him to play. We left the focus on him to return to a general focus into the theatre. Then, somewhere around the downbeat of the third bar of the Vamp, your focus came center. All this will now be reprised with but one change. Then our focus created a zero physical life; now we have a specific to apply to that C spot. (To Miss W) What was nameless before is now your agent, Max. "This is a story about me, Max" will be born upon seeing that C focus at the top of the third bar. Your four-bar Vamp, in the case of "Make It Another Old-Fashioned, Please," is in ad-lib. Looser in tempo, you will have more than sufficient time to play the natal moments of your **Two** that germinate during that sentence. And, remember, you have the *sting* after the fourth bar, so there is no need to rush into the opening of the **Two**. The important thing is to get the arrival of body language from zero as smooth as possible as it peaks out of those last bars of the Vamp.

One more point I want to make. The first performance of a **Five** is always sluggish. The **Two** wants desperately to run the show. To impede that, I will cue you. Knowing your subtext as well as I do, I will be your timer. When you hear my cue, drop whatever you are playing and pick up the signal to move on. *If* you hear it, rest assured that your inner rhythms are not quick enough and increase the speed of the thinking mechanism that contrives your **Two**. Am I making myself clear?

Miss W: Let us hope I won't need that crutch.

DC: I'm afraid, first time around, you will not only need it but crave it. But that is of no importance. Needing it *after* you are weaned is what will concern us. But I feel certain that will not happen. The proficiency of your work has continued to increase. There is no reason to suppose your faculty for fluency will desert you now. But why not begin? In Artistotle's words: "The beginning is half the whole."

Miss W begins her inner monologue (unheard but played), "This is a story about me, Max." DC, as he forewarned, throws her cues, tells her to drop what she is playing, and indicates when to pick up the new beats. She remains alert and malleable. As the final moments of the Rideout are played, this time in combination with the held final note on "rye," DC is still feeding her the cues for "all right . . . reach out now for a cigarette, stay above the landing strip, do not come down, not just yet . . . give in to a feeble admission of failure, and . . . out."

The class applauds Miss W's labor. DC silences the hand.

DC: Try it again and see how much of it can be timed without my aid.

Miss W, unprompted, finds for herself the rhythms that interplayed the **Two** with Mr. Porter's implacable 4/4 time signature. This is achieved after more than one try, but each of her efforts succeeds in a more graceful blending of the one into the other. DC allows her to work out the exercise on her own. No longer in need of the buddy system that sustained her, it is now only a question of perfecting the **Five**.

His Work

Mr. T's **Five**, as before, benefits from his having witnessed Miss W's work. (It is suggested that the reader follow Mr. T's **Two** in chapter 12.) But there are moments in his **Two** that DC would like to place in better-timed niches.

DC: (To Mr. T after cuing him through a first performance of his **Five**) That was a little ragged, I'm afraid.

Mr. T: I'm thrown by hearing your voice cuing me in different places than I've rehearsed.

DC: It is confusing, but your **Two** moves in jerks, stopping and starting and betraying your discomfort with the defined "Air" the composer imposes on those spaces, the duration of which you alone were once master. What was possibly too long hasn't the time now to play itself through, and what was a moment in your **Two** now finds itself cursed with more time than it needs. But, never mind. Let's see what needs to be done to remedy this curable disease. Why don't we take the walkaway out-of-context—the one that sets up the second half of the lyric: "Starting with a cow and a plough and a Frau." You are still using the footwork you employed in the **Two, Three,** and **Four,** when you could pace three to four steps from center to right as you struggle to come up with another idea. Now, you see, the score allows only two beats, two quarter-note beats, to accept what we agree cannot be fit in. What was a walkaway must now be slimmed down to a pivot and a quick return. You do not have time for even *one* step. Just start to turn to go and come back quickly with the fingersnap that sets up the lyric: "It's simply A-B-C."

Mr. T: That's certainly going to be a lot easier. I was trying to keep the walkaway by telling myself I needed it all to get that idea born of a mobile unit doing *Macbeth*.

DC: Now you know you do not have the time and, between us, I think perhaps you were growing a little too fond of that "moment."

Mr. T: Probably. But as you said, the **Two** does tend to constipate one's rhythms. (The class laughs)

DC: I believe I used the word "sluggish" and, as I recall, it had to do with the performance of the **Five** and not the actor. (Further laughter)

Mr. T tries the pivot turn, returning front almost immediately as he grabs for the new idea that creates the life for the fingersnap—all of it combined within the two beats allowed in the score. Improvement increases.

DC: Better. What will make it still better is if you begin the life of the pivot a beat or two sooner in the vocal line "Starting with a cow and a plough and a Frau." Let me see it *on* you when you reach "and a Frau" instead of waiting for "Frau."

Mr. T pivots sooner and the **Five** immediately appears smoother. The class applauds.

DC: Very good. Try it again and again. (To the class) Here is an example of working the exterior physicality as a *staging* problem that must be refined. I would not think of it as an organic moment until my motor system was educated. Which side shall I pivot on? And before that, where must my weight be in order to effect the best rendering of the "business"? Once you have laid that away, you can return to a more *artistic* performance with the knowledge that it will now be *artful*, too. The actor often assumes that if he thinks and feels with complete reliance on *truth*, all else will fall into place. But truth is a many-faceted thing. On the stage "reality," as John Gielgud has said, "is not the same as reality in real life, although it can seem to be."[2] What is often as important is the playwright's (in this case, the composer's) intention and plain, downright dexterity.

   (To the class) I spoke, early in our work, of the odd circumstance in the musical theatre that may find a cast directed by someone who knows nothing about singing and dancing. At that time the point was made within the frame of reference of the audition. By extension, the same director who cast the musical with an untutored eye may now stage it. He can possess other gifts that substitute for his musical innocence, but he will not be able to help the performer when the downbeat of a song arrives. You will be on your own. The choreographer will tell you what to do and where to go, but how to do it will always be your own concern. You are, while singing, as good as what you come up with. The more creative and able you are to "take stage," the more visible you are. The more visible, the more valuable you are—both to the production and to

---

[2] Lewis Funke and John E. Booth, eds. *Actors Talk about Acting* (New York: Random House, 1961), p. 30.

yourself. Now and here is the time and place to perfect sheer craft. You are not too far from what you will experience in an actual musical. The outward appearance of the piece always takes precedence over its inner life. Unlike a play, wherein the shape of things—the interaction of character relationships and the "interior" elements that will give life to the piece—is defined through the rehearsals, a musical receives its shape first. Runthroughs of Act One are not uncommon as early as the third day of the first week of rehearsal, with Act Two staged immediately thereafter. At the end of that first week a director may, and often does, schedule runthroughs every day of the remaining three weeks that are allowed him and the cast. The dancers, by tradition, have five weeks of preparation (one week more than the script), and so the first runthroughs will not include the dancing, but the book and the singing of the score are established early. The orchestra must have keys and piano arrangements in order to be ready with the instrumental score for the first *orchestra reading* that precedes the out-of-town opening.

I mention this now to Mr. T and, through him, to all of you, to make the point that *staging* yourself (an ugly word elsewhere) is not so appalling when you realize that, once cast in a musical, you will be staged from the very beginning. The actor/singer must keep two distinct and mutually exclusive facts in mind. *One:* How well you execute a singing performance—in this case we were triggered by Mr. T's perfecting that pivot and its timing—devolves with positive effect on both you and the musical production you are in. *Two:* If, in a play, content shapes form, one need not reject the musical's notion that the reverse may have equal validity. It is true that most musicals are empty and relatively dependent on staging devices to keep the audience's interest alive. But great musicals possess both. It is not an offense to be an entertainment, but it is offensive if all that pizzazz the actor is asked to do is, like the Emperor's clothes, hiding nothing. Stage yourself, yes, when you have to—as in Mr. T's case—then return and work out the life of the piece that will make the exterior the convex of a rich interior. When you do, it is, after the fact, of small importance which came first.

REVIEW

With Mr. T's performance we can summate the significance of the preceding technical work. Mastery of the **Five** ends the technique section of this volume. Part 2 follows and is concerned with performing. There remains one caveat I must stress. Nothing in this section can or dare be construed as a *performance,* by an actor/singer, of a song. The **Five,** in particular, is surely *not* a performance, in Miss W's case, of "Make It Another Old-Fashioned, Please," or in the subtext Mr. T has created for "A Cow and a Plough and a Frau." It is *performance of a* **Two** on a related lyric and not a *performance of the song.* You have been asked to move continuously throughout the exercise—an activity no one would be foolish enough to indulge in while performing a song. In the **Five** you are concerned not with the *song* but with a technical exercise in body language created from and by an *inner monologue* of a lyric.

Why, then, are the five exercises a part of this learning process? The following reasons explain the need:

1   The actor, the singer, and the dancer are, by nature, uncomfortable when they sing. For all three groups, the empty gesture and the hollow charade are too often the only physical language brought in to dress a song. Now we know that when we *want* to move, we know *how* to move. What we are *thinking* when we sing is all that keeps our bodies alive. What we are *singing* cannot, except in obvious and shallow language, inform our motor systems.

2   Does one do a **Two** every time one picks up a new song? Of course not. Does one do a scale every time one picks up a new piano sonata? No. Does one plié every time one starts to soft-shoe? Not at all. Does this rule out the need to learn scales or work at the barre? Again, of course not. What we speak of as technique is a *means* to an end. Those who make an *end* of technique are identifiable. Their work is noncreative, worshipping as it does at the shrine of know-how.

3   One need not ever do a **Two** on a song to recognize the need to know what a song is about. *What it is about is how the song gets to be sung in the first place.*

197

4 We have said that a **Two** demands that you not stop moving throughout the life of the song. There are many songs that require almost no movement, so eloquent or complicated are their words. Still, the thought processes are concerned with the *significance* of what you are going to say. A **Two** is a string of those thought processes that, in their significance, result in body language. But all thought processes are not, in reverse, **Two**'s. A single color word, or a focus change born of revelation, or a joke that is just around the corner and requires setting up—none of these are **Two**'s, but they are incontestably thoughts that lie in the "Air" spaces of the music that precedes the correspondent lyric.

5 Often, in my studio, when I see a performance that is not interesting enough to look at, I will suggest doing a **Two** in the Bridge, for instance, to spike the eye line of the auditor. What I mean by this is best explained by a sample: Let us suppose you are singing "Where or When" (the song I use at the beginning of classes to play the game of "Essence"). This song does not require physical language. What it speaks about is idea, the idea of déjà vu. There is no heat in the song when it is removed from the musical scene that gave it birth. These factors can make *looking* at the song less interesting than the more engaging experience of *hearing* it sung well. Somewhere around the Bridge, then, it may be wiser to invent thought that can be considered a **Two,** if by such consideration we mean specific thinking that makes you move.

	[Simple physical life]
1ST "8"	It seems we stood and talked like this before— We looked at each other in the same way then, But I can't remember where or when.
2ND "8"	The clothes you're wearing are the clothes 　　　you wore, The smile you are smiling you were smiling then, [Hands up from sides out to "spike" repeat title] But I can't remember where or when. [Hand to brow in confusion]
BRIDGE	Some things that happen for the first time [Down to puzzled surrender] Seem to be happening again.

[Down and out—one at a time]
And so it seems that we have met before . . . .

I hasten to confess the infantilism of the above. I employ it only as illustration and in no way suggest it as a valid garnish for *performing* "Where or When."

Herewith is the essential difference between the acting of spoken dialogue and that of a sung monologue. In acting the actor speaks and then reacts to another actor's line. *Jumping* or *telegraphing* by reacting too soon to what has not as yet been said is considered bad form. In singing, however, there *is* no reaction to another's line.[3] The actor/singer is alone and speaks (sings) without his accustomed cue. But one cannot soliloquize or sing mindlessly. Thought gives birth to language. Where, then, can the thought (subtext) be placed, in order to justify the singing of each line, if not in the space ("Air") that precedes it?

If we regard this as an acceptable premise, we must acknowledge this conclusion: The actor/singer's *script* is in the "Air" of the music, and his reactions are no longer to another man's lines but are the *very lyric of the song itself.*

This, then, is the essence of what I teach: *What the actor literally sings is his reaction to the flow of ideas that move ahead of the lyric and constitute the figurative script of the song.*

What the listener hears is, of course, the song itself. But what he sees is the performer's personal psychological imprint on that song. There is no great vocalism that does not enchant the eye as well as speak to the ear. In the theatre the eye can often fool the ear. The actor/singer's credentials are validated there and become his passport onto the musical stage.

---

[3] One cannot even indulge in a reaction to one's own line. When you are singing, time is strictly parceled out. "Getting on with it" does not permit a thought response to what has *been* said (sung), only to what is *going* to be said (sung).

The actor/singer with nothing on his mind *but* the lyric commits the insane act of mouthing language bereft of thought. It leaves the body self-conscious, since it can only move when the mind tells it to. In consequence, the hands gesture emptily, in the classic manner of the singer who is concerned only with the music and the demands of its vocalism.

Further evidence of the empty mind:

1   The deadly meaningless gesture that, once born and having nowhere to go, dies.

2   Charading the lyric by using the hands to describe what the mouth is saying or, worse, has said. If we grant that idea gives birth to language, physicalization of the text *after* it is spoken is clearly a case of the cart before the horse.

3   Pronoun indication by which the hand(s) points to the singer on "I" or "me" and out to the audience on "you." Sometimes I have asked the actor/singer to indicate the audience when he sings "I" and point to himself when "you" appears in the lyric. On last lines such as the classic "*you* love *me,*" the device works to some odd and witty effect.

We can now move out of the world of technique for technique's sake and into the country where you will spend the rest of your singing life. We have done all that we can to set into motion a solid working knowledge; it is time to apply it. Until now, you sang a song and *did* it as *I* asked you to do it. From here on it is the song, just as the play, that will make its demands on you. How best to make the song come alive and what performing is all about are the broad subjects that comprise part 2.

part two

Performance: Advice to the Songlorn

2

Chapter 16

Advice to the Songlorn

The point thereafter was to arrange for one's own chills and fever, passions and betrayals, chiefly in order to make song of them.

James Merrill

HELD OPINIONS

One cannot codify or evaluate performance. One man's preferred singer is met with disinterest by another. This is a business of volume and variety. The audience, as consumer, has presented to it a diverse assortment from which it may select its favorites. I have refrained from any discussion of which singer, what music, which style, or what sound is good, better, or best because there is no defensible gauge one can apply to singers. But although singing cannot, any more than acting, be reduced to rigid equations, we must at the very least attempt a definition of standards and devices from which the reader can gain a grounding in tenets.

I have emphasized that this volume is meant for the actor who sings—a reader separate from the dancer who sings, and even further removed from the singer who sings. That is not to say that he is, by virtue of his profession, segregated from these colleagues, but it is indisputable that he is not at home in song. Chapters 16–17 are designed to illuminate those dark places in that world of music that so frighten him. What follows are impressions, assessments, and *pensées*, none of them hard and fast rules, and all of them held opinions.

The Coach or the Singing Teacher

There is no doubt that an actor's terror of singing is due in part to the living of a life with no singing in it. What begins with innocence must, if left too long in the dark, turn into mystery. Mystery, synonymous with the unknown, is a breeding ground for fear. To reverse this series, the actor/singer must turn up the lights and begin to see that he can be unburdened of much of his anxiety by singing—singing here, there, in the shower, at work during a break, in his car as an accompaniment to the radio—just plain singing. Get used to hearing yourself making music, even if it strikes your ear as something less than song. Don't allow yourself to be hurt by others' assessment of your vocal adequacy, and if that is not easy for you, sing when you are alone.

Where do you go from here? Two possible avenues of exploration present themselves. Both begin a more serious commitment to the act of singing. Admittedly, everyone can and does sing throughout his or her life, those with bad ears for music no less than incipient Streisands. But only when you are serious enough to indulge in an expenditure of time and money can you claim that a professional involvement separates you from the man-on-the-street singer.

Which of the two roads you choose to travel first depends on your personal work habits. You can hire a pianist or a *coach*, either of whom will play for you—it need only be an hour a week—and afford you the chance to stand on a floor, hear an accompaniment, and sing to it. This act of singing will expose you to further self-knowledge of what you know you know, what you know you don't know, and what you need to know.

The alternate choice is to locate a singing teacher and begin the acoustical study that will help you to produce sound correctly—the earlier in your singing life, the better. Choosing a singing teacher is not the formidable

task actors want to make of it. I suggest the straightforward method: *asking around.* When you hear someone—a fellow actor, a dancer, or a singer—who seems
to have an effortless vocal technique, find out with whom
he or she studies. Nothing advertises a teacher more than
the results achieved by his or her students. There is a pit-
fall here, however. Singing teachers often exert a
Svengali-like influence upon those they teach. You will
seldom hear anyone say anything that is not glowing
about his singing teacher. The theory, I suppose, is that
the actor wouldn't be wasting his time with anyone who
wasn't the best. For that reason alone, ask more than one.
Chances are that you are safer in numbers.

Another point relative to the dilemma of whom to
study with is that every singing teacher, no more or less
than any kind of teacher, need not to be effective in equal
degree with each student. Singing, unlike dancing and
painting, is produced with techniques the eye cannot see.
The teacher cannot *show* you what to do so much as
describe it, and albeit there is only one Rome, there are
many roads taught to get there. If you are a serious student and, after six months, you feel you have learned
nothing, it is reasonable to change roads and try another
way. Do not expect miracles to occur quickly, if at all. But
it does seem to me that, after six months, a teacher should
have effected some degree of progress, and that the student should be aware that it has taken place.

Which road, then, to take first? It depends on you. If
you just want to sing because you like to sing, I would
eschew the singing teacher. They do not teach singing,
but how to sing. The actor may simply want to let a little
music into his life, and a pianist or a coach can be the
proper partner to give reality to this dream. They will not
teach you how to sing (nor should they), and chances are
they will not tell you how to perform the song. But the service they do perform has much value. You will be singing
one song after another, and with each vocal effort the
mystique will lessen. But there are others who cannot do
anything with pleasure until they learn the *how-to* of it.
For them, the choice of a good singing teacher is a wiser
beginning.

With a coach, once your fear of singing is gone, you
will find yourself asking: "Shouldn't I sing better?" At

that point the singing teacher will enter your life. If you opt for the singing teacher first you will finally ask: "But when do I get to sing something?" The coach/pianist is waiting in the wings.

The Accompanist—or Shoot the Pianist[1]

When the actor/singer and the accompanist he has hired—sometimes it is the singing coach—come together, not even Uriah Heep rivals the subservience the first adopts toward the second. Nothing impresses an actor more than the mystery of music, so, by extension, the pianist becomes a master to be obeyed. The singer and the dancer have professional lives that are side by side with that of the pianist, and therefore enjoy an equitable one-to-one relationship with him, but to the actor he is an alien creature to be met with wonder and reverence. There is justification. Most actors have little or no knowledge of music, and the pianist, playing off this ignorance, becomes the preeminent member of an imbalanced duet.

In a learning relationship this is not unfair. The pianist has to cope with possible inadequacy and must work to dissemble it. But there is a residue of deference that lingers when they emerge from the pianist's home front and move into the actor's domain—the theatre. That complaisance at an audition, or anywhere the actor/singer performs, is poisonous. The die, however, was cast long before walking onto the stage. The position of the actor/singer has been psychologically determined by weeks or months of game playing, and it would be close to impossible to reverse the master–slave roles laid down by custom. A great accompanist succeeds by registering the lowest profile. When his work, for any reason, is more interesting than the performance it accompanies, he is not doing his job. Worse, an actor who follows the pianist's bidding is stuck in an absurdist reverse action: the singer accompanying the accompanist.

I have referred to the danger (at an audition) of performing with a pianist with whom you have never sung. It can be seen now that only a singer of marked vocal

---

[1] The reverse exhortation of Oscar Wilde's "Over the piano was printed a notice: 'Please do not shoot the pianist. He is doing his best.' "

refinement can dissociate himself from new sounds never heard before, *fills* that enrapture or ravage the ear and rob him of concentration, and pianistic embellishments that often ornament incompetence at the keyboard. I do not want to appear the enemy of the accompanist. His contribution (piano, orchestra, conductor/arranger) is historic, but I have always found when I sang, and later when listening to great singers, that the song, the singer, and the accompaniment all came together to make *music;* each is an equal fraction of the whole. I have never known a first-rate pianist/accompanist who would not prefer to work with a singer with whom he can rest easy and perform his function without annexing territories that are not rightfully his. When the singer needs more support because of momentary inadequacy, that support is forthcoming only to maintain the integer. This give and take—dedicated to the sublime art of making music—occurs no less in concert halls than in theatres. What I want the actor/singer to realize is this: Performance on the stage is everything. No show, no concert, no nightclub act, and no TV variety program ever succeeded because of the excellence of accompaniment. I have *seen* songs sung by nonsinging actors that were memorable, and I have *heard* songs sung by singers that were stage waits. They had this much in common: I cannot recall the accompaniment of either.

When you embark, then, on the singing experience that now requires a pianist, you may announce, at the outset, your beginner status. (It will probably evidence itself when you first sing, but early confession clears the air.) You are buying the pianist's talent and, as in all mercantile transactions, a bill will be forthcoming. You can be respectful, discerning, attentive, eager to learn, willing to fail, and most of all humorous, but shun gratitude, servility, deference, and those characteristics that, when given a conducive climate, set into motion a relationship doomed to inhabit a country in which real music will never be made.

Choice of Song

There is a trinity of units that comprise the vocal experience: choice of song, style (Oh! that ambiguous catchall) of the singer, and the performance as an entity. In order to put them together in good working order let us take them apart to see how each of the elements works.

We have been choosing songs taken from a bin marked "What Not to Sing." In chapter 4 I discussed what is best left unsung. By now the actor/singer should have achieved that degree of objectivity that makes clear the recessive and dominant characteristics manifested in his work. *Wrong songs* have stressed the recessive; *right songs* from here on will corroborate what the eye sees (dominant), but leavened with the actor's interpretive electives serving as pastel additives to the primary colors.

You may accept with misgiving or reject as worthless so simplistic a division as right and wrong songs, but I know of no professional singer who, upon hearing song A won't respond with "I'm sorry, that's just not for me," and be convinced on sheer gut reaction that song B is "my song."

In the early decades of this century songpluggers, employed by music publishers, would seek out a Jolson, a Tucker, or a Bayes and, through hard-sell and expert pianism, attempt to convince that the song, as plugged, was just what the singer was looking for. The singers, in turn, would move through the myriad music-publishing offices searching for just that song that would serve as possible signature material.[2]

Choice of song, once we have accepted the right and wrong theory as practicable, is defined further by circumstance. Where is the song to be sung? Is it an audition for a musical? If so, how close can choice match the material of the projected score? And within that choice are further Chinese boxes wherein choice will best advertise the actor/singer's strong points and soft-pedal his weak ones. And beyond that, does he want the song to synonymize the script or simply to flabbergast and astonish? Is the song to be sung in a nightclub? A large one or a small boite? Is it to open the act? Be the peak of the act? The finale? The throwaway encore? We should

---

[2] George Gershwin, at sixteen, began his professional career as a songplugger in the office of Remick Music Publishers. Within a year his ability at the keyboard attracted the attention that continued throughout his life, for that awesome pianism—as renowned as his genius for composition—was indicative of his right to be called a composer rather than a songwriter.

always sing a right song, but often *where* a song is sung redefines it from right to wrong.

In this regard the actor and the singer have little in common. The actor, generally speaking, does the play because *it* is "the thing." The singer's life, on the other hand, is forever concerned with the selection of what and what not to sing. The established star may choose the material he prefers to appear in, but this is a concomitant of success. The singer copes with choice from his first to his last day. Success, if anything, makes the choice more hazardous, but one can just as readily say that similar perils lie in the beginning, when the singer's career can be damaged by bad choices.

Relative to choice and of interest to the actor/singer is this rule that does not govern selection so much as supplement it: *You do not have to like the song you choose to sing.* We assume, a priori, that our affection for a song will contribute to the audience's reaction and engender a similar affection. But this hypothesis is not so. Just as the actor, having no particular fondness for a play that turns into a major hit beloved by thousands, still can *play it,* the same can be true of the singer and the song. There is even that point reached where liking a song too much invites an excess of *feeling.* This condition contains its own dangers, as I will discuss in the following section ("Style"). But whether you like it or not does not count it out as a possible choice. I am always taken aback when I assign a song to an actor who, upon hearing my pianist and me perform it, says, "Hey, I *like* that!" It would never occur to me to care one way or another if he did or didn't. The song is assigned for other reasons. If he likes it too much we may be in trouble soon enough. If he doesn't like it, sings it anyway, and gets a job by performing it at a subsequent audition, it will quickly become a favorite. Mount, for performing, as many right songs as you can. Listen to singers and buy records to hear the songs you like—at least until the implicit dangers are identified and conquered.

Style

Singing, no less than any theatre activity, moves on two tracks to gain its effect. What the audience sees and hears bears, at most, no more than a slight resemblance to what the singer is thinking. This is true of a song, and extends all the way up to vocalizing in its most effulgent incarnation: opera. To hear a song or, better, to see and hear it, is exclusive of singing it.

For the actor accustomed to his emotions acting, in part, as dictators of his performance, the surrender of his feelings when he sings—a precondition of early study—is difficult. The adjustment *away from feeling* is made more hazardous because song (music) is a siren song, luring the student on to a reef of emotion where plain and simple vocalizing can be shipwrecked. From the moment feelings take over performance the actor/singer has committed the cardinal sin of joining the audience as a *reactor to,* instead of the *conductor of,* the music.

These two tracks—the seminal inner moment-to-moment thought process that propels the vocalization of the song, and the control of that propulsion—are no strangers to us. We employ them in sport as we do in art.[3] The graceful manipulation and outer manifestation of these two elements in their ineffable combination is what people mean, I suppose, by the word "style" as a descriptive of a singer's work.

Many years ago, a beginner could often be heard to say, "I'm not going to study! I want to keep my own style." It is later in the universal calendar, and today we know that knowledge does not kill style. Style is. And knowledge is power. Without the power of knowledge, style is not erased, but with it, it is illumined, propped up, controlled, and given sanity.

The more I teach, the more I recognize the power of thought and its impress on *doing* as opposed to *feeling.* What the actor *feels* is of little importance to me; what he *does* is everything. I have learned that feelings in singing are most often of shoddy manufacture. Happy songs get sung happily and sad songs sadly by virtue of the cheap emotional reactions set into play by our baser instincts upon first hearing the song. But these are not feelings in the service of the song. They are invalid redundancies.

In addition, the audience will *feel* a song without any

---

[3] W. Timothy Gallwey's *The Inner Game of Tennis* (New York: Random House, 1974) speaks with fascinating synonymity of this very subject, namely, the two selves—the "Teller" and the "Doer."

help from the singer. Music, popular or serious, is a universal language that requires no dictionary. And when we speak of show music and contemporary music, feelings had better be stirred in the listener within seconds after the downbeat, or the song is discarded. Noel Coward's reference (in *Private Lives*) to the potency of cheap music alludes to the arousal of our feelings, often shamelessly, by songs that melt the heart even as they melt the mind.

The audience will respond to the song, each in his own way, just as the song, when first heard, affected the actor/singer. Although it is not important how art—in this case, music—speaks to the listener, in the theatre it assumes significance. The singer wants to control or conduct the audience on a journey through the song. The singer is not only the creator of the song's vocal life, but the manipulator of the listener's feelings and responses. And he must do it with the skill of a practiced lover. In other words, the destination is still Rome and, once there, we can all indulge in our personal feelings about the city, but the road *to* it must be taken by the singer and the audience together. *Which* road is the performer's choice, but the listeners must not be confused once that choice is made.

I am always made uncomfortable by a performance that remains opaque or, worse, misread. The attention of the audience is achieved by the clarity of the actor/singer's intention. They'll *feel* it, rest assured, if you *do* it.

Does all this imply that one must sing without feeling? No. But emotions unchecked, and without knowledge of how they are to be deployed, are enemies. They kill the breath with which we sing, close the throat, and open the sluice-gates of our tear ducts, which, coming full circle, close the throat and kill the breath. It is not the emotional response of the singer but of the listener with which you must be concerned, and the way to the *listener's heart* is through *your head.* What you are doing (thinking) emerges, in part, as language (lyric) from your mouth. If the language heard (the words and the music) is presented through a lucid intelligence, the audience will not only *feel* but feel as *you* do and as you wish for *them* to.

Actors are renowned for playing parts. One says, "I saw him in *Hamlet,*" "I saw him play Lear." Singers reputations are built on "I heard Billie *do* "Strange Fruit," Lena *do* "The Lady Is a Tramp," Judy *do* "Over the Rainbow," Sinatra *do* "I've Got You under My Skin," Cleo *do* "Send in the Clowns." Even when we say an actor *did* a part, the timbre of the word is thinned. Because this is true, we do not say, "I saw Olivier do *Uncle Vanya.* It is not as plangent a description as "I saw Olivier's Vanya," implying that he *was* Vanya, and not that he merely *did* him. But to say "I heard Jolson *do* "Swanee"—well, that says it all.

Chapter 17

Performance

*First say to yourself what you would be, and then do
what you have to do.*

Epictetus

MADE OBSERVATIONS

Performances, in the ideal, are to be witnessed. It is possible to write *about* performance, but description is only the remaindered sifting of subjective editing. When the observer, by virtue of his presence, resorts to description (the party of the second part having been absent at the event), he is no longer the witness but the describer. Held opinions made additionally subjective must give way to made observations, which in their total represent, I suppose, a personal credo. There has been some effort to keep related elements together.

The Height of a Song

Singing what you want (need) to say requires an interior height. When a song stays on the horizontal level that supports dialogue, give it up and make a speech. Whenever a truly first-rate song is dead weight in a musical, the fault is almost certain to be incompetent performance or bad staging. There is the other side of this shameless generalization: A third-rate, brilliantly staged and performed song can stop the show cold in its tracks.

An afterthought: A great song is a great song. When it is not performed well it simply waits around until someone appears who *can* sing it. A song is sized, and it requires someone larger than itself to give it verticality.

Every song seeks its own elevation. You cannot stop its built-in determination to reach the apogee. Well-written songs tend to hit their high point somewhere around the end of the Release or Bridge (never earlier) or into the last "8." (Rideouts sometimes appear to be higher still, but they are not organic parts of the song, only addenda to gain applause or to maintain height by resorting to a mechanical supplement.) The best of singers is not only aware of this height and its placement, but will be *there* moments before to make certain it occurs.

Listen, for the sake of aural illustration, to Cleo Laine's singing of "Send in the Clowns" as she exits, in the Bridge, from "Sure of my lines—No one is there" into "Don't you love farce?" The song is never higher than at that moment. (The last "8" is a gentle dipping, and the additional final "8," "Losing my timing this late in my career," contemplative.)*

To give size its proper emphasis and further indicate the song's elevation, John Dankworth (her arranger and conductor) supplies a key change and Miss Laine caresses the "v" in "love" and follows it with the same elegant stress on the "f" of "farce." No other singer of this song does this with quite the impulse for drama. In fact, most singers ignore this summit and, worse, sing only the one consonant (the "f" of "farce") and allow it to do double duty, as in "Don't you luh-farce?"[1] For the actor/singer, then: Always choose a song less *tall* than you. "Don't Rain on My Parade" requires the forceful life it received from Streisand in *Funny Girl*. "Rose's Turn" from *Gypsy*, a song of even larger proportions, demands a performance of still greater magnitude to contain and control

---

*"Send in the Clowns," music and lyrics by Stephen Sondheim, from *A Little Night Music* (1973). Copyright © 1973 Revelation Music Publishing Corp. and Rilting Music Inc. Used by permission.

[1] Related to this, and germane to it, is the sensible rule that when two explosive consonants follow each other, only the second one need be articulated, as in: "There'll be a hah-time in the town tonight" and not "Ho*t* time," which sounds like a stutterer hung on the sibilance of the letter "t."

its potential to excite an audience. Ethel Merman, aided by Jerome Robbins' expert direction, furnished that volume on both counts.[2]

There are as many *thought processes* to make a song vertical in the second half of its Vamp as there are songs to be sung (see chapter 7). Two simple ones are given here. They are effective and have the virtue of being straightforward.

1   "Listen to me!" cannot only prop up the timid actor/singer but, by the simple act of demanding attention (in *thought*), gains it. The danger here is a weakening of intent by the slight alteration that finds the demand softened to "Listen to me, please!" Ask (in *thought*) an audience to attend you and their natural perversity is fanned. Demand it (in *thought*) and no argument is brooked. "Listen to me!" sans "please" is what you need here.

2   Less heavy, but still weighted with urgency, is an old chestnut that has much to recommend it. "I have a great song to sing for you" conveys an eagerness to share with a wholesome attractiveness of distinct value. It can be altered to "I have a lovely song," "a sad song," "a swinging song to sing for you," but never merely "I have a great song to sing." The pivotal words are "for you."

In both cases there is a catch, of course. One can demand attention or promise an experience, but, following that, the delivery must be made. A "message to Garcia" delivered through and over dangerous obstacles is an insane act if Garcia opens an envelope to discover a blank piece of paper. Promise what you know to be forthcoming—and keep the promise.

Be sure it is *you* singing the song. Do not invent anyone to sing it for you.[3] There is no hiding place in any song you will ever sing. How could there be? You *are* the song.

---

[2] When I draw an example to illuminate a made observation, it is only because the reader may have been a witness to the event or may have access to a recording to corroborate the illustration. Description, as I have said, cannot equal the impact on the eye and the ear of a witnessed performance.

[3] The exception would be an audition the actor/singer would prepare for a specific character role unlike what he appears to be as he comes on stage. This is, however, the single exception to this made observation.

Always stay more important than anything you sing. Another version of this suggestion: Nothing you sing will ever be more important than *you* singing it. If it is, upgrade your acting choices or sing something less important. "I have a great song to sing for you" puts great stress on the words *"for you."* Valuable as they are to remember, the word that is considerably more imposing is "I."

Maintaining importance over a song can be achieved by moment-to-moment thinking. Convey the illusion that you do not know where you are going or what you are going to say, while actually knowing the *curtains for the acts* within the lyric. You should know them, in fact, so well that your *build* to them is why they occur. No more than, in a play, you would be able to perform Act III before Act II and Act II before Act I because of plot development and lack of suitable confrontation, so in singing do you hold sway over the song. Stay away from singing the words and present the song as the *result* of your thinking, and not the reverse. These are the elements that, separate or apart, keep the performer more interesting than what we hear/see him sing.

A further observation made on *importance:* A well-written song continues gaining importance as it proceeds, the second "8" being more interesting than the first, the Bridge or Release more valuable than the second "8" but less so than the last "8." This is elemental to the art of lyric writing. Remember that you, too, must continue to gain importance as you sing the song. Each "8" must not rest on the energy levels of the "8" that preceded it. Realize that the song is continually ascending toward a peak. Your thinking (performance) must increase in energy (thinking) to maintain that state of thrust. I have referred to all vocalization of songs as revelations that occur to the actor/singer at the same moment the audience hears them. Whether these revelations are subjective or objective makes little difference, since both are being realized *now*. A splendid example of this is the performance of Rex Harrison singing "I've Grown Accustomed to Her Face." Instead of information delivered to the audience—a choice rich in dullness—we *see* a man enduring the anguish of a revelation of dependency upon Eliza

Doolittle, who, a moment before, Higgins protested was but "an owl sickened by a few days of my sunshine! Very well! Let her go! I can do without her! I can do without anybody! I have my own soul! My own spark of divine fire!" This pain is not realized until Higgins/Harrison runs out of bluster. Then we *hear* a lovely ballad, but what we *see* is a man in defeat, surrendering not only to the first passion of his life but to the pain of the loss of self-control effected by a woman. Beautiful as the song is, it cannot draw our attention away from *him*. Here is a perfect example of a great song sung more greatly still.

An actor/singer may choose to do a song in any way he pleases. Only one limit is placed on the flow of his creative imagination: His "handle" (choice) must be at the service of the song, the lyric illuminated by the actor's performance of it. What is confusing to the eye, what is provocative, easy to misread, opaque, or unclear, must go, no matter how good you feel doing your number. The number you are doing is the song you are singing, and not the idiomatic meaning of that phrase.

What Not to Sing

Made observations impel me to restrain the actor from choosing to sing *loser* songs or songs in which he elects to *play the loser*. In my own experience I have never met a director or a hirer at a musical audition who can distinguish between a loser and someone playing the part. Tell them out front that you are a failure and you will never brook an argument. Self-pity, too, is to be eschewed. What is impressive is the countless number of songs that can find expression in this choice. All songs of loss, e.g., the Verse and all of the Chorus minus the last "8" of:

"A Foggy Day," music and lyrics by George and
   Ira Gershwin, from the *A Damsel in Distress* (film, 1937).

"Without Love," music and lyrics by Cole Porter,
   from *Silk Stockings* (1955).

"But Not for Me," music and lyrics by George and
   Ira Gershwin, from *Girl Crazy* (1930).

and songs of love unrequited:

"Love Look Away," music and lyrics by Richard
and Oscar Hammerstein II, from *Flower Drum Song*
(1958).

"Why Was I Born?," music and lyrics by Jerome
Kern and Oscar Hammerstein II, from *Sweet Adeline*
(1929).

"Little Girl Blue," music and lyrics by Richard
Rodgers and Lorenz Hart, from *Jumbo* (1935).

These are examples of songs not to be unsung, but not to
be loser-sung. They are aided in that positive cause by the
addition of wit, knowledge gained, and evidence of survival. Observe Fred Astaire sing "By Myself" (music and
lyrics by Arthur Schwartz and Howard Dietz, from *Between the Devil* [1937]) in the film *The Band Wagon* and
you will learn more about choice and style than you will
from watching all the blue lights thrown on all the blue
ladies and gentlemen stuck with and in the blues.

Performance vs. Staging

Once choices are made, do not rigidify their exterior
appearance. Freeze your thinking and the *doing* of it will
take care of itself. I confess to a certain sadness when I
see a performer stage his life in a song in order to store up
courage and diminish the risk of failure.

There is a distinct separation, however, between the
words "performed" and "staged." Staging, unlike the
techniques outlined in chapters 11–15, is performed *on*
the beat and not *before* it. Choreographers *stage* songs. In
choral numbers staging is necessary not only for appearance's sake but as a preventive for anarchy.
Sometimes a choreographer, especially if he is doubling
as the director, will stage the soloist ("I want you to do
this here and do *this* here and in the second '8' cross and
do *this* here"). The choreographer's defense: "If I don't
tell him what to do he won't do anything." Nothing advertises the state of the aridity of the musical theatre today
more than this simple truth. Just as the great stars of the
past in the theatre and in the pop field were never in need
of, and would have resisted, this sort of staging, so does
its presupposed presence make a judgment of sorts on
the talent that requires it.

Staging, of course, can be a valuable asset for creating excitement. Michael Bennett (*Company, Follies, A Chorus Line*), Bob Fosse (*Sweet Charity, Pippin, Chicago*), and Patricia Birch (*A Little Night Music, Candide, Grease*) are masters of the art of presenting the song in such a manner as to gain maximum visual impact. But at an audition—where the actor/singer has none of the trappings and all of the vacuum in which those trappings will later be placed—staging inverts to disadvantage. Decoration is destroyed by the high visibility of its mechanics. Better to do nothing than to present an undeviating staging of yourself. At the worst, *nothing* leaves open to question whether, had you wished to, you could have done *something*.

A final word on staging: Film and television, guilty of bestowing celebrity with haphazard aim, feeds into the theatre, film, and the large Las Vegas club scene those stars who can sell the tickets but seldom the song. Unless these new talents are impelled by personal drive to perfect their craft, the stager's imprint on the action will continue to be indispensable. The inevitable judgment made on a performer by his peers will not be based on his ability but on his stageability. An unchecked deterioration of standards of excellence can only be arrested by the performer himself. The eagerness of the press and public to confer fame and place value on what is mediocre should have no effect upon the artist. We work with standards of our own making. It has never been of greater importance than now to maintain those criteria.

Your Way with a Song

And a last reference to choice: What impels an actor/singer to elect one way instead of another to sing a song is better left, for explanation, to the gods. Sometimes I am caught up by the daring and the imagination of the singer and realize again that every song I have ever heard is new when newly sung. Not to resist the pun, I once watched Tony Newley sing Cole Porter's "It's All Right With Me" (from *Can-Can* [1953]) posed, for no reason I could determine, as Rodin's "Thinker," and found him and the song original and effective. Would I or you have thought to sing it thusly? No. Do I even suggest it be sung henceforth in this somewhat self-conscious manner? No.

But for the three or four minutes during which he and the song were a part of each other, it unquestionably held sway over the audience. In point of fact, choices of an oppositional tone to the lyric occasionally have merit. This is especially true in the case of comic material, where the temptation to be and "do" funny is plainly counterproductive. In an interview with Philip Roth after the publication of his novella *The Breast,* in which a man literally transmutes into the book's title, Mr. Roth said his goal was "to resist exploiting an idea in large part because the possibility is so apparent. It strikes me that what is most obvious is thus the least promising way of treating a character in a situation. If the joke was there before I even began, I thought perhaps the best thing was to stand it on its head by *refusing* to take it as a joke." The italics are mine and reference is to the novel, but as exegesis it is applicable to singing a song.

Oppositional choice can also be applied to the musical arrangement of a song. Streisand's "tempo di dirge" on "Happy Days Are Here Again" remakes a standard into a new listening experience. I have often up-tempoed ballads with similar striking results. (Rodgers and Hammerstein's "All at Once You Love Her," from *Pipe Dream* [1955], and Cole Porter's "I Am Loved," from *Out of this World* [1950], are two examples of the slow-to-fast conversion.) What guides you in these cases is a simple desire to give new life to a song by "standing it on its head." Taste is the limiting agent. Effect for effect's sake may backfire. Remember, oppositional choices of any kind are guilty until proven innocent.

OFFERED SUGGESTIONS

How much does one move and how much physicality does a song need to gain its life? Unlike the depth of the ocean and the height of the sky, there are definable limits we can set for ourselves. These reflections and others relevant to a topic as general as *performance* demand a modulation from made observations to the meeker key of offered suggestions.

Movement

What a song says and how it says it can determine how much movement is necessary. "I Wish I Were in Love

Again" (Richard Rodgers and Lorenz Hart, from *Babes in Arms* [1937]) has a complicated lyric that requires absolute attention in order to get the gist and the joke. Movement of any kind would upstage the verbal Niagara. "I Still See Elisa" (Frederick Loewe and Alan Jay Lerner, from *Paint Your Wagon* [1951]) has little verbal splendor, but what it says is so affecting that an older man, singing of a wife long since dead with all his passion for her still very much alive, need not move at all for the song to be most touching.

At the other extreme are the songs that say nothing and therefore require uninterrupted movement: "I'm Gonna Wash That Man Right Outa My Hair" (Richard Rodgers and Oscar Hammerstein II, from *South Pacific* [1949]) is valid only as an accompaniment to a self-administered shampoo. On the other hand, "Don't Rain on My Parade" (Jule Styne and Bob Merrill, from *Funny Girl* [1964]) and "Rose's Turn" or "Everything's Coming Up Roses" (Jule Styne and Stephen Sondheim, from *Gypsy* [1959]) are just too exciting to deliver without moving.

Between these extremes are songs with a density that demands lacquering of body language on to the lyric (see chapter 15). Ballads, such as:

"Smoke Gets in Your Eyes," music and lyrics by
Jerome Kern and Otto Harbach, from *Roberta* (1933).

Songs of strong conviction:

"Some People," music and lyrics by Jule Styne
and Stephen Sondheim, from *Gypsy* (1959).
"That Great Come and Get It Day," music and
lyrics by Burton Lane and E. Y. Harburg, from *Finian's Rainbow* (1947).

Songs of entreaty:

"Hurry! It's Lovely up Here," music and lyrics by
Burton Lane and Alan Jay Lerner, from *On a Clear Day You Can See Forever* (1965).

Songs of a professed rhythm:

"I Got Rhythm," music and lyrics by George and
Ira Gershwin, from *Girl Crazy* (1930).

Songs of dancing skill:

"(I've Got) Shoes with Wings On," music and
lyrics by Harry Warren and Ira Gershwin, from *The
Barkley's of Broadway* (film, 1948).

This last-named group of material not only requires
movement but, after a Chorus sung, comes the Chorus
danced. Dancing is a numbers game and its study is one I
recommend to all actors who are working in a musical
ambience. The dance, fencing, the gentler martial arts,
and even the gymnasium workout all introduce the actor
to his body and its coordination. Even were the actors
never to dance, such study would not be a wasted experience. Alexander Pope said that "those move easiest
who have learn'd to dance." But if the actor cannot dance
well, dancing less than well is a terpsichorean embarrassment. Continue singing in public. As for the other, my offered suggestion is: belly up to the barre.

There are songs of low height, such as "How Are
Things in Glocca Morra?" (Burton Lane and E. Y. Harburg, from *Finian's Rainbow* [1947]) and "A Very Special
Day" (Richard Rodgers and Oscar Hammerstein II, from
Me and Juliet [1953]), and this particular grouping seems
too fragile to support heavyweight movement, subtextual
or staged. The physicality mirrors the simplicity of the
statement.

There are songs of great height, such as "Gimme a
Pigfoot and a Bottle of Beer" (music and lyrics by Wesley
Wilson; Northern Music [latest publishing date: 1962])
and "Ridin' High" (Cole Porter, from *Red, Hot and Blue!*
[1936]), and you move when you sing them or you just
aren't singing them. And there are contemporary rock
songs, with movement so inherent that if it doesn't come
to you instinctively, you shouldn't be singing them at all.

Hands

Hands reveal what we might be wiser to conceal.
Some valuable offered suggestions:

1   When you first begin to layer body language on to
a song, inhibit the "high and wide" of it by the mental
construction of wall and ceilings that provide an *imaginary* encasement for you on the stage. I suggest, at the

start, narrow corridors that forbid hands moving too wide away from you and a ceiling, no higher than the nipple line, that will restrain them from working around and in front of your face. You can always widen the walls and raise the ceiling, but choice will be impelled by reason and not mindless whim.

2   Interior decoration wisely resists symmetry. In singing, asymmetry, as applied to moving hands, dispels the impression on the eye that half of you is a mirrored image of the other half. Uniformity of gesture tends to be too tranquilizing. In the theatre we are concerned with the attention of the audience, not with its tranquilization. Practice is recommended. The arbitrary activity given one arm in opposition to the movement given to the other makes for habit patterns that will evidence themselves when you are singing.

3   Hands can be moved as mere decoration—an embellishment and not an expression of significant body language. When the gesture is only a beau geste it moves in more graceful design *before* (in the "Air") and not *during* the line. When hands come to rest in an open position away from the sides—not high or too wide—in time to *frame* an important lyric, a joke perhaps, or the title of the song heard for the first time, decoration (arising from no significant thought process) passes for style. As performers coarsen, the need to decorate disappears, but there will always be those who do it well and who pass as stylists even though their work is simply decorative.

4   Do not frame a title more than once. Many songs proclaim their titles two, three, and even four times within a Chorus. It is valid to *freeze-frame* the title when it is first heard. Subsequent repeats should not only *not* be framed but should be layered over with body language (a mini-**Two**?) to get you moving. Remember, a repeat line is a moment of stage wait. There is nothing new to *hear* and now we need something to *see*. Sing the title, but in your thinking rewrite it to create movement. An example: "It Never Entered My Mind."

Once I laughed when I heard you saying
That I'd be playing solitaire,
Uneasy in my easy chair.

(TITLE 1) It never entered my mind.
Once you told me I was mistaken,
That I'd awaken with the sun
And order orange juice for one.

(TITLE 2) It never entered my mind. ["What a laugh! It was
absolutely out of the
question."]
You have what I lack myself,
And now I even have to scratch my back myself.
Once you warned me that if you scorned me
I'd sing the maiden's pray'r again
And wish that you were there again
To get into my hair again.

(TITLE 3) It never entered my mind. ["My God! How far I've
come!"]

"It Never Entered My Mind," music and lyrics by Richard Rodgers and Lorenz Hart, from *Higher and Higher* (1940). Copyright © 1940 by Chappell & Co., Inc. Copyright renewed. International copyright secured. All rights reserved. Used by permission.

5   Coming from another tangent into the language spoken by the singer's hands during the act of singing leads us, surprisingly, to the subject of sexuality. Unlike acting, wherein the actor is clothed in and behind the role he plays, and even more distinct from dancing, an art that apotheosizes rather than arouses and makes of the body a metaphor for all that is poetic, singing—both for the singer and for each member of the audience—becomes a highly personal and sensual experience. It is a shared condition most apparent when one recalls the effect of Frank Sinatra, Elvis Presley, the Beatles, or any current pop idol on their contemporary teenage audiences. Sexuality is the intent of the singing game being played. The physical language needs no dictionary to make clear its meaning. Its statement is sung out and outspoken. But even in less obvious arenas the condition exists, although it may not be shared or even intended. The singer, by the very act of singing, denudes himself and is elevated to extraordinary summits. Any singer can testify that he often is aware of changes that occur in his body metabolism when he is performing. On the receiving end, the spectator indulges in *his* own reactions, some of which are defined strictly within the perimeters of his sexual fantasies. One tends to scrutinize

the singer in a cool but nevertheless intimate manner. Attention is paid to the body, since it is presented to us as open, giving, and seemingly available. The actor/singer, made aware of this built-in distraction that may muddy what he wishes the audience to see, can manipulate his body language in such a way as to cool or heat the delivery of the song and, by so doing, conduct the spectators' attention toward or away from their personal mental meanderings. Let us agree that music, in its *vocal* statement, creates a sexual environment of which the actor/singer must be made alert. Like the movie camera that instructs our eye and orders what it is to see, the performer on a stage dictates focus. When he sings he must learn to protect himself not only from disinterest but from distractions as well.

For example, when a comfortable stance is chosen by the actor/singer because no physical language is necessary (weight on one leg in an at-ease position), hands can be said to be at zero. This position is defined in three variations that readily come to mind: hands at sides, hands clasped low in front, hands clasped behind. Each of these positions, although defined as zero, possesses a shaded language. Hands at sides can be said to imply absolute zero: nothing. Hands clasped low in front seem to convey a conversational tone. Ad-lib verses moving in the rhythm of speech appear friendlier in this less-zeroed zero. As an offered suggestion, and therefore arguable, hands clasped low in front achieve this conversational aspect because they cover a part of the body the performer does not permit to be scrutinized, thereby dictating the allowable facade of intimacy. The third variation, hands clasped behind, for the opposite reason bares the body totally to view. By so doing it presents a more alluring and permissible physical line of sight. I repeat: All three positions of the hands say nothing by themselves, but they can go from zero to zero-plus to plus-zero with interesting effect and increasing intimacy if, for example, they progress in that order when singing a Verse that moves from strict exposition to more personal information.

It can be said that hands reveal (subtext) and conceal. In either case, what they *do* advertises the expertise of the actor/singer's craft, for what they do is controlled by what is on his mind.

6 In the beginning, when you are free to *do* what you think valuable, restraint is served by never *doing*, were it excised, what would not be missed. The platonic notion that beauty of style depends on simplicity obtains in singing as well as in art.

Feet

In chapter 7 I described feet as the betrayers of thought. Muddy your thinking and your hands and feet will advertise it. When you know what you are doing or, better, what you are going to do, they can be trusted to furnish you with all-out support.

Where you stand at an audition is in that ideal geography: downstage center. Must one always stay there to achieve maximum importance? No. Songs begin there, surely. But your feet can take you wherever you care to go if the journey keeps the song alive. Lateral moves can add visual value to material that, due to length, would suffer from an excess of immobility. Remember, however, that the pitfalls are obvious. You may be singing beneath a worklight whose glow to the left and right of you ranges from semi- to total darkness. When the stage is lighted or daylight permits a widening of your playing field, there is definite gain in traveling. I have seen interesting audition performances that dared an exit, on the Rideout, to the L or R, but, as I have remarked, the greater the dare risked, the greater risk of failure. But if you can carry it off, there is an advantage to be scored.

As for *upstage* moves, I try to shun them. We have seen that singing seeks the most downstage placement to gain its vertical urgency. Shifting "up" adds distance between you and the audience that disserves by cutting you down to a shorter size. You become less visible and, worse, lose some degree of control of the house. But if you feel you must move upstage, a good rule of thumb is to *increase* the size of your physical statement. Your hands and, in particular, the importance of the interior energy (thinking) that governs the height and width of your arms should be turned up to do effective battle with the inevitable shrinking that is the consequence of an upstage move.

The overriding impulse is always to service the song

and make its effect on the eye more interesting. If you keep that in mind, you can move up, you can go R, and you can go L, but you will never go wrong.

Don't's

   I am content to repress my own likes and dislikes when, bearing witness to a student's performance of an assigned song, I act as editor of the work. What the actor/singer does *with* a song is his own affair; how well he does it is our mutual concern. The inhibition of personal preferences, however, suffers some degree of strain when I observe what he does *on* a song. Execution is the child of invention and its appearance may ill-advertise the parent. This kind of editing requires a gentle hand. All of us tend to respond unfavorably to criticism of our appearance even when its concern is only for appearance's sake. What we are we know we are; of what we look like we remain forever unknowing. I offer these prefatory sentences as a setting for three—and only three—personally held aversions for that which performers show exceeding affection:

   1   Self-indication of the pronouns "I" and "me" (see chapter 9).
   2   The flashing smile that accompanies, in mindless partnership, the words "happy," "glad," "pleased," "joy (ous)," "merry," "cheery," and their synonyms. Perverse motive can effect a provocative reading, as in:

Like a straying baby lamb
With no mammy and no pappy
I'm so [smile] unhappy
But oh, so [no smile] glad.

   3   The *shrug*. To avoid ambiguity: Do not shrug. If body language is the exterior manifestation of your interior thinking, the shrug expresses indifference, doubt, aloofness, and other dispensable outer layers of a performer's psychological clothing. The figurative relative degree of importance determines whether a statement will be spoken or translated into a lyric and sung. If a song sings of what is most, not least, significant, a shrug,

by its very definition, is to be excluded from all body language. The "who cares?" look of it is a dangerous indication offered by the singer to the audience as a suggested response.

Props

If we accept the idea that all language springs from two distinct channels mutually related but exclusive of each other, then the proper handling of a prop proceeds from a *third* script. Without it, the prop's attribution to the main (spoken or sung) script is forfeited, whereupon the prop appears to inflate until the witness sees nothing *but* the prop.

Years ago I heard a story, ascribed to the eminent actor Joseph Schildkraut, in which he recalled an incident in his youth when he was away at school in Austria. With each appearance he made in a school play he would beseech his father by letter to come to see him act. The father, Maurice Schildkraut, being an actor of great renown and of oversized passion for the theatre, refused, on the grounds that children in plays were of disinterest to him whether or not one of them was kin. But at last the old man agreed to attend a school production of *King Lear* in which his son, then no more than fifteen, was appearing as Lear himself. Whether curiosity or conscience persuaded him to change his mind we cannot know, but the sight of the boy in grey wig and penciled-in wrinkles must have caused him great pain. Finally, unable to watch his son stroking a hooked-on long white beard, he rose from his seat, raised his arms and eyes heavenward for an answer from the deity, and cried out, "Beard! Where are you going with my son?!"

The story has been told and retold and now may be more fiction than fact, but its relevancy still leavens the laugh with the pain of acquired knowledge: We must subjugate a prop or it soon becomes our master. The actor/-singer who wants to hold, light, and smoke a cigarette while singing a song had better first learn how and when to accomplish what, under social conditions, may be an easy coordination but, under the more sophisticated demands made on our breathing mechanism, may menace and disallow the production of sound. Playing with eyeglasses or handkerchiefs, getting in and out of coats—these activities are obtrusive until they are the result of a third script that will punctuate what we hear by beguiling the eye.

When a prop has its own script it can be an asset to the song's performance. Just as ignorance of its power upstages the nervous amateur, knowledge of it proclaims a professional.

I can recall a performance of Rodgers and Hart's "Did You Ever Get Stung?" by an actress of deserved recognition in the theatre who constructed it in my studio as an exercise in the handling of props. She put on and adjusted furs and then, in the second "8," removed a compact from her bag, extracted a lipstick, and freshened her make-up. Powdering her nose, carefully placed in the spaces of the lyric that permitted it, was reserved for the Bridge:

Did you say, "She lives for me!
This is it, now at last?"
You bit! You were it!
You got hit by the blast!

"Did You Ever Get Stung?," music and lyrics by Richard Rodgers and Lorenz Hart, from *I Married an Angel* (1938). Copyright © 1938; renewed 1965 Metro-Goldwyn-Mayer, Inc., Culver City, California. Rights throughout the world controlled by Robbins Music Corporation. International Copyright secured. Made in U.S.A. All rights reserved. Used by permission.

The rim-shot we placed after the last word was punctuated with the closing of the compact, releasing the excess powder around her face and making the word "blast" a miniatomic explosion. The last "8" and Rideout extensions were sung as she put on her gloves and so timed as to achieve her readiness to exit at the last moment of the Rideout, which, in fact, she did. The song became a valuable audition piece for her, but I doubt if those who saw it ever realized how difficult that smooth precision had been to accomplish. Mastering the *business* had not been made easier by the relentless 2/4 time signature. Spaces that allowed physical activity were tightly defined within the song. But it was unquestionably the third script (moving the props) that set off the second script (thought process) and triggered the first script (the lyric) that, all together, created the perfect setting for Rodgers and Hart's lovely gem.

A single idea for a prop to illuminate, one that will live as a piece of stage business for a moment and then dies, leaving you with an inert inanimate object while you continue singing a major part of the song, is not enough justification to keep it in. A prop attracts the eye. It must be taught its place. Nothing—not even the song—can be permitted to take attention away from you. When a prop *knows* its place and helps to illuminate what you are singing, let it live. When it is no more than a distraction, kill it.

Focus

Some songs, written with the objective "you" in the lyric, have an explicit unifocus (see chapter 1). "Send In the Clowns" is an example: "Me here at last on the ground, *you* in mid-air." The "you" here is directed exclusively to a center focus by virtue of the fact that the song belongs to the "you" from its beginning down to "Well, maybe next year."

The "you" in "If *you* feel like singing, sing" has the same *explicit* "you" in the lyric, but its *implicit* connotation is the Southern *you'all* or the French pronoun *on*. Focus, then, is wherever eye communication is made and should *spot* to as many parts of the house as one can contact without appearing lunatic.

The impulse to make the song you are singing more important and to invest urgency in its telling can result in what I call pushing *against the fourth wall*. Pressing on a spot by staring at it or boring into it with drill-like eyes to convince us that there is someone there has a contrary effect: The more pressure, the more I suspect *nothing* is there. Let us agree that the theatre (audience, auditioner, or the spot[s] you sing to) is *there*. Insisting on the focus will not make it *more* there. The credibility factor is heightened by your *reactions to what or whom you see*. I believe there is a life out front because I can read its presence on you. Emphasis on this simple truth gives the lie to it. If you see it you will react to it. If you *do* you seeing it, I will mistrust the very impulse that induced the push against the fourth wall.

I have noticed that once the actor/singer is taught how to spot and the importance of a center focus is accepted by him, he trades in his rolling eyeballs for the new model—uninterrupted commitment to that C lifeline. Songs that are house numbers but are sung only to center or L, C, R never realize their full size-potential. This recommended adjustment should be made: All songs belong to the theatre and the theatre is *anywhere you choose to play to.* Only when a song forbids it—when the "you" is to one person alone and singing to more than one explicit "you" would offend or imply a capricious commitment to the C—or when a spot change might present the singer in confusing fickleness are there prohibiting limitations on playing the house. Why, if these restrictions are not present in the script, create a prison for yourself when you are free to go where you will?

The method I use to train the actor to consider that there are other spots besides C is only a technical one. L of C and R of C are asked to play double roles in house numbers only because spots are infinite in number—one can relate *anywhere* through the fourth wall and to *anyone*—but one cannot teach focus with margins of such unlimited choice. This much can be said that is constant and true of all house numbers:

1.   Important lines, e.g., the first line of the Verse, the last line of the Verse, the first line of the Chorus, the first line of the Bridge (Release), and the last line of the Chorus, in their complete subject and predicate, should be addressed to C.

2.   Once this is set into the performance we know where we need not be C, namely: the lines that precede those in C. They can be focused anywhere we care to go (see chapter 9).

3.   It is a good idea to vary relating to one spot, L, R, C, or to any point of focus, *by seeing no one in particular and everyone in general,* just as you would speak to many people without contacting the eye of any one person. This roving focus or panning effect can add importance to the line that follows it if it is spotted to a specific place in the theatre. Practice will make sense of focus and reintroduce the actor/singer to what he does intuitively when he speaks to one or to many listeners.

232

Learning the Song

It is a universal understanding that what is implied by the phrase "to learn a song by heart" is the committing of words and music to memory. The parochial meaning is more inclusive. Memorization involves choices of phrasing, both of music and lyric, to allow for maximum clarity of the words and melody and for husbanding the breath required in the vocalization of long-arced musical lines and Rideouts. Also, I have referred to the *freezing* of those interior cues that will reveal *what the song is about*—these cues moving ahead of the sung line not necessarily to invent constant physical language, but always to accommodate the script and its interpretation.

The "Air" in the song, considered all too often as instrumental fills to be waited out, should be added as another element to be memorized, for it is within those defined spaces that phrasing and the inner monologue will be housed.

"Air" comes in all sizes. Sometimes shorter than the time it takes to snap one's fingers, it can also be of considerable length, and only concentration on a created subtext during the playing-out time precludes "Air" pockets. The singer must not only know the *duration* but the *relative importance* of each "Air" space. The following list (an offered suggestion) places "Air" in the order of its importance:

1   The Vamp, from Belltone to maximum length, is the primary nonsung music in every song you sing. The graceful exit from a place where singing what you have to say would be bizarre into a country where it is not only the sane but the inevitable thing to do—this alone justifies its leadoff position.

2   The Rideout. Contained here are the reverse of the conditions inherent in the Vamp: how to avoid a precipitate splashdown out of the song into a world where sung/speech is not sanctioned.

3   The "Air" that separates the Verse from the Chorus, the third most significant within the

body of the song. This fill marks the end of
the passive exposition and the start of what
is active (the Chorus) in the lyric—why, in fact,
you sang the Verse to begin with. In the
language of the playwright, it is the attack of the
play.

4   The "Air" that follows the second "8" of
the Chorus and elevates the song into the Bridge or
Release. (If no Verse was sung, this "Air"
would move up a peg and follow the Rideout in
relative importance.)

5   The "Air" that ends the Bridge and takes
us into the last "8"—the denouement hell-bent for
resolution (see "Send In the Clowns" at the
beginning of this chapter).

6   Last, the "Air" between the first and second "8"s. Despite its ultimate position in the list,
this "Air" energizes the second "8" up and
over the heat level of the first "8" and
establishes, within the body of the Chorus, the
first illustration of the impulse to make more important the need to continue.

Suggested Songs for the Actor Who Can Sing

In a study experience there is value for the novice ac-
tor/singer to choose a song that *sings* in broad Brahmsian
phrases. The song functions as a vocalise since it can contain, in its melody, vocal problems the neophyte has been
solving with a singing teacher, while at the same time
moving him away from exercises that are all technique
and no music.

If the actor/singer has a voice of some distinction,
this kind of song offers the composer, lyricist, and director the opportunity to *hear* as well as *see* a performance,
thereby providing audition material of double value.
Here, as offered suggestions, are some song titles chosen
at random to illustrate genre and nothing more:

"Lonely Town," music and lyrics by Leonard
Bernstein and Betty Comden and Adolph Green,
from *On the Town* (1944).

"In the Still of the Night," music and lyrics by
Cole Porter, from *Rosalie* (1937).

"Here I'll Stay," music and lyrics by Kurt Weill
and Alan Jay Lerner, from *Love Life* (1948).

"Dancing in the Dark," music and lyrics by Arthur
Schwartz and Howard Dietz, from *The Band
Wagon* (1931).

"Out of This World," music and lyrics by Harold
Arlen and Johnny Mercer, from *Out of This World*
(film, 1945).

"The Song Is You," music and lyrics by Jerome
Kern and Oscar Hammerstein II, from *Music
in the Air* (1932).

The familiar arias from *Porgy and Bess* (1935),
music and lyrics by George and Ira
Gershwin and DuBose Heyward.

"I Got Lost in His Arms," music and lyrics by
Irving Berlin, from *Annie Get Your Gun* (1946).

"Will He Like Me?," music and lyrics by Jerry
Bock and Sheldon Harnick, from *She Loves Me* (1963).

"With So Little to Be Sure Of," music and lyrics by
Stephen Sondheim, from *Anyone Can Whistle* (1964).

"April in Paris," music and lyrics by Vernon Duke
and E. Y. Harburg, from *Walk a Little Faster* (1932).

"I'll See You Again," music and lyrics by Noel
Coward, from *Bitter Sweet* (1929).

"Night Song," music and lyrics by Charles Strouse
and Lee Adams, from *Golden Boy* (1964).

"A Quiet Thing," music and lyrics by John Kander
and Fred Ebb, from *Flora, the Red Menace* (1965).

Last words: These songs and their categorical cousins
cannot be cheated vocally—they must be sung. *Caveat
actor/cantor.*

HELD OPINIONS

Chapter 1 of this volume is concerned with words. Let me tie off loose ends on the same subject with some held opinions.

Poetical Lyrics

Lyrics, as with light verse, are governed by the laws of poetry and prosody, the demands of rhyme, metrical structure, stanzas ("8"s), and, in song, vocal prerogatives.[4] Unless an actor has had experience in the verse plays of Shakespeare, Molière, Jonson, and Congreve, or in the plays of our own time by T. S. Eliot and Christopher Fry, for example, singing will be a new and alien act of communication.

We have spoken of the *second* script that silently spins out the text's significance. It is imperative in the creation of this flow of cues that the thought patterns unwind in our customary speech, the vulgar and idiomatic thinking being our defense against the spoken (sung) poetry. Nothing congeals the mind and body more than singing a lyric that expresses itself in language far loftier than straight-talking lingo. For illustration, this lovely song that demands a second script with the common touch or the performer early on turns to cement:

Out of my dreams and into your arms
I long to fly.
I will come as evening comes to woo
a waiting sky.
Out of my dreams and into the hush
Of falling shadows
When the mist is low and stars are
breaking through
Then out of my dreams I'll go
Into a dream with you.

"Out of My Dreams," music and lyrics by Richard Rodgers and Oscar Hammerstein II, from *Oklahoma* (1943). Copyright © 1943 by Williamson Music, Inc. Copyright renewed. International copyright secured. All rights reserved. Used by permission.

[4] Most lyricists are not happy to publish their work apart from the related melodic lines upon which the lyric was laminated. They maintain, with some justification, that were the words intended to stand alone, they would quite probably have been created in another manner and with different results.

The Doo-Wahs

On those rare occasions when you are asked to hum a phrase or, worse, *doo-wah* it, avoid an empty mind at all costs. Humming is a self-conscious effect only when it is accompanied by a hummed thinking process. One hums on a closed "n" or "m" but never with a closed mind. *Doo-wahs* and their variations are easier to deal with. They are as mindless as a hum but, because they appear in upbeat rhythmic arrangements, the resulting sense of free-swinging fun helps fill the empty head. Another point in favor of the *doo-wahs* and the *doo "break"*: It is usually assigned to the choral ensemble, in which case you are free of it. Like a disappearing species, it is becoming extinct and, when it achieves that end, you will be freer still.

Diction, Phrases, Words

The first script, the lyric itself, from the pen of a Gershwin, Harburg, Lerner, Sondheim, Hart, Fields, Hammerstein, Dietz, Harnick, et al., is a monument of pithy, sententious, witty, elegant, punned, sentient, romantic, unsentimental light verse set to music. The actor/singer is advised to heighten not only his vocal powers but his sense of language as well.

1   Diction. Nothing infuriates more than the strain of trying to hear what is being sung. In the beginning exhaust the muscles that articulate sound and shape it into language. A tired face is a small price to pay for the contented ear that can hear without resorting to guesswork and "What did he say (sing)?"

2   Vowels, when sung, make the music of the word. The consonants that surround the vowel make the word. Remember to finish the word by exaggerating the final consonant. You may discover that what seemed too much to you was just enough for the listener. Again, you can always make less of too much.

3   Rather than thinking of the verbal line as *one nonstop flow of words,* sharpen your awareness of:

Although Ira Gershwin has been published (*Lyrics on Several Occasions* [New York: Viking, 1959), the collection is only a sampling of his output and the book itself more a reminiscence than a corpus.

a) the phrase within a phrase. Example: the last "8" of Ogden Nash's "Roundabout":

Then it's roundabout and roundabout
And roundabout once more   (✔)
As you pray again
Each day again to soar [no breath]
On *your way(,)*[glottal stop] again   (✔)

It's roundabout once more.

"Roundabout," music and lyrics by Vernon Duke and Ogden Nash, from *Two's Company*. Copyright © 1946 Warner Bros. Inc. Copyright renewed. All rights reserved. Used by permission.

b) the qualifying words that define and resist the dying fall (explained at the end of this chapter):

When the sky is a bright *canary yellow* . . . ."

"A Cockeyed Optimist," music and lyrics by Richard Rodgers and Oscar Hammerstein II, from *South Pacific* (1949).

c) the lovely surprise of a *twist,* as in Larry Hart's classic homonymnal hymn:

You are so fair,
Like an oriental vision;
But you won't make that decision.
You're not quite fair.
I'd pay your fare
To Niagara Falls and back, too,
But you never will react to
This love affair.
You are the crepes suzette
I should get
On my bill of fare
But if you love me not,
Flower-pot,
See if I care!
See how you'll fare
If you keep on playing rover
When I come to think it over,
You're only fair.

"You Are So Fair," music and lyrics by Richard Rodgers and Lorenz Hart, from *Babes in Arms* (1937). Copyright © 1951 by Chappell & Co., Inc. International copyright secured. All rights reserved. Used by permission.

The last-line twist not only takes back the all-out rave of the first line, but rejects the homonym for a word of different meaning, although spelled the same.

Phrasing Postscripts

The preceding section began with names and adjectives in series. Here, the last four bars of Mr. Hart's Verse for "My Funny Valentine":

Thou noble, upright, truthful,
Sincere and slightly dopey gent: (✔)

phrased with a degree of sensitivity to the build of favorable adjectives to the final pejorative one:

(✔) Thou noble(,) [glottal stop]
upright [one "t," the "t" of "truthful"]
truthful
Sincere and(,) [glottal stop] slightly *dopey* gent: (✔)

In chapter 3, "Phrasing," I suggested that a breath, when needed, can be taken *before* a preposition with little or no damage to the language, e.g.:

When my slippers are next (✔)
To the ones that belong (✔)
To the one and only beautiful girl (✔)
in the world.

The three indicated possibilities (one or two are sufficient to make the Rideout robust) will serve the actor/singer with an adequate supply of breath.

This rule has one exception: When the verb combines its infinitive with a preposition, e.g.: to tell to, to work in, at, or for, to sing to or for, to cry for or about. In all such cases, the verb and the preposition should *not* be

separated and the breath should be taken as *early after*
as possible, for example, "to tell to me," "to work in an
office," and so on.

A phrasing postscript: One cannot sing without
breath. Dissension among singing teachers is par for the
course in voice production, particularly when study arrives at secondary techniques, but there is total accord on
this primary obligation: You must breathe in order to produce sound. And when sound on varying pitches creates
a flow of continuing intervals (the vocal line), the inspired breath and the singer's control of its expiration
share equal importance. I have emphasized that, no matter the plotting of your phrasing, it is imperative that you
breathe when you need a breath. Relative to this injunc-
tion: Accustom yourself always to breathe at the expense
of what has *just been said (sung)*. For example (refer to
plotting of the phrasing for "The Most Beautiful Girl in
the World" in chapter 3), if in:

When my slippers are next
To the ones that belong (✓)
To the one and only. . . .

you choose to forfeit the breath after "next" and keep the
one after "belong" (as marked here), remember that the
song is still *a tempo*. Do not linger on the word "belong."
You are robbing time from the minimal space available
to gain breath for "To the one and only. . . ." It would
be better to cut short "belong" (breathing at the expense
of what you have just sung) and have sufficient breath for
what you are going to sing. An audience is less aware of
what they missed than of what they are missing.

Bad English—Good Lyrics

In all languages certain words, when juxtaposed, can
be misapprehended by the listener. A *glottal stop* between the two words restores the original meaning and
prevents nonsense:

And the world discovers
As my book(,) ends. . . .

and scatological solecism:

Isn't(,) it romantic?

Her(,) ears?
They're ordinary ears. . . .

"It's a Nice Face," music and lyrics by Cy Coleman and Dorothy Fields, from *Sweet Charity* (film, 1970).

It's(,) not where you start,
It's where you finish. . . .

"It's Not Where You Start," music and lyrics by Cy Coleman and Dorothy Fields, from *Seesaw* (1973).

I'm wearing my heart(,) on my sleeve. . . .

Lyrics often take on the appearance of German syntax or of a Latin pony ("throw the horse over the fence some oats"), although when the lyric is sung the awkwardness is unnoticeable. A few examples:

You've got what Adam had
When he with love for Eve was tortured.
She only had an apple tree,
But you, you've got an orchard!

"You've Got that Thing," music and lyrics by Cole Porter, from *Fifty Million Frenchmen* (1929). Copyright © 1929 Warner Bros. Inc. Copyright renewed. All rights reserved. Used by permission.

The convolution in the first couplet proves that all is fair in love, war, and in this case, rhyme.

One *says*, "Someday the man I love will come along," but *sings*:

Someday he'll come along,
The man I love. . . .

and:

And so, all else above,
I'm waiting for the man I love.

"The Man I Love," music and lyrics by George and Ira Gershwin, from *Lady Be Good* (1924).

Again, for rhyme's sake, the phrase "above all else" has its sequence juggled to "all else above."

This convention demands that your thought-energy continue until the end of the sentence, for it is there you will find the subject or the active verb. If, for example, the performer does not know that it is the "man I love" who will come along someday, the ear of the listener will hear the *he* in "Someday *he'll* come along," but his eye (understanding) will have to wait until the *who* is verbalized. Until then, it could be anyone from the IRS down to the Grim Reaper. This is another example of the need to think ahead or to reverse the line in your mind, but never to be nose-to-nose with the unraveling of a lyric.

The Effects of Rhythm

Music may be described as a lamination of melody onto a harmonic structure couched in specific rhythms.[5] Within a bar of music two beats have given names: the *downbeat* (always the first beat of the bar) and the *upbeat* (the beat that precedes the downbeat). By virtue of its primary placement, the downbeat is the dominant beat of the bar, while the upbeat is weak and seeks to resolve into the new downbeat. In 4/4 time, the *first* and the *third* beats are considerably stronger than the second and fourth beats, as in a march:

downbeat		upbeat		
1	2	3	4	
left	right	*left*	right	etc.[6]

The accented force of the downbeat and the weakness of the upbeat are manifest in every bar of music, no matter the time signature. This is important to know. Lyrics, even those of first-magnitude writers, will frequently have a weighty or qualifying word falling on an unac-

[5] See chapter 2. The harmonic support for the melodic line has been omitted from this book. Its domain does not require inclusion here, although vocalization can be richer when the singer's knowledge of music is not superficial. It is also undeniable that innocence of the chordal element of a song in no way prohibits effective interpretation.

[6] A simplistic reduction: When these accents are reversed and the second and fourth beats in the bar given the stress, while the first (the downbeat) and third beats are made recessive, the basic pattern that informs jazz is indicated:

| 1 | 2 | 3 | 4 | 1 | 2 | 3 | 4 | | etc. |

One can almost hear the fingersnap and the toe tap that illustrate the point.

cented beat. The performer must bring a conscious energy to its articulation or it will disappear with little or no trace. For example: "Whose broad stripes and bright stars," extrapolated from our anthem, is in 3/4 time. "Whose broad" is crammed into the upbeat that precedes the downbeat "stripes." Giving "broad" its due is almost impossible, most of us settling for the approximation: "Whose braw stripes." I use this example not to beg for an upgrading of the singing of our anthem, but because the reader is familiar with the text and the musical line that sets it. There are countless songs you will sing wherein the same awkward accents appear. It is wise to *white-light* the weak word by a vocal stress on the vowel and the end consonant (if there is one). Left unlighted, it remains, unheard, in the darkness: "Whose br(awd) stripes and bright stars." It is unncessary to single out "stripes." Its placement on the downbeat affords it the power of the first beat of the bar.

The Dying Fall

In the reading of verse the English actor is often said to have an advantage over his American counterpart. Shakepeare's language and the King's English find him at home in shared indigeneity, whereas the American, accustomed to *his* lingua franca, is beyond salvation. I do not want to debate the issue, but there is one *melody* in spoken American English—the dying fall—that pollutes our spoken language and, in a singing context, works outright damage to the text. Read the preceding sentence out loud and it becomes evident that every sentence we speak ends on a tonal downer. Even this sentence drops on the very words *tonal downer.*

The dying fall is poisonous because the integral verbal point of the line you are singing most often is heard at the end of the lyric phrase, when not only the penchant for the dying fall occurs, but energy (thought) and breath supply, being in partnership, are both waning. Begin to practice a conscious resistance. Sing the line with this intention:⎯⎯⎯rather than⎯⎯⎯. You will hear a new method of delivery that not only gains and holds the attention of the ear, but brings serendipitous line readings. I have heard "Change Partners" sung innumberable times. The first "8" is always performed:

Must you dance ev'ry dance
With the same fortunate man?
You have danced with him since
    the music began—
Won't you change partners and
    dance with me?

The accented *"dance"* justified by the active, if not obvious, nature of the word. Not for Fred Astaire. He sings
the last line: "Won't you change partners and dance with
me?," resisting the dying fall and, at the same time, sug-
gesting that the key notion in the phrase is not *dancing*
but rather *with whom*.
    When the melodic line rises at its end, the dying fall
is denied. And sometimes the composer scores the money
word on a vocal climb to insure its audability, as in the
penultimate line of the last "8" of "I've Got Rhythm." But
the first "8" needs a firm defiance against the dying fall:

I got rhythm
I got music
I got my man
Who could ask for anything *more?*

The word "more" is a qualifier of the word "anything." It
isn't "anything" we could ask for but anything "more"
than rhythm, music, and a lover. Outwitting the dying fall
lights the valuable word in the phrase. Who could ask for
anything more?

Chapter 18

The Limits of Study

> . . . Where is the wisdom
> we have lost in knowledge?
> . . . Where is the knowledge
> we have lost in information? . . .
>
> T. S. Eliot

CLAIMED CONVICTIONS

Held opinions yielded to made observations, which surrendered to offered suggestions. Here, for purposes of rounding out, some claimed convictions.

I have written at some length in the Preface about the need for study and the subsequent need to discontinue it. In my studio the time for ending study is instituted by me, but the decision is made mutually by both the student and myself. What defines it? The study of performance in a controlled environment (class) becomes an unnecessary expenditure of time, energy, and money when the actor/singer evidences no problem in learning and getting on to the stage an effective performance of any song assigned to him. Then, and only then, do I suggest the end's beginning. There is some resistance some of the time, but this is more a manifestation of the end of a summertime romance than a dispute over the assessment of evidenced skill.[1]

[1] Held opinion: Singing is a sensual act of personal statement. The journey the actor takes in my studio from the terror of singing a song to the rapture of

It is my claimed conviction that study possesses damaging reverse values when it continues beyond that point where ignorance of the subject is not the motivating impulse. This position is not popular and I am asked to defend it by opponents whose heated antagonism is due to misunderstanding rather than disagreement. Clearly I do not regard the study of *dance* or *singing* as closed-end efforts. Any education that trains muscles to do a bidding that either would not be done or would find them too underdeveloped to do is one that requires ceaseless application. When I speak of study I refer to *performance* alone, particularly the performance of songs and the degree of proficiency applied to the singing of them. Study need not continue after that point in time when the actor/singer is able to secure work by virtue of his skill. An hour of singing before strangers under conditions determined by a professional ambience is worth one hundred hours of performance in a controlled environment monitored by a teacher.

When one of my students and I say goodbye to each other, I find myself making a silent prayer that he will forget everything I have taught him. Nothing saddens me more than to hear a producer, a director, or a casting agent tell me that they guessed I taught someone they had seen. The ultimate achievement must be a letting go followed by the continuing search for self in your work. This recollection of Joseph Fuchs, the eminent violinist, of his teacher Franz Kneisel, with whom he had studied from the age of twelve until he was nineteen, is pertinent:

Kneisel said, "You've been with me now almost seven years. You have enough. Go out into the world, do what you can. There's so much I taught you. Remember—if you keep 25 percent it's enough. If you keep 50 percent, it's not as good as 25. If you keep 75, you're in danger. And if you keep 100, then God help you."[2]

---

singing himself is somewhat primal. Coupled with this metamorphosis is the intensity of the interaction between the singer and his classmates. Lasting friendships, romances, and even marriages have resulted from the intimacy created by the making of music.

[2] From an interview with Fuchs by Joseph Horowitz, in the *New York Times*, November 11, 1977.

Singing for your supper is the ideal.[3] If consistent op-portunities do not present themselves, hire a pianist once or twice a month, depending on his availability and the size of your pocketbook. Spend an hour singing the songs you want to keep from growing stale—songs you will use for future auditions or engagements. What is important is that *you* are now the judge of your work. You are singing and beginning to trust that what you feel is good, and to lay those foundations upon which you will build your personal criteria. These standards will change as you change. They will surely be strained by the demands placed on you in the marketplace, where politics often becomes the better part of wisdom. But the work will be measured against your idiosyncratic gauge and not that of a teacher.

[3] Today, in the major cities across the country, there is a new scourge on the show-biz land: the production in which everyone is paid but the cast. The "showcase" label propounds the justification that to be seen is reward enough. Thus the performer assuages his conscience. I remain unconvinced. Get paid, even if it is only a token gratuity. Payment for services separates the amateur from the professional. In a not dissimilar context, Alexander Woollcott, in an essay on actors and streetwalkers, said: "The two oldest pro-fessions in the world—ruined by amateurs." *Shouts and Murmurs: Echoes of a Thousand and One Nights* (London: Parsons, 1923).

Chapter 19

Rideout

But all good things must come to an end, and so one must move forward into the space left by one's conclusions.

John Ashbery

Where is the musical theatre heading? Its roots and evolution have been defined, but the future is not readily construable. Soaring costs deal death blows to experimental efforts and justify recourse to revivals.[1] But revivals are stopgap measures that contain their own law of diminishing returns. The Broadway and summer-stockpile will, in time, be exhausted and leave the enterprising producer no other expedient but to bring back, in the name of nostalgia, that which closed only yesterday or, better still, to revive the revivals. In either direction lies a death.

A revival holds significance for audiences old enough to cherish the memory of the original. As the mean age of the audience decreases and represents a

---

[1] From a column in *Daily Variety*, dated November 25, 1977, entitled "Quality of Theatre on the Decline," by Bill Edwards: "As for musicals, that field is practically dominated by revivals and holdovers with the only new one this season being *The Act*, which can hardly be called musical comedy . . . . High cost of production is always the reason given for either not taking a chance on a new show or reviving such proven material as *The King and I* and *Hello, Dolly.*

greater fraction of the whole who share no particular bias for the subject matter, box-office receipts will, by reflection, diminish. Of equal relevance will be the increasingly alien sound of the music. The farther the show tune, with its structured lyric, slips into the past, the more a score flirts with the loss of relatability.

Apart from the ephemeral rock musical, the one distinguishing characteristic of our musical theatre is its sublime disinterest in contemporaneity. I do not intend this as a judgment, but the widening gap between theatre music and the "pop" sound must be recognized as an inevitable choice factor to be faced by our future score writers. The old show tune, as a song form, is no longer a viable expression. It seems to me to have fulfilled its purpose by filling out its perimeters to overflowing. New theatre music not only reprises what has been written before but, with few exceptions, does not do it half as well. There is a nagging fear, too, that we are drawing ever closer to that place where all combinations of melody and rhythm will have been depleted. After all, the scale and interval variations are finite, and what then? As for rock, country, middle of the road, and other collateral music, I have referred, in the Introduction, to its ineffectivity as a theatre *sound*. The dilemma remains.

If cost sheets are considered the cause for today's famine, ways and means must be found to bring down the damages. Broadway need not be considered the ne plus ultra. Size need not be the measure of worth. Production need not be a recall of Ziegfeld to define excellence. And affectionate criticism of size and production need not be suggestive of quality.

Regional theatres would appear to be a fertile breeding ground for tomorrow's musicals. There exist, even now, many prestigious plants throughout the country with audiences attuned to more daring fare. The houses are smaller, obviating the need for large dancing and singing Choruses. In general, the first-magnitude theatres share a common goal—the presentation of meaningful theatre in a climate unfettered by old formulas. I see no reason why new musicals should be treated as creative efforts less worthy than new plays, and new composers, lyricists, and librettists afforded less opportunity to be heard than new playwrights. What is on a writer's mind is of equal interest whether the final statement is spoken or sung. We must begin to accept musical theatre with the respect due it. It is not a term of opprobrium to call an entertainment an entertainment. Neil Simon entertains and enlightens. Stephen Sondheim does the same.

Of late there has been a noticeable increase in the production of opera made possible through the sharing of expense by more than one municipal opera company. The production can play in those home cities that have carried a portion of the cost, thereby diminishing the treacherous cost risk, while at the same time affording a longer life for the piece, gaining a larger audience to hear it, and giving the singers the chance to enrich their performances. Perhaps a banding together of regional theatres might occasion similar rewards. The performers would inherit the increased run of work very much in the manner of the old Fanchon-Marco vaudeville circuit. We have the creative and interpretive talents to seed this kind of organized plan. It is an act of appalling waste not to afford our musical theatre artists the same opportunity for public expression as we do our new playwrights.

The musical theatre, if it is to survive, must continue to evolve, just as the mittel-European operetta metamorphosed from a song form only singers and buffo-comedians were able to vocalize,[2] down or up to the show score in which interpreters with less vocal skill and more ability to illuminate text are at home.

The best of the scene today employs the actor who sings (Rex Harrison, Robert Preston), the singer who creates character (Cleo Laine, Barbra Streisand, Liza Minnelli), and the dancer who can do both (the supreme Fred Astaire and the casts of *A Chorus Line* and *West Side Story*). This trinity, a hybrid offspring, gives evidence of the ever-growing maturity of the musical in the last twenty-five years. How fitting that so democratic an interaction of song, play, and movement became this coun-

---

[2] When operettas are revived today it is Sills we see in *The Merry Widow* and *Die Fledermaus* and, in recordings, the splendid likes of Tauber, Sutherland, Schwartzkopf, Wunderlich, and Gedda whom we hear.

try's most significant contribution to world theatre, and how important that this three-way egalitarianism be furnished with the proper inducements to make possible a continuing creative adulthood.

The musical deserves salvation. There is always much to dance and sing about. Our lives require the veracity of song. One *Fiddler on the Roof* affects and haunts more disparate audiences than any so-called "play of the moment." One *Threepenny Opera* sings all we have to know about man's inhumanity to man.

Young talent must be heard and seen. We cannot have a musical statement without an arena in which it can be shaped and articulated. Without such an arena we are all stuck with hollow remountings of shows with nothing to say/sing, sentimental juvenilia that says/sings it forgettably, or the cacophony of the contemporary Tin Pan Alley sound in which nothing is said/sung in anything approaching a literate voice. This volume is a by-product of the *new* musical theatre because it speaks to latter-day immigrants into the country of song and dance. It will be our loss if these future citizens come together on the dole and not the stage.